The Subtext of Form in the
English Renaissance

The Subtext of Form in the English Renaissance

PROPORTION POETICAL

S. K. HENINGER, JR.

The Pennsylvania State University Press
University Park, Pennsylvania

Library of Congress Cataloging-in-Publication Data

Heninger, S. K., Jr.
   The subtext of form in the English Renaissance : proportion poetical / S. K. Heninger, Jr.
     p.   cm.
   Includes bibliographical references and index.
   ISBN 0-271-01070-3 (alk. paper) — ISBN 0-271-01071-1 (pbk. : alk. paper)
   1. English poetry—Early modern, 1500–1700—History and criticism—Theory, etc. 2. Aesthetics, Modern—16th century. 3. Aesthetics, Modern—17th century. 4. Renaissance—England. 5. Narration (Rhetoric). 6. Proportion (Art). 7. Literary form. 8. Poetics. I. Title.
PR535. A34H46   1994
821'.309—dc20

                                         92-44786
                                           CIP

Published by The Pennsylvania State University Press,
Barbara Building, Suite C, University Park, PA 16802-1003

It is the policy of The Pennsylvania State University Press to use acid-free paper for the first printing of all clothbound books. Publications on uncoated stock satisfy the minimum requirements of American National Standard for Information Sciences— Permanence of Paper for Printed Library Materials, ANSI Z39.48–1984.

CONTENTS

LIST OF ILLUSTRATIONS

The woodcut initials at the opening of each chapter are reproduced from John Lyly, *Euphues: The anatomy of wyt* (London, 1578), with permission by the British Library.

Introduction

This work bears the title of an essay in the strictest sense of the word. No one is more conscious than the writer with what limited means and strength he has addressed himself to a task so arduous. And even if he could look with greater confidence upon his own researches, he would hardly thereby feel more assured of the approval of competent judges. To each eye, perhaps, the outlines of a given civilization present a different picture.

—*Jacob Burckhardt*[1]

rudently in these sentences opening *The Civilization of the Renaissance in Italy,* Burckhardt recognizes the tentativeness of cultural history and acknowledges the subjective element in historiography. It's a good place for all of us to start. Reconstruction of a distant past is at best partial and vulnerable to revision, and the project is made more difficult because even familiar facts may be interpreted in different ways and interrelated to produce various patterns.

I too am writing essays in cultural history, an attempt to identify the largest and most compelling features of English art (music, poetry, painting) during the sixteenth century. And I too feel the cautions and constraints confessed by Burckhardt. Especially in our poststructuralist environment, recovering the past has been fundamentally problematized by the assault on positivist historiography. We cannot ignore the arguments of Michel Foucault, Jacques Derrida, Hayden White, and Richard Rorty, to name just the leaders of the dissent. The course of human events is char-

1. *The Civilization of the Renaissance in Italy: An Essay,* trans. S.G.C. Middlemore, 3d ed., rev. (London: Phaidon, 1950), 1.

acterized by heterogeneity and disruptiveness—by the turbulence of competing discourses—rather than by continuity; and any account of those events is inevitably a human construct conditioned by the interests of the narrator. I have no wish to deny the premises of this attack or to refute its conclusions about historiography.

I am concerned, however, to avoid its counterproductive consequences. Traditional historiography has assumed that the past is in large part knowable and that it can be objectively recovered. But there is a growing consensus that nonpolemical history is impossible, with a concomitant feeling of frustration. A reliable account of former times lies beyond us. And not only is every history vulnerable to basic revision, but every theory of historical writing has been exposed as fallacious. We have only arguments that refute other arguments.[2]

The source of this quandary lies, I believe, in the error of mistaking epistemological problems for ontological certainties. Admittedly, we cannot know the past completely and accurately in every detail, and consequently our reconstruction of it is necessarily erroneous. This is a difficulty of knowing, however, and we are not warranted to extrapolate from these epistemological matters and jump to the ontological conclusion that the past is a cipher—not only unknowable, but inconsequential and even nonexistent. The act of knowing is relative to a perceiving subject, but the object of the inquiry enjoys an autonomous existence. The proclamation of Elizabeth as queen, for example, occurred quite apart from William Camden's—or any other historian's—recapitulation of it. Because historians cannot fully replicate events in a written text, then, does not prove that there is no such thing as history.

The point can be adumbrated in the now-ubiquitous dictum iterated upon the authority of Derrida: "History cannot exist independent of the text that inscribes it." If by "history" we mean the written reconstruction of an event by a human agent, the statement is self-evidently correct. But we are not justified in going beyond this admission and construing "history" to mean that which actually took place at a time in the past. Clearly, the objective reality of what actually takes place need not wait for its inscription in a written record. Those who wish to prove the relativism of history have tacitly changed its definition from "what has actually happened" to

---

2. For a candid shot of the rapidly deteriorating situation as this book goes to press, see Lawrence Stone's review of G. R. Elton, *Return to Essentials: Some Reflections on the Present State of Historical Study* (Cambridge: Cambridge University Press, 1991), in *Times Literary Supplement*, 3 January 1992, 3.

"what is later recorded in a historical narrative." Under the poststructuralist aegis, the argument that history cannot exist *hors texte* is, in fact, tautological, with a conclusion assured by the specious definition of its terms.

The crux I wish to highlight lies in the acceptance or rejection of an objective reality, a reality apart from author, text, or reader. Only a handful of poststructuralists have faced this crux directly and wrestled with its consequences. In the course of discrediting authoritative paradigms that literally predict fulfillment, though, the most rigorous deconstructionists have followed their arguments to the extreme of denying even the possibility of an objective reality. Neither a text nor a historical era has semantic stability. And this, it seems to me, is what finally separates poststructuralism from structuralism and its other predecessors. Poststructuralism is most clearly novel in its ontological premises and breaks with the Western tradition most decisively by refuting the transcendent signified that is posited by logocentrism in its many manifestations.

The present paralysis in historiography affects also literary studies—not only by rendering suspect the writing of literary history, but also by questioning the possibility of assigning meaning to a text. Traditional hermeneutics assumes that a text has a knowable meaning which can be recovered by a reader. But that also is under attack. In the preface to *Of Grammatology* Derrida makes the operative analogy between an earlier time and a text: "The age already in the *past* is in fact constituted in every respect as a *text*,"[3] and therefore reading either of these congeries of disparate data involves the same problems. Both epochs and texts contain concealed, marginalized, subversive elements that prevent totalization and preclude a stable, definitive interpretation.

The result of this threat to hermeneutics has been an increasing tendency to view the text as a system of signs that never reaches closure and consequently through an infinite series of deferrals escapes decipherment. The text becomes an indeterminate activity devoid of any capacity for particular meaning. Whether or not this result is theoretically inevitable, the practice, reductively, has led to the cul-de-sac of self-reflexiveness. Every text reflects upon its own processes and provides, at best, no more than an allegory of reading itself.[4] While the victory of poetics over hermeneu-

3. Trans. Gayatri Chakravorty Spivak (Baltimore: Johns Hopkins University Press, 1976), lxxxix.

4. As Paul de Man says on his first page, "Whether a further step . . . can be taken should not *a priori* or naïvely be taken for granted" (*Allegories of Reading: Figural Language in Rousseau,*

tics has given a boost to literary theory, this victory has undermined the plausibility of interpretation, not to mention its fashionableness.

Of Grammatology and its adherents have been very much in mind as I have written my own book. I have been attracted by both the continuities and the incongruities between Elizabethan and poststructuralist positions. Furthermore, I have been challenged by the feasibility of applying post-structuralist principles to the analysis of artifacts from a fundamentally— even belligerently—logocentric culture. In many ways the Elizabethans pre-pared for our contemporary world and belong to it. But also there are gross and irreconcilable differences between their ontological postulates and our own. So is it possible to say anything cogent about an earlier culture by applying principles that would have been anathema to it? Is poststructuralist analysis appropriate to texts from a premodern, essentially logocentric era? Is deconstructing a Renaissance text an exercise in irrelevancy, and there-fore futility? The answers to these questions are complicated, but hopeful.

Derrida's attack on logocentrism encompasses the assault on both pos-itivist historiography and hermeneutics. My concern, however, is not to refute Derrida and the deconstructionists, and certainly not to rail against their influence. There has been enough acrimony and handwringing, and it is time to move on.[5] Rather, I hope to take advantage of poststructural-ist insights and go beyond them in order to demonstrate a theory and praxis that preserve interpretation while eluding the limitations of posi-tivism as well as the pitfalls of poststructuralist thought.

Ultimately, practical (even political) concerns impel my defense of hermeneutics. The negation of hermeneutics removes any purpose for lit-erary studies, because a text without meaning is also without interest, except as a hypostatized object. Like an item of scientific investigation, it can be analyzed and I can learn *about* it; but I cannot interact with it, mentally or emotionally. I cannot assimilate it into my personal mind-set. More seri-ously, a text without meaning is also without influence on society, and there-fore without practical value. It cannot be contextualized. Analysis by decon-struction becomes no more than an intellectual exercise, a sanitizing, aestheticizing, and disempowering of the text. So I am concerned to devise a means of recuperating sixteenth-century English culture in such a way as to legitimize interpretation. I am not willing to forgo reading as enlight-

---

Nietzsche, Rilke, and Proust [New Haven: Yale University Press, 1979], ix), to which I shall return (page 108 below).

5. For a window onto the current state of affairs, see John M. Ellis, *Against Deconstruction* (Princeton: Princeton University Press, 1989), esp. preface and chaps. 1, 6, and 7.

enment, even enlightenment of a humanistic sort. To do so is to neutral-
ize the text, deprive it of effect, exclude context, and ignore the realpolitik.

Rather than pitting hermeneutics and poetics against one another, then,
as Paul de Man has done, and without privileging one at the expense of
the other, I want to license meaning in Renaissance texts in order to explore
their negotiations within the larger culture. After all, that is what Derrida
does in *Of Grammatology*. By his own account, "It is a question of a reading
of what may perhaps be called the 'age' of Rousseau" (lxxxix), and in part
2 he proceeds, despite denials, by telling us what Rousseau's texts mean.

I take my subtitle from George Puttenham's *Arte of English Poesie* (1589).
Puttenham devotes the second of his three main sections to what he calls
"proportion poetical," a phrase designating those formal features of a poem
induced by metrification, including the length of lines, the stanza form,
and the rhyme scheme. It is clear that such features are of fundamental
importance for Puttenham. They are, in fact, the source of beauty in the
poem and the basis for any ethical instruction of the reader. Aligning himself with a venerable tradition of defining the good, the true, and the beautiful in terms of mathematical ratios—a tradition grounded in platonist
discourse and revitalized for the Renaissance by Leon Battista Alberti—
Puttenham begins his first chapter: "It is said by such as professe the
Mathematicall sciences, that all things stand by proportion, and that without it nothing could stand to be good or beautiful."[6] Over the door of
Plato's Academy an inscription had denied entrance to anyone not trained
in mathematics—basically, the quadrivium later codified by Boethius: arithmetic, geometry, music, and astronomy. So Puttenham's opening sentence
announces allegiance to the classical lore of Plato as it had been institutionalized in Western culture.

Puttenham's next sentence, however, augments pagan authority by adding
the weight of Judeo-Christian doctrine: "The Doctors of our Theologie to
the same effect, but in other termes, say: that God made the world by number, measure and weight." Puttenham cites here a commonplace of the
Renaissance, an extract from the Book of Wisdom (11.21) found in many
discussions of poetry, painting, and music, and visualized in the familiar
image of God as a geometrizing deity with extended compasses setting
aside a circular portion of the abyss for his creation (see Fig. 28). Puttenham

6. *The Arte of English Poesie by George Puttenham*, ed. Gladys Doidge Willcock and Alice Walker
(Cambridge: Cambridge University Press, 1936), 64.

activates an ancient and revered discourse that recognizes proportion not only as the source of aesthetic properties, but of meaning itself. Formal features of an artistic work express the immaterial, hidden, and otherwise inexpressible ideas that in the platonist ontology underlie and sustain the transient world we inhabit.

This orthodox aesthetic persisted into the Renaissance and by means of adaptive modification has survived until our own century. With remarkable tenacity, formal features in works of art have endured as nonverbal signs, a subtext of form.[7] Gradually, however, beginning in the fifteenth century and quickening with time, a radical aesthetic emerged to accommodate the new ontology that assigned ultimate being to the sense-perceptible items of objective nature. The consequence has been a fundamental rethinking of what an artifact might represent and of how that representation might be achieved.

In this study directed toward England I pursue some of the ramifications of this shift when the orthodox and the new were most nearly in equilibrium. I have not attempted a comprehensive examination of the changes, nor do I claim that my hypotheses are exhaustive. Rather, I explore a few topics that in my judgment reveal the dynamics as well as the significance of this confrontation between conservative and radical worldviews. The result is five interrelated essays that constitute the chapters of this book.

As a way of laying out the salient questions, I begin by surveying the changing conception of Renaissance studies in the last hundred years and by noting the problems of periodizing in history. I conclude at the end of Chapter 1, provisionally, that the Renaissance can best be identified as that period when a radical, materialist aesthetic competed on equal terms with an orthodox, theocentric aesthetic. In consequence, analysis of any artifact from the period produces at least two competitive readings: one grounded in the *logos* as the sole referent for validation and evaluation (what is commonly called logocentrism), and the other grounded in a reality of matter and its palpable phenomena (what I call "hylocentrism").

7. I must distinguish my "subtext of form" from what Alastair Fowler has called "literary numerology" (*Triumphal Forms: Structural Patterns in Elizabethan Poetry* [Cambridge: Cambridge University Press, 1970], x). In numerology the meanings assigned to particular numbers are arbitrary, usually grounded in mysticism or mythology. The semiotic system of numbers that I invoke may also be seen today as culturally induced, but in a logocentric culture it would have been deemed natural, even divinely ordained. In the resultant poetics, formal features reflect the cosmic forms employed by the deity in the creation of our universe, and the numbers rarely exceed the numeral 12. In literary numerology, by contrast, the numbers are regularly much larger: for example, 666 the number of the beast and 108 the number of Penelope.

Successive chapters then elaborate this hypothesis, addressing from different directions the issues raised by poststructuralists and gradually shifting from the more orthodox position to the more radical. Chapter 2 displays the imperatives in the culture that promoted logocentrism and authorized a subtext of formal features that serve as nonverbal signs. Chapter 3 shows how these logocentric imperatives produced the fourteen-line sonnet as a means of encoding theological and philosophical optimism, and how later sonneteers played off the subtext of form against the verbal system of the poem. Chapter 4 reveals how companion poems became the testing ground for logocentrism versus hylocentrism, and how the debate became genderized. Chapter 5 explains how the introduction of perspective in painting licensed the use of similar strategies in literary narrative, so that framing devices allowed construction of a fictional reality to coexist with actuality.

As the chapters progress, I move from a focus upon those artifacts that support the logocentric culture by expressing it through formal features (such as metrics in poetry and proportion in the plastic arts), to a focus upon those artifacts that challenge and subvert the conservative culture by offering an alternative reality in a fiction. The ability of fiction to deconstruct the actual world by producing an alternative reality with truth-value is the final metamorphosis for the subtext of form during the Renaissance. The book is designed to exemplify the dual presence of both logocentrism and hylocentrism throughout the period when it is considered synchronically; and yet, when considered diachronically, the Renaissance moved from a dominant logocentrism to an incipient hylocentrism.

1 Romancing the Renaissance
The Perils of Periodizing

Even historiographers (although their lips sound of things done, and verity be written in their foreheads) have been glad to borrow both fashion and, perchance, weight of the poets.

—*Sir Philip Sidney*[1]

fter the last two decades of revisionist history, is the term "Renaissance" still viable in scholarly discourse? It persists in our language to indicate a period in European history roughly from the mid-fourteenth century in Italy to the mid-seventeenth century in England. Lately, however, use of the term has been challenged. Several difficulties have been noted, initially by those who question the advisability, or even the possibility, of periodizing history. Human events occur in uncontrolled succession and bewildering profusion, so to segment history into quasi-coherent entities such as the Renaissance or the Middle Ages or the Enlightenment is an artificial exercise that inevitably distorts. More recently (and most pointedly), because the Renaissance has been identified with logocentric humanism and recognized as a male-dominated culture, a determined attack has been mounted by those who subscribe to a variety of poststructuralist theories: the Marxists with their sympathy for the

---

1. *A Defence of Poetry*, in *Miscellaneous Prose of Sir Philip Sidney*, ed. Katherine Duncan-Jones and Jan van Dorsten (Oxford: Clarendon, 1973), 75.22–25. Later citations of this text will include page and line numbers, as here.

oppressed, the deconstructionists with their rejection of positivism, and the feminists with their attention to the marginalized. Some propose using the phrase "early modern Europe" as an alternative.[2]

Increasingly, in fact, there is a tacit accusation that anyone using the term "Renaissance" approves of the elitist imperatives that determined such a culture and wishes today to perpetuate its hegemony. So debate over the appropriateness of the term has decidedly political overtones. The phrase "early modern Europe," by intention, also indicates a political position, though an opposite, liberating one.

But there are problems also here. Those who use "early modern Europe" annex the Renaissance to the present, making everything since the Middle Ages, in a totalizing way, "modern." Even worse, they may be guilty of suggesting continuity, with the "early" modern period being the forerunner of what is classic modern. The untidy Foucauldian view of history, the basis of the objection to "Renaissance," is thereby similarly violated.

In any case, those who use "early modern Europe" evidently adopt a retrospective view of the period and see it in light of the present—not necessarily as the cause or the antecedent of the present, but as a congeries of data having no greater validity than any other directly observable phenomena. The past can be dealt with only as though it were present, only as it *is* present. The purists in this group, backed by a carefully argued theory refuting the positivist assumption that we can objectively recover the past, argue that we are able to know the past only through the questions that *we* formulate. History, as Hayden White concludes, is no more than a literary fiction of our own construction.

Use of the phrase "early modern Europe" announces this poststructuralist position, while it implicitly denounces logocentrism and its multifarious effects. In the poststructuralist view, use of the term "Renaissance" exalts a Eurocentric and phallocentric culture artificially constituted *post facto* by older, white, male historians who wish to prolong their political advantages, and therefore it must be abolished. The debate is serious and consequential.

The debate, however, is also reductive, because it polarizes the discourse and confines each side to a constricted position. There are other possi-

2. For the most comprehensive and compelling argument for the use of "early modern Europe," see Leah Marcus, "Disestablishing the Renaissance: New Directions in Early Modern Studies," in *Redrawing the Boundaries of Literary Studies,* ed. Stephen Greenblatt et al. (Modern Language Association, forthcoming).

bilities, according respect to the past while pushing for reforms in the present. I prefer the term "Renaissance" (albeit warily), for reasons I shall soon elaborate. In addition, I am prepared to laud the notable achievements of humanism, including the political institutions nurturing the intellectual and religious freedom that has produced poststructuralist thought. Our record is not to be totally decried. At the same time, however, I see no ineluctable progress in human affairs, and a simple trust in divine providence is no longer creditable. In the face of daunting problems, therefore, improvement lies in our ability to fashion a view of the human condition appropriate to our times. Debate over use of the term "Renaissance" encapsulates that struggle. Not surprisingly, it has become a focus of scholarly contention.

My particular argument, though, is that unless we know the past, its abominations as well as its successes, we run the danger of repeating its mistakes. The most naive of political positions is to relegate the past to the unknowable, and therefore to the disregardable. Revising the Renaissance so that it reflects our own concerns may give us a feeling of control over the present as well as the past, but it is a self-indulgent and ultimately pointless exercise. While the Renaissance—or, for that matter, any period in our history—is not a coherent entity that can be neatly reconstructed in accordance with the scientific model for describing a body of verifiable data, there are rewards in learning what we can about it. Facts (in the literal sense of "that which has been done") with varying degrees of certitude can be accumulated and interrelated; and as more information becomes available, the resultant hypotheses about history can be reviewed and updated.[3] There is no complete picture that we can reconstruct, piece by piece—a preexistent paradigm to be fulfilled. But neither should we acquiesce in the self-defeating notion that what we can know is, at best, subjective and therefore relative—and, probably, indeterminate. Such annihilation becomes a front for cynicism or a license for mayhem. Neither attitude will be productive within the university community or the larger society. Let's see, then, if we can find a path that skirts the old positivism while it avoids the new nihilism.

The Renaissance looms so bright on our cultural horizon that it has received perhaps a disproportionate share of scholarly attention. A large number

3. For an overlooked but valuable book that set the stage for the poststructuralist critique of historiography while avoiding its excesses, see Murray G. Murphey, *Our Knowledge of the Historical Past* (Indianapolis: Bobbs-Merrill, 1973).

of the most formidable reputations are based upon investigations into it:
E. H. Gombrich, Paul Oskar Kristeller, Erwin Panofsky, George Sarton, C.
S. Lewis, and Ernst Cassirer, to name just a few. Those giants still roam the
hermeneutic landscape. And yet the conception of Renaissance studies
has shifted radically in the last century.

Already by 1860 Jacob Burckhardt had elaborated the notion that certain changes originating in Italy during the fourteenth century permeated
Western Europe, giving both the period and the region a distinctive character. Burckhardt called this movement "the Renaissance"; and reflecting
Hegelian notions of human progress, he characterized it most concisely
as the emergence of the individual with a political consciousness.[4] Using
a wealth of carefully organized detail, he proposed a totalizing vision of a
heroic culture. He blithely assumed that a period known as the Renaissance
was identifiable as a coherent entity.

Burckhardt told us *what* the Renaissance was, but there remained uncertainty about its beginning. So next came the question, when was the
Renaissance?—a question recognizing the difficulty of setting temporal
limits in the continuous flow of time but not raising doubts about its actual
occurrence. In the opening paragraph of his monumental seven-volume
study published between 1875 and 1886, J. A. Symonds ventured a sug-
gestion: "We use it [the term 'Renaissance'] to denote the whole transition from the Middle Ages to the Modern World; and though it is possible to assign certain limits to the period during which this transition took
place, we cannot fix on any dates so positively as to say—between this year
and that the movement was accomplished."[5] Yet, pressed to be precise,
some proposed the fall of Constantinople in 1453 as its starting date, while
others pushed it back to Petrarch, and even Giotto and Dante. No consensus has ever been reached.

But determining the start of the Renaissance proved easy compared to
determining its end. Did it terminate with widespread adoption of the scientific method in the seventeenth century? With the triumph of reason in
the eighteenth century? With the industrial revolution in the nineteenth
century? With the rejection of prescriptive paradigms in the twentieth century? Has it ended yet?

4. William Kerrigan and Gordon Braden have recently reargued Burckhardt's essential
position, acknowledging a circular return; see *The Idea of the Renaissance* (Baltimore: Johns
Hopkins University Press, 1989), esp. 4-17. See also Charles Trinkaus, "Renaissance Ideas
and the Idea of the Renaissance," *Journal of the History of Ideas* 51 (1990): 667–84.

5. *Renaissance in Italy*, 2 vols. (New York: Modern Library, n.d.), 1.3.

Growing tired of that irresolvable debate and recognizing that our dating depends upon how we perceive the Renaissance, scholars then turned to the substantive question, What salient features grounded in historical change allow us to set the Renaissance apart from other periods? This discussion centered around the meaning of the term itself. Did the Renaissance signal a rebirth of the classical world after the dark ages of medieval scholasticism leading to a pagan humanism, or did it merely recognize the retrieval of certain classical texts that were added to the libraries of the learned without disturbing the main thrust of Christian authority?[6] Issues of radicalism and orthodoxy, of continuity and disruption, moved to the forefront.

Increasingly, the Renaissance was seen as the efflorescence of humanism, so the dispute focused upon the nature of the humanistic enterprise. Kristeller saw humanism as essentially a philological movement, Hans Baron characterized it by a dedication to civic virtue, while Eugenio Garin emphasized the importance it assigned to education. This debate was joined by Douglas Bush, who insisted that Christianity be factored into the discourse; humanism implied *Christian* humanism. Wallace K. Ferguson, posing as a synthesizer, saw in the Renaissance the birth of private enterprise: he characterized it by the development of a money economy to replace the feudal, agrarian economy of the Middle Ages, accompanied by an expanding urban society.[7]

But the difficulty of this last question addressing the nature of the Renaissance quickly broadened into a general, theoretical issue: Can we define a Renaissance at all (or, for that matter, any other period)? Any limits we set, temporal or ideological, depend upon the criteria we use in making the determination. And that realization poses an epistemological problem: How do we know that our definition of the Renaissance has any validity? Might it not be merely a product of our methodological assumptions? Hayden White culminates this line of thought by arguing that historians make their data conform to preexistent modes in the culture, such as comedy or tragedy or romance, in order to familiarize the unfamiliar and make it understandable.[8] Is our definition of the Renaissance any more than an artificial construct to explain what we claim to know about the period? Or

6. An influential study is Erwin Panofsky, *Renaissance and Renascences in Western Art* [1960], 2d ed. (New York: Harper/Torchbooks, 1969), esp. chap. 1.

7. "The Reinterpretation of the Renaissance," in *Facets of the Renaissance,* ed. William H. Werkmeister (New York: Harper/Torchbooks, 1963), 14–17.

8. "The Historical Text as Literary Artifact," in *The Writing of History: Literary Form and Historical Understanding,* ed. Robert H. Canary and Henry Kozicki (Madison: University of Wisconsin Press, 1978), 41–62.

rather, more honestly, what we choose to know? Already by 1948 Ferguson, in his painstaking retrospective of conceptualizations of the Renaissance, expressed the hope that "by viewing this phenomenon through the eyes of successive generations we might be able to see it for ourselves a little more clearly and completely, with a greater awareness of the subjective biases that tend to make us see it in this or that light."[9]

Recognizing these "subjective biases," must we not admit that any view of the Renaissance is unavoidably influenced by our own allegiances? As Jean E. Howard recently declared: "It seems necessary to abandon the myth of objectivity and to acknowledge that all historical knowledge is produced from a partial and a positioned vantage point."[10] Must not our view of the Renaissance, therefore, be fallacious, a fiction reflecting twentieth-century assumptions, even our own vested interests? Is it possible to reconstruct a past without malicious as well as egregious error? Louis Montrose in the most pointed manifesto of the new historicism explains: "Integral to this new project of historical criticism is a realization and acknowledgment that the critic's own text is as fully implicated in such an interplay as are the texts under study"; and he renounces "the illusory quest of an older historical criticism to recover objective, authentic, or stable 'meanings'."[11] Since we cannot know the past, is it not pernicious to propose a discussion of it in any terms other than our admittedly immediate and partisan ones?

And moving from politics to philosophical speculation, how do we know that a distinct event which we can identify by its own name even took place? Doesn't entertaining the possibility that we can define (both in the sense of delimit and characterize) a period in the past smack of intellectual presumption and folly? Given the inaccessibility of reliable data, our inferences are perforce illusive. The inevitable question formulates itself: Was there ever such a thing as "the Renaissance"?—a skeptical query that extends epistemological uncertainty until it undermines the validity of our evidence.

This series of questions charts the course of our own intellectual history over the last century from Victorian positivism, through existential angst, to poststructuralist indeterminacy and nihilism.[12] And this last observation leads to the conclusion that not only is history culturally determined, as

9. *The Renaissance in Historical Thought: Five Centuries of Interpretation* (Boston: Houghton Mifflin, 1948), 386.

10. "The New Historicism in Renaissance Studies," *English Literary Renaissance* 16 (1986): 22–23.

11. "Renaissance Literary Studies and the Subject of History," *English Literary Renaissance* 16 (1986): 7–8.

12. It is Paul de Man who most eloquently and convincingly leads us to this nihilism; cf.

Hayden White would have it, but also any theory underpinning historiography is equally a product of its times. Theories of history as well as history itself are little more than fashion.

Such a conclusion can then be taken in two opposite directions. We can dismantle history and the theories that license it: we can say that history and historiography are both no more than fabrications of the human mind, and therefore have no ontological validity, no authority. We can argue along with Montrose that there are no objective, authentic, or stable meanings to be recovered. Or we can make the Marxist argument insisting upon the potency of social context: we can say that historicity is a necessary dimension of any event, present or past, and that understanding any event, artistic or political, requires reconstruction of the circumstances which surrounded it. We can look for documents and hypothesize about occasions that anchor texts in actual occurrences.

In literary studies the new historicists have vacillated and tried to ignore this crux, sometimes denying an objective reality and at other times insisting upon the potency of extraneous circumstances. When expedient, they proceed in one direction with the deconstructionists; but just as readily, they troop in the other direction with the Marxists.[13] In consequence, I see the new historicists on an uncertain course, veering recklessly between

---

Blindness and Insight: Essays in the Rhetoric of Contemporary Criticism (New York: Oxford University Press, 1971), esp. chap. 1; and "The Resistance of Theory," in *The Pedagogical Imperative: Teaching as a Literary Genre*, ed. Barbara Johnson, Yale Studies in French 63 (New Haven: Yale University Press, 1982), 3–20. David Simpson has sought a way out of the shambles: "Literary Criticism and the Return to 'History'," *Critical Inquiry* 14 (1987–88): 721–47. For a denial of any breach between "old" and "new" historicism, see the Introduction by Heather Dubrow and Richard Strier to *The Historical Renaissance: New Essays on Tudor and Stuart Literature and Culture*, ed. Dubrow and Strier (Chicago: University of Chicago Press, 1988), 1–12.

13. Sensing the contradiction, Montrose counters by arguing the desirability of having it both ways ("Professing the Renaissance: The Poetics and Politics of Culture," in *The New Historicism*, ed. H. Aram Veeser [New York: Routledge, 1989], 15–36). Montrose links "the linguistic and the social" in correlative dependency, in what he calls "reciprocity and mutual constitution" (15); and he happily, if unwarrantedly, concludes: "Formal and historical concerns are not opposed but rather are inseparable" (17). But if the linguistic is defined in Saussurian terms as a system of differences only and in Derridean terms as the incessant deferral of meaning—as Montrose does when he denies the possibility of "objective, authentic, or stable" meanings (14 above)—then the inability of the text to mean renders it sui generis, irrelevant to everything except itself, and therefore impotent. "The propositions and operations of deconstructive reading," Montrose claims, "may be employed as powerful tools of ideological analysis" (15). But since in deconstructive reading, self-reflexively, the text becomes merely an allegory of reading itself, correspondingly when deconstructive reading is applied to historical data, that congeries of phenomena too will prove to be only

opposite dangers—a veritable Scylla and Charybdis that threaten not only the well-being of the crew, but also the safety of the cargo. On one side lurks the Scylla of deconstruction, prepared to snatch and destroy the precious text by rending it into dismembered gobbets; while on the other side the Charybdis of Marxist theory waits furtively to ingest it whole, sucking it down into the maelstrom of cultural studies.[14] Will our valiant voyagers make it safely to Ithaca? And back at home, will they find waiting for them faithful Penelope (a.k.a. the old historicism)? Tune in next decade, and find out—although the experience of Kerrigan and Braden may be prophetic. Meanwhile, however, the hermeneutic enterprise is in grave peril. Whether deconstruction or Marxism predominates, the text is consumed, demolished.

I therefore hope we can chart a safe passage through these curiously complementary dangers. What we need, of course, is a prudent way of periodizing, so that a text survives the ravages of deconstruction without being lost in the culture that accompanies and informs it.[15] Floundering forever in the roiling waves of indeterminacy leaves us just there: floundering.[16]

We have all had plenty of warnings about the perils of periodizing. Culler states flatly, "The identification of historical sequences, while an inevitable and indispensable aspect of literary study, is not just open to oversimplification; it is itself an act of oversimplification."[17] As Ferguson had earlier conceded, "It is an arbitrary construction imposed upon the unbroken flow of historical actuality."[18] More recent theorists, concen-

---

about itself—that is, it will prove to be a particular instance without further significance or application. For a stringent critique of Montrose's essay, see Hayden White, "New Historicism: A Comment," in the same volume, 293–302. For a more hopeful way of dealing with the problem, see Geoff Bennington and Robert Young, "Introduction: Posing the Question," in *Post-Structuralism and the Question of History*, ed. Derek Attridge, Bennington, and Young (Cambridge: Cambridge University Press, 1987), 1–11. See also, in the same volume, Jonathan Culler, "Criticism and Institutions: The American University," 82–98.

14. The impasse is elegantly described by David Quint, "Introduction," in *Literary Theory/Renaissance Texts*, ed. Quint and Patricia Parker (Baltimore: Johns Hopkins University Press, 1986), 15–16.

15. Gary F. Waller has incisively formulated the contretemps in "Author, Text, Reading, Ideology: Towards a Revisionist Literary History of the Renaissance," *Dalhousie Review* 61 (1981–82): 418–21.

16. A case in point: Montrose, "The Elizabethan Subject and the Spenserian Text," *Literary Theory/Renaissance Texts*, 303–40.

17. Jonathan Culler, *The Pursuit of Signs: Semiotics, Literature, Deconstruction* (Ithaca: Cornell University Press, 1981), 65.

18. *Historical Thought*, 393.

tratedly in the journal *New Literary History,* have dwelt upon the distortions that periodizing inevitably induces and have made it the cardinal sin of historiography.[19] These warnings are especially pertinent to Renaissance studies because historians have been most assertive in debating the autonomy of that period, which is also particularly vulnerable to predators.

We can, in fact, periodize the Renaissance right out of existence. Not only is it a potential casualty of poststructuralist theorizing, but it is susceptible to eradication also in the very practice of writing history.[20] The Renaissance can be seen as the end of an earlier era, the consummation of the Middle Ages. It is Augustinian Christianity renovated by humanism. Conversely, the Renaissance marks the origin of a new era, the beginning of modern Europe. For the first time the self-aware individual affirms personal rights in a secular, nationalistic state. The commonplace that the Renaissance serves as an age of transition, already enunciated by Symonds in the statement on page 12 above, implies this dissolution. The Renaissance itself disappears, distributed between its antecedents and its aftermath.

Such is the state of Renaissance studies today. We hear a cacophony of voices—sometimes despairing, sometimes angry. There are those who throw up their hands, saying we cannot reconstruct the past and therefore refusing to try. Here are the words of Richard Waswo, justifying his refusal to objectify history: "I fear that the past can be made to speak with no other voice than that of the ventriloquial present."[21] There are those who say the Renaissance has previously been defined in terms of an elite without taking into account the oppressed, or even the popular (these are the Marxists). Others say the Renaissance has been defined without due acknowledgment of the anomalous and the perverse (this is the deconstructive position). Others still, often adopting the Marxist and deconstructive arguments, say the Renaissance has been defined without recognition of half the population who were marginalized through gender

19. Individual issues of *New Literary History* have been devoted to the problematics of literary history: see "Is Literary History Obsolete?" 2.1 (1970–71): 7–192; and "On Writing Histories of Literature" 16.3 (1984–85): 447–679. The journal has also printed separate articles on this topic too numerous to list. For a dispirited but clear-eyed current assessment, see David Perkins, *Is Literary History Possible?* (Baltimore: Johns Hopkins University Press, 1992).

20. See Karl H. Dannenfeldt, ed., *The Renaissance: Medieval or Modern?* (Boston: Heath, 1959).

21. *Language and Meaning in the Renaissance* (Princeton: Princeton University Press, 1987), x.

discrimination (these, of course, are the feminists).[22] Previous accounts ignore the excluded and the subversive, the very elements that brought about change. Finally, some are beginning to say that scholars working in the Renaissance have interpreted texts in such a way as to reinforce a male ideology and thereby continue to support genderized attitudes in our profession.[23] Renaissance studies themselves have been elitist (the Marxist view) and reactionary (the deconstructive view) and patriarchal (the feminist view).

All of the above can find suasive grounds for their arguments.

Yet, it is difficult to forgo the project of identifying the Renaissance; and the term, despite efforts to the contrary, remains in use. The persistence of the term, which implies a substantial entity to serve as its signified, suggests that more is involved than merely custom or convenience. This term denotes an occurrence of perpetual consequence. There is more than just a personality difference between Aquinas and Voltaire: they are responding to fundamentally different cultural environments. Something decisive happened between their points in time, it is useful to give that something a name, and the name generally agreed upon is "the Renaissance." We can group together a set of related historical phenomena and call them by a collective label, just as we group together literary works and say they represent a corporate entity, a genre, at the same time recognizing that a genre can be identified only by virtue of its disparate constituents.

In fact, not to identify and characterize important events in the past is dangerous as well as naive. To intellectualize them out of existence is to make rewriting the past available to anyone, for whatever ulterior motive. If we can argue that there was no such thing as the Renaissance, we can argue also that there was no such thing as the Inquisition. Abominations disappear along with the rest of objective reality. In the same vein, we can argue away the Nazis and prove that World War II is misperceived, if it happened at all. As Stuart Schneiderman observes of Jacques Lacan's response to the war, "Doubtless he knew that the best way to think the unthinkable

22. Particularly pertinent here is Joan Kelly, "Did Women Have a Renaissance?" in *Women, History and Theory: The Essays of Joan Kelly,* ed. Catherine R. Stimpson (Chicago: University of Chicago Press, 1984), 19–50. See also *Rewriting the Renaissance: The Discourses of Sexual Difference in Early Modern Europe,* ed. Margaret W. Ferguson, Maureen Quilligan, and Nancy J. Vickers (Chicago: University of Chicago Press, 1986), esp. "Introduction," xv–xxxi; and Elaine V. Beilin, *Redeeming Eve: Women Writers of the English Renaissance* (Princeton: Princeton University Press, 1987), esp. "Introduction," xiii–xxiv.

23. E.g., Mary Nyquist, "Textual Overlapping and Dalilah's Harlot-Lap," *Literary Theory/Renaissance Texts,* 341–73; and Carla Freccero, "The Other and the Same: The Image of the Hermaphrodite in Rabelais," *Rewriting the Renaissance,* 145–58.

was first to empty it of all content."[24] And consider this conclusion reached quite gratuitously by de Man in an essay on literary modernity: "The bases for historical knowledge are not empirical facts but written texts, even if these texts masquerade in the guise of wars or revolutions."[25] My generation, though—the one that fought in World War II—was very much imbued with the Spenglerian notion that those who do not know history are condemned to relive it. The veracity of our data about that catastrophe cannot be shaken by epistemological maneuvers claiming that wars are only texts rendered invalid by necessarily subjective interpretation. I still have a small white hexagonal tile picked up from the rubble of Hitler's bathroom in Berchtesgarten.

So I lean toward the tarnished view of history as a recoverable past that we ignore at our peril. Some have willfully, even guilefully, declared the past unknowable in order to discredit any alternative to their own ahistorical position, in order to assert their own hegemony over a heritage that, if we cannot control, we can at least annihilate. Just as Roland Barthes slew the author in order to license the reader, so they obliterate the past in order to legitimize radicalism. But in the realpolitik such blindness is more likely to lead to further excesses than to constructive insight.

I am not prepared to accept the scientific model, however, and say the Renaissance exists as a monolithic event that can with patience be fully reassembled. There is no big picture we can put back together piece by piece. We live in a poststructuralist environment, and of course we face problems in historiography. But I believe these problems can be addressed effectively and actually turned to advantage. The poststructuralist critique of positivism can be put to valuable use. We can deconstruct the Renaissance in such a way as to give it a distinct identity.

First, I want to stop the clock and think of the Renaissance as something other than a durational stretch of time with a beginning and an end. To use Saussurian terms, I want to think of the Renaissance as a synchronic system, rather than a diachronic one. I view the Renaissance synoptically, with all of its constituent phenomena simultaneously present. I think of the Renaissance as a space rather than a time.[26]

24. *Jacques Lacan: The Death of an Intellectual Hero* (Cambridge: Harvard University Press, 1983), 175–76.

25. *Blindness*, 165. De Man's essay is in large part an advertisement for Nietzsche's advocacy of the "ability to forget and to live *without* historical awareness" (146).

26. This spatializing of the Renaissance may be justified by noting what happened to the writing of history during the period. The traditional chronicle, an account of events unre-

In fact, I will adopt a phrase of Foucault and conceive the Renaissance as "an epistemological space."[27] Such a space, be it noted, does not prescribe a fully determined set of circumstances. Quite the contrary. It is not a status quo, but an interval, a potential susceptible to incursion. It designates a field for activity, a common ground where competing discourses come together to confront, challenge, and subvert one another. But in such a space, although it provides a matrix for change, change itself does not occur.

This achronicity avoids any notion of continuity, while it precludes the description of the Renaissance as a coherently totalized entity. I recognize that my epistemological space encourages a confrontation of adversarial ideologies—thereby, I hope, placating the Marxists. I also admit, even welcome, the anomalous and the marginal—thereby, I hope, satisfying the

---

lentingly sequential, was confronted by a new mode that distributed history among localities in a regional survey. The confrontation is epitomized by William Harrison's *Description of England,* published with Holinshed's *Chronicles* in 1577. Other examples in sixteenth-century England include William Lambard's *Perambulation of Kent* (1576) and John Stow's *Survey of London* (1598); see William Keith Hall, "A Topography of Time: Historical Narration in John Stow's *Survey of London,*" *Studies in Philology* 88 (1991): 1–15. The trend to deconstruct the temporality of history by spatializing it was further developed in elaborate new atlases with maps offering a great deal of historical information, such as Christopher Saxton's atlas of the English counties (1579) and John Speed's *Theatre of the Empire of Great Britain* (1611). For the same trend on the Continent, note the Galleria delle Carte Geografiche in the Vatican (1580–83); cf. Iris Cheney, "The Galleria delle Carte Geografiche at the Vatican and the Roman Church's View of the History of Christianity," Southeastern Renaissance Conference, University of Kentucky, Lexington, 8 April 1989. The new deconstructed history with maps proved extremely popular, as evidenced by the many editions of William Camden's *Britannia* (illustrated with maps after 1607) and Michael Drayton's *Polyolbion* (1612).

27. Michel Foucault, *The Order of Things: An Archaeology of the Human Sciences* (New York: Pantheon/Random, 1970), xi. At basis, Foucault and I are following Ferdinand de Saussure in his distinction between synchronic and diachronic linguistics. Saussure first wishes to ignore the changes in a language through time in order to study it as a contemporaneous system (what he calls "a linguistic state"), although he recognizes the impossibility of excluding the temporal dimension: "In practice, a linguistic state occupies not a point in time, but a period of time of varying length, during which the sum total of changes occurring is minimal. It may be ten years, a generation, a century, or even longer" (*Course in General Linguistics,* trans. Roy Harris [London: Duckworth, 1983], 99). Saussure does not deny diachrony (cf. 78), and therefore his linguistic theory does not prescribe exclusively an ahistorical methodology, as some invoking his name have assumed. For him, synchrony with its insensitivity to change is simply one of two viable choices, each with liabilities; and he adopts synchronism first in order to allow the consideration of a language as a self-consistent, fixed system of signs. But he later devotes an entire section to "diachronic linguistics" (139–81).

In my nonlinear historiography I have been influenced also by Jacques Derrida, esp. his comments on history in *Positions* [1972], trans. Alan Bass (Chicago: University of Chicago Press, 1981), 56–60.

deconstructionists and feminists as well. Obviously, the Renaissance as I have conceived it invites deconstruction. As our model we can follow the definitive deconstruction of Zeno's paradox offered by Derrida.

Zeno the Stoic, like the sect that he founded, dealt with objective reality not by intellectualizing it out of existence, but by recommending an impassive indifference to it. All circumstances must be endured with the same equanimity. Toward this end, he set out to demonstrate that change, despite all appearances, cannot occur, and he took as his exemplary case the flight of an arrow. We think of an arrow as traversing a distance, moving from point A to point Z, undergoing change. But since an arrow must be in some precise location at each moment of its trajectory, its flight is not continuous motion, but rather a series of discontinuous positions. In actual fact, at any given moment in its flight the arrow is fixed in space, and there is no way to account for how the arrow moves from one position to another. It seems to move, but there can be no explanation for its motion. In consequence, Zeno logically concluded, motion—and its concomitant, change—is only illusory.

In this instance, logic is inconsistent with our experience: we observe that the arrow does move; and being empiricists in a materialist culture, we discredit Zeno. But while Zeno's argument is patently unreasonable, it is extremely difficult to refute, and therefore it is often called a paradox. Derrida, though, has exploded the premises of Zeno's argument. And rather than seeking to counter it, he sets about exploiting it for his own deconstructive purposes.[28]

Derrida accepts Zeno's premise that at any moment the arrow is fixed in a circumscribed location, motionless. But he goes on to note that implicated in this position is a past which has led the arrow to this point, as well as a future which will carry the arrow beyond it. The arrow's position as an entity disappears, becoming no more than a function of this past and future. The momentary position of the arrow becomes no more than the dimensionless point where past is demarcated from future. Each point in the arrow's flight, then, actually indicates a rupture, a moment of discontinuity where past and future come together and delimit one another. Derrida reveals the binarism inherent in the individual moment, which (like Foucault's epistemological space) becomes a matrix for change.[29]

28. I rely upon the skillful reconstruction of Derrida's argument by Jonathan Culler, *On Deconstruction: Theory and Criticism after Structuralism* (Ithaca: Cornell University Press, 1982), 94–95.

29. My post-poststructuralist analysis of the Renaissance can draw sustenance also from

Notice, though, how Derrida's adaptation of Zeno's paradox eludes narrativity—that is, it removes temporality as a factor in the course of events. The state of affairs at any moment is described in an abstract way that is true for every moment, so the movement from point A to point Z becomes a series of identical occurrences independent of sequentiality. Analysis of any moment is equally valid for every moment, since every particular moment comprises in the same way both past and future. Just as important, notice that each of these opposing entities is operative at all times; neither can ever be excluded or ignored. Any moment within the Renaissance implicates a past that stretches backward into the Middle Ages as well as a future that extends forward to our own day.

At the risk of being simplistic, I shall now characterize that past and that future.[30] The past stretching backward into the Middle Ages is dominated by an idealist ontology defined by Christianized platonism. The ultimate constituents of its reality, that to which all else must be referred for meaning, are the essences in Plato's world of being or, when Christianized, the attributes of God in a neoplatonist heaven. For the Renaissance the past was essentially a logocentric culture that recognized the originary authority of Christ as *logos*.[31] In contrast, the future stretching forward to our own day is dominated by a materialist ontology defined by empiricism.[32] The ultimate constituents of its reality, that which provides the source for all truth, are the components of physical nature. To describe this culture I have devised a term to be symmetrical with "logocentric": I call it "hylocentric," based upon the Greek ὕλη, the word that Aristotle used to designate matter.

---

the history-of-ideas study by Rosalie L. Colie, *Paradoxia Epidemica: The Renaissance Tradition of Paradox* (Princeton: Princeton University Press, 1966). While eschewing any notion of a zeitgeist, Colie demonstrates that the Renaissance is characterized by "a paradoxical mode of perception which deliberately intermixed material from very different categories—such as, in ontology, 'being' and 'becoming'" (xii–xiii).

30. By making a space for the Renaissance in the flow of events I have, inevitably, reduced the past to a monolithic entity, and have done the same for the future. The present is brought into existence to the discredit of both past and future, which may in turn be analyzed as "epistemological spaces." Saussure had a similar problem of defining diachronic linguistics as anything other than a succession of discrete "linguistic states."

31. For a concise description of this culture, see Edgar de Bruyne, *The Esthetics of the Middle Ages*, trans. Eileen B. Hennesy (New York: Frederick Ungar, 1969). For an update, see Umberto Eco, *Art and Beauty in the Middle Ages*, trans. Hugh Bredin (New Haven: Yale University Press, 1986). For the importance of *historia* in this culture, a concept that persisted into the Renaissance, see Stephen G. Nichols, Jr., *Romanesque Signs: Early Medieval Narrative and Iconography* (New Haven: Yale University Press, 1983).

32. For the opinion of an art historian on this point, and the resultant praxis he adopts,

Each moment of the Renaissance, then, comprised a past with a reality grounded in platonic essences, but also a future with a reality grounded in the phenomenal world. Always operative and equally viable was an orthodox logocentrism as well as a radical hylocentrism. Although logocentrism and hylocentrism are mutually exclusive as philosophical systems, each of these options was simultaneously available in the culture—indeed, they were equally unavoidable, and neither could be disregarded. In consequence, when interpreting an artifact of the period we must take into account both paradigms. A poem, for example, participates in two discrete, though intersecting, discourses: one governed by the logocentric rules of idealism, and the other by the hylocentric rules of empiricism.

My analysis of the Renaissance as an epistemological space indifferently hospitable to both logocentrism and hylocentrism is especially useful for illuminating the interrelationship among the arts in the Renaissance. Although the fine arts were not yet segregated as a class, certain arts— notably music, poetry, and painting—were highly developed and widely practiced. Within the coordinates of logocentrism and hylocentrism we can readily devise a taxonomy for these arts.

Today in the backwash of Romanticism we are likely to think of music as the purest expression of the creative ego and the arouser of emotions. Certainly, music is an acoustic event. But in the theory of music that the Renaissance inherited from the Middle Ages it was conceived as a system of mathematical ratios addressed to the reason, the *ratio,* of the percipient. The tuning system itself, by legend going back to Pythagoras, was derived "rationally" from relationships between the first four integers: 1, 2, 3, 4.[33] It comprised a finite scale of eight notes determined by arithmetical calculation—what we still call an octave; and harmony consisted of proportions between these mathematically determined points on a continuous scale of sound. Mathematical ratios could be realized not only in harmony—that is, in the relationship between the pitch of notes—but also in rhythm, in the relationship between the duration of notes (for example, whole notes, half notes, and quarter notes). So music was conceived as a system of mathematical ratios, and it was "rational" in the sense that it was aimed ultimately at the reason (the *ratio*) of percipients rather than

---

see Martin Kemp, *The Science of Art: Optical Themes in Western Art from Brunelleschi to Seurat* (New Haven: Yale University Press, 1990), 1.

33. See my *Touches of Sweet Harmony: Pythagorean Cosmology and Renaissance Poetics* (San Marino, Calif.: Huntington Library, 1974), 95–97.

the body's faculty of hearing.[34] Music activates the inherent mathematical forms in the human soul as Timaeus had explained them (*Timaeus* 35A–37C), causing it to reverberate sympathetically and thereby awakening an awareness of its own nature as a microcosm participating in the divine scheme of things. This theory also underlies the efficacy of David the psalmist when he played before the deranged Saul.

To the extent that poetry exhibits mathematical ratios, it also submits to this theory and enjoys this efficacy, as the prototype of David's psalms indicates. If poetry is defined as metrified language, it assimilates to music. The metrics of a poem are comparable to the measures of a musical composition.

The long-lived and indefatigable Thomas Churchyard (c. 1520–1604), who began publishing during the reign of Edward VI and lived into the reign of James I, represents the older generation of Elizabethan poets still writing under the assumption that poetry is closely allied to music. Despite the literalness with which he treats his subject matter and the pedestrian quality of his verse, Churchyard doggedly clung to the doctrine that poetry is identified by its metrification. *Churchyardes chance* (London, 1580), for example—a miscellany of clumsy epitaphs, epigrams, and extended lyrics— was put together as a new year's gift for Sir Thomas Bromley, the Lord Chancellor, and in the dedicatory epistle Churchyard talks about the usefulness of poetry as a respite from burdensome responsibilities. It has restorative powers because of its harmony. "The minde," he warns, "wearied with over long labours, and sadde motions of the spirite (that through continuance, maie dull the senses) is sharpened and made better at commaundement, when chaunge of pastymes with some pleasaunt exercises hath eased the bodie, and refreshed the memorie" (a3v–a4). To this end, he continues, "I have tuned all my notes and songes worthie the hearyng, into one kind of voice and order." Churchyard makes his pitch for a readership on the basis of being a "Musition"; like David playing before Saul,

34. See Manfred F. Bukofzer, "Speculative Thinking in Mediaeval Music," *Speculum* 17 (1942): 165–80; Bruce R. Smith, "The Contest of Apollo and Marsyas: Ideas About Music in the Middle Ages," in *By Things Seen: Reference and Recognition in Medieval Thought,* ed. David L. Jeffrey (Ottawa: University of Ottawa Press, 1979), 81–107; and Andrew Hughes, "Music, Western European," in *Dictionary of the Middle Ages,* ed. Joseph R. Strayer, 13 vols. (New York: Scribner's, 1982–89), 8.578–95. For a full exposition of the discipline of music at the opening of the sixteenth century, see Giorgio Valla, *De expetendis, et fugiendis rebus opus* (Venice, 1501), e6–m8. The difference between music to be apprehended by the soul and music to be heard by the ear may be exemplified by the difference between Gregorian chant and a Liszt sonata. In Keats' refined opinion, "Heard melodies are sweet, but those unheard / Are sweeter" ("Ode on a Grecian Urn," 11–12).

he will bring harmony to the soul distracted by business. His aesthetic assumptions and his very vocabulary derive from a conception of poetry as a musical (i.e., metrified) art.

Therefore, not surprisingly, Churchyard entitles a later volume *A musicall consort of heavenly harmonie (compounded out of manie parts of musicke) called Churchyards charitie* (London, 1595), dedicated to Robert Devereux, earl of Essex; and in a prefatory epistle "To the generall Readers," he voices the same sentiments using the same vocabulary (A4). This volume is not a miscellany, though, but a joining together of two dissimilar long poems: first, "Churchyardes charitie" (pages 1–23), a descant on "charity" in the Christian sense of universal love (or, rather, the paucity thereof), written in rime royal; and second, "A praise of poetrie" with a separate title page (pages 25–43), written in the ballad stanza.

In "A praise of poetrie," Churchyard (purportedly in echo of Sidney) insists that the poet must inculcate virtue, and he achieves this aim by his poetic skill:

> As though a sweete consort should plaie
> On instruments most fine
> And shew their musicke evry waie
> With daintie notes divine.
> . . . .
> Not farsed full of follies light
> That beares ne poies nor weight
> But flying cleere in aire like flight
> Whose force mounts up an height.
>
> (pages 33–34)

Churchyard concludes: "Such poets Sidney likes." But given the obsolescence and redundancy of Churchyard's verse, it is no wonder that his presumptuous gifts of poetry to the power brokers of the realm went largely unrewarded.

Nevertheless, the assimilation of poetry to music persisted as a strong imperative in the culture; and poetry, like music, automatically activated the logocentric doctrine. For their interpretation the metrics of a poem must be referred to the Christianized platonic reality, because the ratios of metrical forms are grounded in such idealism—as Churchyard says, their "force mounts up an height." The more capacious mathematical patterns informing a poem—such as an annual calendar or the seven days of creation—also have signifying power and as logocentric signs must be similarly interpreted.

Conversely, however, to the extent that poetry is descriptive, producing pictorial images referrable to the material world, poetry approaches the plastic arts. Poetry is related by its sense-based properties (especially the production of verbal imagery) to painting, and requires an empiricist epistemology. Sidney proposed a poetics of "speaking pictures," primarily depictive and narrative. In this hylocentric aesthetic the existence of the artistic work rests in its palpable phenomena; and therefore, since the phenomena as perceived are disjunctive and diverse, the artistic work submits to deconstruction.

In a strictly hylocentric culture where matter is the ultimate reality, meaning can be generated only by reference to the objects of physical nature. A literary work can mean, therefore, only so far as it describes the world we know from sense experience. A poem, although it may retain a metrical arrangement, becomes a word-picture relying upon accurate description, such as Thomson's *Seasons;* and in contrast to the logocentric lyric, the meter and rhyme are applied merely as decoration after the subject matter is laid out. The metrics lose their power to signify. Quite predictably, the novel *in prose* becomes the more comfortable mode of literary expression. It can describe without the encumbrance, without the embarrassment, of metrics. And Aristotle's formula for mimesis, the imitation of the actions of human beings, is adapted to serve as a license for describing human beings in action. *Poetike* becomes primarily a descriptive and narrative art.

The point, quite simply, is that poetry through its formal properties approximates music; while by virtue of its depictive capacity, poetry assimilates to painting. Moreover, because of this connective position in the family of the arts, poetry in the Renaissance was exalted above its siblings. Poetry was at once both musical and painterly, activating the soul by its metrics at the same time it stimulated the mind's eye with its images.

Any poetical artifact, therefore, must be analyzed for both its musical and its painterly components. Put another way, for its full interpretation any poem must be read within the context of the logocentric aesthetic, which allies poetry to music, but also within the context of the hylocentric aesthetic, which allies poetry to painting. As a result, the poem produces two different, perhaps competitive, readings: one where formal properties are the primary textual data, and another where primacy is assigned to the language that produces images referrable to physical nature. Formal properties acquire meaning in accordance with an idealist ontology; verbal images acquire meaning in accordance with an empiricist ontology, where transmission through sense perception introduces a subjective element of play that licenses ambiguity and unpredictability.

Furthermore, we must recognize that each of these disparate aesthetic programs encodes an ideology. The logocentric aesthetic asserts the doctrine that Christ is the *logos,* the primordial signified lying behind all the signifiers in the book of nature. The logocentric aesthetic is orthodox, authoritative, patriarchal. In contrast, the hylocentric aesthetic assumes that the ultimate referent for meaning is not Christ as *logos,* but rather the random phenomena of material objects. The hylocentric aesthetic is radical, relativistic, and nongendered. Just as the formal properties of poetry serve, however unwarrantedly, as a metonym for God's providential scheme, disruption in a literary work is a metonym for uncertainty, anxiety, alienation, and despair.

An exercise will show how my proposal works in practical exegesis. My exemplary text is a poem by the earl of Surrey, which in Tottel's miscellany is given the title "Description of Spring, wherin eche thing renewes, save onelie the lover."[35] Actually, Surrey adapted a well-known sonnet by Petrarch, so by intertextuality it incorporates an undeniable past. But it also creates a continuous present in which we participate, so it implies as well an ongoing future. My analysis explores the epistemological space occupied by Surrey's lines.

The soote season, that bud and blome furth bringes,	a
With grene hath clad the hill and eke the vale;	b
The nightingale with fethers new she singes;	a
The turtle to her make hath tolde her tale.	b
Somer is come, for every spray nowe springes;	a
The hart hath hong his olde hed on the pale;	b
The buck in brake his winter cote he flinges;	a
The fishes flote with newe repaired scale;	b
The adder all her sloughe awaye she slinges;	a
The swift swalow pursueth the flyes smale;	b
The busy bee her honye now she minges;	a
Winter is worne that was the flowers bale.	b
And thus I see among these pleasant thinges	a
Eche care decayes, and yet my sorow springes.	a

35. *Songes and sonettes,* ed. Richard Tottel (London, 1557), A2v.

At first glance, this is a simple, straightforward statement by a mourning lover who recognizes that nature enjoys renewal in the spring, a renewal in which he does not take part and therefore which makes his anguish all the more painful. As twentieth-century readers conditioned by the empiricist aesthetic, we note its careful and extensive description of nature, a spring replete with flora and fauna.[36] Not only are animals in abundance, but also the birds and the bees, and even fishes and snakes. A luxuriant and sensuous world. The older among us, trained in New Criticism (the acme of the empiricist aesthetic), are likely to call this language "imagery," and we might comment upon its "affectiveness," upon how it elicits a buoyant response from the reader. No complications, no problems in the first twelve lines. As for the last two lines—well, the reversal in sentiment is what we expect in the concluding couplet of a sonnet. The lover, full of despair, a concomitant of mortality, separates himself from the rest of nature reveling in renewed vitality. The scholar in us nods knowingly: Oh, yes! this is an old theme in love poetry, going back at least as far as Ovid. Spenser was later to employ it as the overarching motif to provide organization for *The Shepheardes Calender,* his twelve eclogues proportionable to the twelve months concluding with Colin Clout's farewell to his world. This reading of Surrey's poem, attentive to its language and its verbal images, occurs under hylocentrism where the empiricist aesthetic applies. This reading results from scrutiny of the painterly qualities of the poem. It is the future implied in Surrey's moment.

This reading, however, fails to take note of a whole category of textual data: the formal properties of the poem. But they cry out for attention. What, for example, is the signifying power of its anomalous rhyme scheme comprised of only two sounds? Was Surrey doing more than simply imitating Petrarch when he chose to compose a fourteen-line poem, a quatorzain? What can we make of the way the last word, "spring," takes us back to the poem's opening phrase, "the soote season"? Does the blatant alliteration do more than call attention to the artifice? Surely such care, evident in the production of such diverse formal properties, is not accidental, or even casual. Surrey expended considerable effort to sophisticate his poem with a variety of forms with semantic potential quite apart from what the language of the verbal system might say. To ignore these nonverbal signs is to exclude a sizable and prominent portion of the textual data.

36. William A. Sessions makes the usual observation: "The poetic text itself becomes a landscape, as it were, of solid actuality"; and again, "[Surrey's] landscape is actual and concrete" (*Henry Howard, Earl of Surrey,* Twayne Series [Boston: G. K. Hall, 1986], 55–56).

They constitute the musical qualities of the poem, and to interpret them aright we must apply the logocentric aesthetic.

Let's begin with the most aberrant nonverbal sign, the rhyme scheme. It is an extraordinary alternation of only two rhymes, concluding in a rhymed couplet. The peculiarity and artfulness of such restricted patterning demands interpretation. Surrey is paraphrasing an earlier poem, a sonnet of Petrarch, but the original exhibits none of this cunning: it conforms to one of Petrarch's familiar rhyme schemes involving five sounds. Surrey's reduction from five to only two is notable, then, if not unique, and he must have consciously decided upon this artifice. But what does it mean?

When this nonverbal sign is referred to logocentric principles, its significance becomes obvious. The alternation between a and b rhymes is an ideogram for time, represented regularly as a binary system of alternating states, such as the opposites of day and night comprising the diurnal unit of time. But more is implied here. While day and night taken together define a unit of time, they also perpetually follow one another, so that in their continuous succession they extrapolate to eternity.[37] Similarly, the annual unit of time, the year, can be represented as a binary system comprised of opposites, spring and winter, as Shakespeare does in the songs between the cuckoo and the owl at the end of *Love's Labor's Lost*. Those contraries also, repeated in endless succession, eventuate in eternity.

And that temporal motif underlies the dynamics of Surrey's poem. The spring-world, emerging from winter, undergoes renewal and will continue this cycle ad infinitum—a realization that makes the lover's mortal finitude all the more debilitating. The finality of the rhymed couplet sounds like a death knell. Moreover, in the couplet the focus of attention shifts dramatically. For the first time the persona steps forward into full view and speaks of himself in the first person. The matter-of-fact description of physical nature gives way to the emotion-charged outburst of an individual. We move from an objective reality to the subjective realm of human perceptions and responses. This transport from objectivity to subjectivity indicates a disruption that serves as a metonym for the lover's despondency and fear of death.

Rather than signaling a simple end, however, the two rhymed lines of the couplet represent a stasis, a point where change no longer occurs. Motion has been allayed, subsumed into the ultradynamics of perfection. The two rhymed lines by their coherence and sameness reveal the arrival

37. See Milton's lines that serve as epigraph to chapter 4 (page 119 below). Sidney has one sonnet with only two rhyme words, which perhaps not wholly by chance are "night" and "day" (*A&S* 89).

at an absolute. The lover, along with eternal nature, has been assimilated into the logocentric ideal. Limited to the mortal sphere, the lover can see only debility and defeat; but viewed *sub specie aeternitatis,* he participates unknowingly in the providential scheme as it unfolds in the course of kind. Contrary to his own perception, he will ultimately enjoy salvation, everlasting bliss beside the throne of God.

This participation in time—a time that through dilation reaches to eternity—is confirmed by the oxymoronic last words of the poem: "sorrow springs." "Sorrow" is identified with baleful winter, and yet surprisingly it "springs," a pun on its seasonal opposite. This is a curious choice for the last word if the poem is to end in despair. But of course "springs" returns us to "the soote season that bud and blome furth brings," the opening of the poem. The double alliteration of "sorrow springs" and "soote season" confirms this continuity, this endless repetition. Alpha and omega coincide. In the end of the lover lies his beginning. As a later poet puts it, "Death, be not proud."

The optimism of this reading is consistent with—I will even say, predicted by—Surrey's choice of the quatorzain as his stanza form. We hylocentrists don't think of the fourteen lines of the sonnet as having the power to signify, but this form is highly significant to a logocentrist. As I explain in chapter 3 (pages 73–78 below), the nonverbal sign of the quatorzain's form is theologically optimistic. No matter if the division into octave and sestet is obscured, as in Surrey's poem. There is in the quatorzain a persistent and irrefutable subtext expressed in this form, an affirmation of God's love and mercy. The arrangement of octave and sestet with concluding couplet assures eventual arrival in the presence of God. The form itself promises salvation.

The significance I assign to the mathematical arrangement of the octave/sestet is corroborated by a reexamination of the alternating rhyme scheme of Surrey's poem. If we take an *a* and *b* rhyme together to represent one unit, like day and night represent the diurnal unit of time, we have six such units. There are six *a-b* units, analogous to the six days of creation. But these six units eventuate in a seventh unit of a different order. The final couplet rhymes *a-a;* there is no longer change. This last unit, of course, represents the sabbath. Again, we arrive at a beatific stasis, rejoicing in the presence of the deity. The optimistic form of Surrey's rhyme scheme reiterates the inherent optimism of the fourteen-line sonnet.

This pious reading of the poem, licensed by the logocentric aesthetic and full of hope, is evidently at odds with our first reading under the auspices of the hylocentric aesthetic. The painterly properties of Surrey's poem lead to one reading: although the lover participates in a natural world that enjoys renewal, he does not possess this capacity for self-perpetuation; so his body will suffer dispersal among the ever-changing phenomena of physical nature. But the musical properties of Surrey's poem lead to a contrary reading: because the lover participates in the infinitely repeated cycles leading to eternity, he (like nature) enjoys beatitude and, unbeknownst to him in his mortal and pessimistic state, is destined for heaven.

Which shall we choose—the optimistic or the pessimistic reading? Are the two meanings reconcilable? Is reconciliation desirable? Why not disparate, alternative readings? That is, pluralism. Is pluralism theoretically justifiable or practically feasible? What is a reader to do with mutually exclusive readings, each valorized by a viable poetics? These questions form the nub of the discourse in the essays that follow.

To conclude here, though, let me return to the somewhat easier task of defining the Renaissance. My proposal, quite simply, is that the Renaissance may be defined as the time during which literary works exhibit this dual referentiality, a reference simultaneously to both a logocentric and a hylocentric reality. The Renaissance is that period, whatever the actual years might be and in whatever geographic area, when the logocentric *and* the hylocentric ontologies were both operative and equally available to artificers, regardless of the medium they worked in.

As a result, we find this urge for dual referentiality affecting the other arts as well as poetry. There were musical compositions that imitated sounds experienced in actual circumstances, bringing music under the alien jurisdiction of the hylocentric aesthetic. Already in the fourteenth century Guillaume de Machaut had experimented with natural sounds in his songs, and Clément Janequin in the sixteenth century composed long chansons based upon bird calls, street cries in Paris, sounds of the hunt, and noises heard in battle. From the opposite direction, in painting, Alberti invited us to view the picture as a window through which we see actual nature. But in the same treatise he introduced single-point perspective and demonstrated that all objects in space are interrelated by mathematical laws which, though invisible, are nonetheless irrefragable and verify a single, comprehensive authority. Painting was placed under the alien jurisdiction of the logocentric aesthetic, as evidenced by the harmonious composition of the most admired works by Raphael.[38]

38. In addition to Raphael, Piero della Francesca and Leonardo da Vinci were early to utilize the proportional relationships in the perspective construction to harmonize their

Most readily of all, though, the Renaissance can be identified as the period when poetry was equally musical and painterly, and when poets exploited the semantic potential of signifying in both ways.

---

paintings—to imbue them with musical significance and ally them with the Pythagorean tuning system; see Martin Kemp, *Geometrical Perspective from Brunelleschi to Desargues: A Pictorial Means or an Intellectual End?*, Proceedings of the British Academy 70 (London: Oxford University Press, 1985), 95–101: "Leonardo felt that he was dealing with a form of visual music, which he expressed most tellingly in the *Last Supper,* where the ratios of the widths of the tapestries on the wall plane are $1 : 1/2 : 1/3 : 1/4$" (100).

According to Francisco de Hollanda, Michelangelo in a conversation of 1539 disapproved of Flemish painting because of its verisimilitude and lack of formal features: "In Flanders they paint with a view to external exactness. . . .They paint stuffs and masonry, the green grass of the fields, the shadow of trees, and rivers and bridges, which they call landscapes, with many figures on this side and many figures on that. And all this, though it pleases some persons, is done without reason or art, without symmetry or proportion." The great artist insists upon a subtext of form to give the painting rationality, and he continues: "For good painting is nothing but a copy of the perfections of God and a recollection of His painting; it is a music and a melody which only intellect can understand" (Hollanda, *Four Dialogues on Painting* [1558], trans. Aubrey F. G. Bell [1928] [Westport, Conn.: Hyperion, 1979], 16). Well into the seventeenth century, Henry Peacham subscribed to this theory; echoing Aristotle's statement that plot is the soul of tragedy (*Poetics* 1450b40), he says: "Symmetry or porportion is the very soule of picture" (*The art of drawing with the pen, and limming in water colours* [London, 1607], C2v).

2 Socrates and His Versified Aesop
The Subtext of Form

Poesie is a skill to speake & write harmonically: and verses or rime be a kind of Musicall utterance.

—George Puttenham[1]

 n 1591 Sir John Harington contributed to the venerable tradition of what he called "Heroicall Poesie" by publishing a verse translation of the *Orlando Furioso*. Clearly apprehensive about the reception of his work, he prepared a preface that exposes the conflicting currents in literary theory near the end of the sixteenth century.[2] Neo-Aristotelians such as Julius Caesar Scaliger and Philip Sidney, adopting the novel hylocentric aesthetic and identifying poetry with mimesis, had licensed a new sort of fictive narrative, acceptably in prose. At the same time, however, the logocentric imperatives requiring metrical form were still in force, and the lyric was at its high point. As Harington puts it, repeating a platitude of the day, there are two disparate elements in a poem: "that principall part of Poetrie, which is fiction and imitation; and . . . the other part of Poetrie which is verse" (204.11–13). At risk on one side was

---

1. *Arte of English Poesie*, 64; cf. 8.
2. G. Gregory Smith, ed., *Elizabethan Critical Essays*, 2 vols. (London: Oxford University Press, 1904), 2.194–222. Later citations of this text will include page and line numbers.

the truth-value of the new fiction; and on the other, the necessity for the conventional rhyming and versing.

As a conscientious man of letters, Harington had consulted the appropriate authorities, and he stakes out a mediating position in the debate. He makes it clear that he has read Sidney's *Defence of Poesie,* even though at that time it existed only in manuscript, and he follows Sidney's lead in defending poetry against its detractors. Harington is mindful also of Puttenham's *Arte of English Poesie,* which (as Harington observes) had been published a scant two years earlier. So he relieves himself of the need to deal with the "definitions of a Poet and Poesie, & with the subtill distinctions of their sundrie kinds; nor to dispute how high and supernatural the name of a Maker is" (196.12–15)—all topics that Puttenham as well as Sidney had satisfactorily covered. This disclaimer clears the way for Harington's central concern: the continuing requirement of metrics in a literary work. His uneasiness is evident in the brusqueness with which he pretends to be disinterested: "Least of all do I purpose to bestow any long time to argue whether *Plato, Zenophon,* and *Erasmus* writing fictions and Dialogues in prose may justly be called Poets, or whether *Lucan* writing a story in verse be an historiographer, or whether Master *Faire* [i.e., Phaer] translating *Virgil,* Master *Golding* translating *Ovids* Metamorphosis, and my selfe in this worke that you see, be any more then versifiers" (196.18–25).

What is at stake, of course, is the very definition of poetry. Is poetry to be defined essentially as metrified language, a verbal system disposed according to formal features that organize the sounds to approximate music, as the orthodox aesthetic would have it?[3] Or instead is poetry to be defined by "fiction and imitation," a narrative with a plot devised by a maker, as neo-Aristotelians had begun to argue vociferously? Aristotle himself had brought the question to crisis. In the *Poetics* he had made mimesis the sine qua non of poetry, disallowing verse as sufficient or necessary. Furthermore, to exemplify his point Aristotle had declared that Empedocles was no poet even though he had composed in meter, while Herodotus would still be a historian even if transformed into verse

3. The basic document for such a tradition is Augustine's *De musica;* see Robert J. O'Connell, S.J., *Art and the Christian Intelligence in St. Augustine* (Cambridge: Harvard University Press, 1978), chaps. 3–4. For a study of how Augustine's *De musica* informs medieval and Renaissance prosody, see William H. Pahlka, *Saint Augustine's Meter and George Herbert's Will* (Kent, Ohio: Kent State University Press, 1987). For the earlier period, see also Robert R. Edwards, *Ratio and Invention: A Study of Medieval Lyric and Narrative* (Nashville, Tenn.: Vanderbilt University Press, 1989), esp. chap. 1.

(1447b16–23, 1451a36). During the late Renaissance, Scaliger (whom Harington mentions prominently) had confused the issue by betraying Aristotle and asserting with bluster that, although the poet may well be a maker, he is a maker of verses, not plots.[4] Sidney had leapt into this fray and, while respectful of Scaliger, had returned to Aristotle's strict definition of poetry as mimesis. "Poesy," he explains, "is an art of imitation, for so Aristotle termeth it in the word μίμησις" (79.35–36). And to reinforce his position, a few pages later Sidney says by way of negative definition: "It is not rhyming and versing that maketh a poet" (81.33–34).[5] Puttenham invokes the controversy in the first paragraph of his treatise; but, no doubt because of honest confusion rather than a wish to conciliate, he waffles: "The very Poet makes and contrives out of his owne braine, both the *verse* and *matter* of his poeme, and not by any foreine copie or example, as doth the translator, who therefore may well be sayd a versifier, but not a Poet" (3; italics mine).

In his nervous statement about who may be rightly called a poet or a historiographer (196.18–25, quoted above), Harington feels the need to confront these contentious issues. He is especially wary of being called a mere versifier and no poet, so his statement bristles with the new vocabulary devised to debate the nature of poetry. He is familiar with the derivation of "poet" from ποιεῖν (to make), as Sidney had recalled in the *Defence*, and with Puttenham he accepts Sidney's observation that "we Englishmen have met with the Greeks in calling him a maker" (*Defence* 77.35–36). In addition, the poetics implied by this term had generated a neologism, "fiction," similarly derived from a classical language and meaning "that which has been made."[6] "Fiction" comes from *fictus*, the past participle of *fingere*, the Latin cognate of ποιεῖν. With the sense of "making" in accordance with Aristotelian mimesis, "fiction" implies an imitation (but not replication) of nature that encapsulates a universal truth: what might be or should be according to probability or necessity (*Poetics* 1451a36–38).

Moreover, Harington plays with the ambiguity of *historia*, recognizing that the word implies both history as a record of actual occurrence and

4. *Poetices libri septem* (Lyons, 1561), 202, 210–11.

5. For a full account of Sidney's complex attitude toward metrification, see my *Sidney and Spenser: The Poet as Maker* (University Park: Pennsylvania State University Press, 1989), 239–46.

6. Harington was fond of the new word "fiction," and he later uses it as an appositive for both the Aristotelian term "imitation" (204.11–12) and the rhetorical term "invention" (204.16). For Harington, in fact, the three words were almost synonymous; cf. 207.25–26.

history as fictive narrative, a "story."[7] Plutarch had licensed this ambiguity in "How the Young Man Should Study Poetry,"[8] an essay that Harington soon mentions by name; and Spenser had sorted through its implications for the poet when he distinguishes between the "historiographer" and the "poet historical" in the letter to Ralegh appended to *The Faerie Queene*. Although Harington evidently hopes to preclude dismissal as a mere "versifier," he nonetheless shies away from pursuing these issues to a conclusion and instead refers his reader to Sidney's *Defence*, where "[such questions] are discoursed more largely, and where, as it were, a whole receit of Poetrie is prescribed" (196.26–30).

In this context of apologizing not just for poetry, but specifically for rhyming and versing, Harington retrieves a bookish topos from the antique world. It comes in an extended discussion of Plato, who had been ambivalent about poetry, sometimes extolling it as a sacred fury while at other times decrying it for immorality. Nonetheless, as many in the Renaissance observed, because of his mythmaking Plato himself could qualify as a poet, even though he never wrote in meter. As Harington says, "*Plato* still preserved the fable,[9] but refuseth the verse" (203.33). Harington's primary purpose, though, is to justify the use of meter in poetry; so while he concedes that Plato wrote only prose, he recalls that Plato's mentor, Socrates, had spent considerable effort to compose in meter. Harington brings this passage on Plato to a triumphant conclusion by grandly stating: "Yet his master *Socrates* even in his old age wrote certaine verses, as *Plutarke* testifieth" (204.13–14).

This is the topos that interests me: "*Socrates* even in his old age wrote certaine verses." What curious bricolage! Socrates, of course, left no writings, much less anything in meter. So to hear that he wrote verses in his old age is quite a surprise. But Sidney, too, had been diverted by it. Even while declaring an allegiance to Aristotle, Sidney contrarily condones rhyming and versing. And as he warms to the task of defending poetry by listing the famous men who have patronized poets or who have themselves been poets, Sidney repeats our topos: "Even the Greek Socrates, whom Apollo confirmed to be the only wise man, is said to have spent part of his old time in putting Aesop's fables into verses" (109.11–14). The context of the topos in Sidney is simi-

---

7. Later Harington speaks of "historical narration, either true or feigned" (202.7), the usual adjectives used by Elizabethans to distinguish between historiography and made-up fiction.

8. See my *Sidney and Spenser*, 173–77.

9. "Fable" (L. *fabula*) was at this time the preferred term for Aristotle's μῦθος, what we usually call "plot."

lar to that in Harington. By citing Socrates' versification of Aesop, Sidney creates an intertextual space in which he not only expresses his praise for poetical making, but also valorizes what metrics contribute to the mimesis.

When we pursue Harington's citation of Plutarch, we find the reference in the essay that Harington and Sidney had been reading, "How the Young Man Should Study Poetry." And we can readily understand why they had pored over this section of the treatise: it deals with Plutarch's defense of poets from the charge of lying (16A–C). Of course poets lie, concedes Plutarch, because the truth is too stern to bear. Consequently, in the good cause of wooing the gentle reader to well-knowing, the poet is allowed a certain license to mitigate actuality in order to produce an attractive story: "Fiction, being a verbal fabrication, very readily follows a roundabout route, and turns aside from the painful to what is more pleasant." Moreover, confirming Aristotle, it is this fiction that gives poetry its special quality: "For not metre nor figure of speech nor loftiness of diction nor aptness of metaphor nor unity of composition has so much allurement and charm, as a clever interweaving of fabulous narrative (μυθολογία)." And at this point, out of context and subversive to his own argument, Plutarch cites our topos: "This explains why Socrates, being induced by some dreams to take up poetry, since he was not himself a plausible or naturally clever work-man in falsehood, inasmuch as he had been the champion of truth all his life, put into verse the fables of Aesop."

Harington's source gives more particulars than he. Plutarch specifies that the verses written by Socrates were a metrical rendition of Aesop's fables. And not surprisingly Plutarch here, as so often, serves to popular-ize Plato. Plutarch in turn had picked up this odd bit of information from one of Plato's most poignant and memorable dialogues, the *Phaedo* (60B–61B), widely known among Christian humanists because of its assurances about the immortality of the soul. In the *Phaedo*, a narrative of Socrates' final hours, the reference to his metrified Aesop is incidental, and at first glance puzzling. Socrates, who previously had composed no poetry, spent his time in prison turning Aesop's fables into verse in response to some persistent dreams. But to what purpose?

According to Phaedo's account, Socrates on the last day of his life was sitting on his bed and talking to his friends. He had not yet drunk the hem-lock, although the passage under scrutiny introduces the discussion about the soul's immortality which leads Socrates to meet his death willingly. Xantippe holding their infant had taken her final farewell amid much grief. After her departure, Socrates rubs his legs, sore from being bound, and offers an impromptu lecture on pain and pleasure. He comments upon their complementarity—how they are opposites, and yet how they inevitably follow one another; and he speculates aloud:

> *Aesop,* if he had taken notice of the thing, would have composed a Fable of it, namely, that God, when he attempted to reconcile these two Enemies, *Pleasure* and *Pain,* making War each against other, but could not effect it, bound their heads together, so that where either comes, the other also must follow, as seemed to me even now.[10]

These musings by Socrates remind Cebes of something he has recently heard and prompt him to interrupt. "Many have asked me," Cebes says, "concerning the Poems you have of late made, particularly the Fables of *Aesop,* you have turned into Verses, and a Hymn to *Apollo*: for what reason you composed those Poems, since you came into this place, when you never before addicted your self to Poetry." To Cebes, one of the most devoted disciples, Socrates then replies:

> I have done this . . . to make trial, what might be the sense of some Dreams, and to know if they injoyn'd me this kind of *Music.* For very often heretofore in my life, the same Dream occurred to me; when appearing to me sometimes in this, sometimes in that figure or representation, it still inculcated to me the same thing: alwaies saying, study *Music Socrates,* and practise it . . . for as much as Philosophy is the noblest and most excellent *Music.*

Socrates asserts a belief in dreams, which throughout his life had directed

10. I quote from the earliest English version of the *Phaedo*: Plato, *His Apology of Socrates, and Phaedo,* trans. anon. (London, 1675), 90–93. Baldassare Castiglione drew from this portion of our topos: "Socrates saith well in Plato, that hee marvaileth that Esope made not an Apologus or fable, wherin he might have fained that God, since hee coulde never couple pleasure and sorrow together, might have knit them with an extremitie, so that the beginning of the one should have beene the end of the other. For wee see no pleasure can delite us at any time if sorrow goeth not before" (*The Book of the Courtier,* trans. Sir Thomas Hoby, ed. W.H.D. Rouse, Everyman's Library [London: Dent, 1928], 89).

Sidney read our topos in Plutarch's essay, but he may have known it also directly from Plato. For evidence that Sidney was otherwise familiar with the *Phaedo,* see John Gouws, "Fact and Anecdote in Fulke Greville's Account of Sidney's Last Days," in *Sir Philip Sidney: 1586 and the Creation of a Legend,* ed. Jan van Dorsten, Dominic Baker-Smith, and Arthur F. Kinney (Leiden: Brill, 1986), 65–66.

him toward proper action, and he readily submits to their authority:

> I thought it safer, not to depart from hence, before I had . . .
> performed my Vow; obeying my Dream, by making Verses. The
> first Poem I made therefore, was to that God whose Feast this
> was.[11] After that devout care of God, conceiving it decent for a
> Poet, if he ought to be reputed worthy of that name, to com-
> pose Fables, not orations; and being my self unskilful in the art
> of inventing Fables: I therefore made an Essay upon the Fables
> of *Aesop*, which I had by me.

In the context of this long passage from the *Phaedo,* then, Socrates metrifies
Aesop in order to satisfy a divine command to produce music, which he
equates with philosophy. Philosophy, in fact, "is the noblest and most excellent *Music.*"

The Greek word translated here as "music" is μουσική—literally, whatever is produced under the aegis of the Muses. Regularly in Plato, as in
most Greek authors, the term implies not simply melody and harmony,
but also a verbal text. It is, in fact, closer to what we today mean by "poetry"
than to what we mean by "music." The poet accompanied himself on a
lyre, like Orpheus—or, to use an example from the Bible, like David the
psalmist.[12] For the Renaissance syncretist, Homer singing was the prototypical poet/musician.[13]

11. That is, Apollo. In his life of Socrates, Diogenes Laertius records what he claims to be
the opening of this hymn and two lines of verse purportedly the beginning of a fable by
Aesop (*Lives of Eminent Philosophers*, 2.42).

Late in the seventeenth century Socrates' Aesop was still a viable topos in squabbles over
ancient texts. Richard Bentley used it to argue that what we have are not fables by Aesop,
but spurious tales of a later date; see William Wotton, *Reflections upon Ancient and Modern
Learning . . . Also, A dissertation upon the Epistles of Themistocles, Socrates, Euripides, &c. and the
Fables of Aesop, by R. Bentley* [1698], 3d ed. (London, 1705), 457. For Charles Boyle's caustic
refutation of Bentley, see Boyle, *Dr. Bentley's Dissertations on the Epistles of Phalaris, and the
Fables of Aesop, Examin'd* (London, 1698), 236–40.

12. Renaissance humanists quickly co-opted this tradition in order to explain the ability
of the Bible to bring the Christian to godliness. Aldo Pio Manuzio published a quatrain
lifted from Arator and frequently repeated:

> Metrica vis sacris non est incognita libris,
>   Nam psalmos lyrici composuere pedes.
> Exametris constare sonis in origine linguae
>   Cantica Jeremiae, Job quoque dicta ferunt.

(The force of metrics is not unknown in the Holy Scriptures, for the psalms

The full implications of this incident in the *Phaedo* now become apparent. Socrates, like Harington after him, recognizes two distinct and perhaps incongruous elements in a poem. There must be a fable (narrative); but just as necessary, to fulfill the prescription for μουσική, there must also be meter (formal properties like the measures of music). Aesop's fables in a prose version lacked music, and therefore fell short of philosophy. To endow Aesop's prose with truth-value, however, required no more than metrifying the language. The meter transmutes narrative into μουσική, placing it under patronage of the Muses. Thereby Socrates followed the divine dictate of his dreams, and the writing of poetry accords with his lifelong practice of studying philosophy and speaking only the truth.

One final point before leaving the *Phaedo*. Note that Aesop's fables exist prior to Socrates' transformation of them. The prose text is anterior to the metrified version and literally prescribes it. Socrates' versified Aesop is a derivative of the original. But yet, for Socrates a narrative even as overtly didactic as a fable was deficient in truth-value if not accompanied by the supplement of meter. Rather than being incidental, then, meter is essential, the sine qua non of poetry that claims to purvey truth. Socrates makes the prose fable a subset of, and therefore inferior to, the metrified version. By a reversal so important to a deconstructionist, it is the verse that gives value to the prose. It is the supplement that authorizes the original.

In the platonist system, in fact, priority is regularly given to formal properties, and mathematical forms become a major means of signifying. The basis for this practice can be found in the *Timaeus*, the only text of Plato known directly during the millennium between the classical world and the Renaissance. That momentous dialogue offers a cosmogony in which cre-

---

are composed in lyric measures. And in their original language the lamentations of Jeremiah as well as the complaints of Job are said to have consisted in hexameters.)

(*Poetae Christiani veteres*, 3 vols. [Venice, 1501–4], 2.aa1v)

For the original text in Arator, see the dedicatory verses to Pope Vigilius that he placed before "In apostolorum acta, libri duo," published in *C. Juvenci, Coelii Sedulii, Aratoris sacra poësis* (Lyons, 1553), 226. For a later version, as well as cogent discussion of it with references to both Christian and classical authorities, see Marcantonio Natta, "De poëtis liber," in *Opera* (Venice, 1564), fols. 110–14.

13. For an invaluable study of this tradition, see Claude V. Palisca, *Humanism in Italian Renaissance Musical Thought* (New Haven: Yale University Press, 1985). For its earlier manifestations, see John Stevens, *Words and Music in the Middle Ages: Song, Narrative, Dance and Drama, 1050–1350* (Cambridge: Cambridge University Press, 1986), esp. 13–47 and 375–409.

ation proceeds as the deity imposes insubstantial forms upon preexistent matter to produce the items that comprise our universe, much as Socrates imposes meter upon the prose of Aesop.

Even after the platonist tradition was Christianized, this act of creation served as the model for all creative acts, including the composition of poetry. In such a poetics a poem is necessarily composed in meter because formal properties are intrinsic, and the readiest way a poet can manifest the requisite proportions and harmonies is by rhyming and versing. A line in the biblical Book of Wisdom, repeated endlessly by the literati as well as theologians and natural scientists, proclaims: "God created the universe according to number, weight, and measure" (11.21). And with an amplitude of gesture, syncretists applied this dictum to the Timaean demiurge as frequently as to the Hebraic-Christian Jehovah. It was almost as often applied to the poet.[14] The poet also composes according to number, weight, and measure—unless, Sidney notes admonishingly, "number, measure, order, proportion be in our time grown odious" (100.32–33). So in this poetics, poetry is defined as metrified language. A poem is comprised of well-weighed syllables. It is a mathematical system reflecting celestial beauty, since the poet is a Timaean maker. Shakespeare began as an apprentice in this school; and even at the end of his career, he considered his plays to be a species of poesy and felt compelled to write in meter. Milton, as we know from his preface, was struggling with the cultural demand for rhyme as late as *Paradise Lost*.

Plato's *Timaeus*, then, describes the prototype for the creative act and

14. Cristoforo Landino, a Florentine platonist cited by Sidney (*Defence*, 121.15), provides the conventional comparison:

> Just as God arranges His creation—that is, the visible and invisible worlds which is His work—according to number, measure, and weight (as the prophet proclaims *Deus omnia facit numero, mensura, et pondere*), so the poet constructs his poem with the number of metrical feet, with the measure of short and long syllables, and with the weight of sententious sayings and of passions.
> (quoted from my *Sidney and Spenser*, 181)

Puttenham's "Second Booke, Of Proportion Poetical" (*Arte of English Poesie*, 64–136) is, of course, a compendium of the resultant poetics; cf. also 6–9. This orthodox discourse persists today; for a handsome example, see Gyorgy Doczi, *The Power of Limits: Proportional Harmonies in Nature, Art and Architecture* (Boulder, Colo., and London: Shambhala, 1981). For a survey of recent scholarship on how this discourse affected the Elizabethans, see P. J. Klemp, "Numerology and English Renaissance Literature: Twentieth-Century Studies," *Bulletin of Bibliography* 40 (1983): 231–41. For a discussion of how this discourse conditioned early stringed musical instruments in Europe, see Kevin Coates, *Geometry, Proportion and the Art of Lutherie* (Oxford: Clarendon, 1985). For a statement of this discourse in surrealist art, see Salvador Dali's *Sacrament of the Last Supper* (1955) in the Chester Dale Collection of the National Gallery of Art in Washington, D.C.

delineates the forms that the creating deity imposed upon preexistent matter. In general terms, he proceeded according to numerical principles of proportion or, more musically, of harmony.[15] Specifically, the deity utilized the tetrad pattern, which reconciles two pairs of opposites to produce a dynamic but stable arrangement of four basic qualities: hot, cold, moist, and dry.[16] These are the irreducible constituents of the cosmos, and from them derive the four elements, the four humours that comprise the human microcosm, the four seasons of the year, and so forth. The tetrad, in fact, is the fundamental pattern that underlies each of the multifarious systems which make up our universe. By means of this repeated pattern, the demiurge produced an integrated array of correspondences that obtain throughout creation. The result is a vast complex of natural metaphors.

The tetrad itself, though, has no substance. It is immaterial, and cannot be perceived by mortal senses except through its imprint upon matter to produce physical systems. Such thinking is difficult for us, but a more familiar example will help. In a textbook of geometry, the figure of a circle does not represent a particular, concrete circle, but rather the concept of a perfect circle. The form printed on the page that we perceive with our sense

15. In his "Table Talk" (8.2), Plutarch transmitted those principles from the *Timaeus* of greatest pertinence here; see the section, "How *Plato* is to be understood, when he saith: That God continually is exercised in Geometry," *The morals*, trans. Philemon Holland (London, 1603), 767. The *Timaeus* was assimilated by early Christian writers such as Augustine, Isidore of Seville, and Bede, and its doctrine was found everywhere in the Renaissance.

Quoting Boethius, John Dee in his "Mathematicall praeface" to Euclid provides a cogent example in English: "All thinges (which from the very first originall being of thinges, have bene framed and made) do appeare to be Formed by the reason of Numbers. For this was the principall example or patterne in the minde of the Creator" (*The elements of geometrie*, trans. Henry Billingsley [London, 1570], *1). Then in the spirit of Plato's *Phaedrus* (246A–247C), which describes the human soul as a winged creature, Dee exhorts his reader to "arise, clime, ascend, and mount up (with Speculative winges) in spirit, to behold in the Glas of Creation, the *Forme* of *Formes*, the *Exemplar Number* of all thinges *Numerable*." Dee here is drawing upon Heinrich Cornelius Agrippa, *Three books of occult philosophy*, trans. John Freake (London, 1651), 170–72. (This text was first completely published as *De occulta philosophia libri tres* [Cologne, 1533].) Cf. also Saint Augustine, *De libero arbitrio voluntatis: St. Augustine on Free Will* [2.11, 16], trans. Carroll Mason Sparrow, University of Virginia Studies 4 (Charlottesville: University of Virginia Press, 1947), 63, 71–72. For the vigorous continuation of this tradition into the seventeenth century, see William Ingpen, *The secrets of numbers: According to theologicall, arithmeticall, geometricall and harmonicall computation* (London, 1624). Of course, it was by contemplation of such numbers/forms/ideas that, as Sidney put it, the mind is lifted up from the dungeon of the body to the enjoying its own divine essence (82.26–27). Later in the *Defence*, though, Sidney reveals ambivalence toward this tradition and jokes about it (93.22–24).

16. On the tetrad, see my *Touches of Harmony*, 160–74; and *Cosmographical Glass: Renaissance Diagrams of the Universe* (San Marino, Calif.: Huntington Library, 1977), 99–110.

of sight is only a crude visualization of the ideal circle involved in the geometrical proof. Similarly, the forms in the platonist realm of essences can be reduced to material representation in palpable objects, though they themselves are not material.

The tetrad, then, is an insubstantial form. It is, to be accurate, no more than a potential, a schematic representation of relationships which may be realized in actual objects, but which exists prior to and independent of matter. This is what Plato meant by the word *idea*. His term *idea* translates to our word "form," which similarly should be understood to signify a potential of relationships rather than physical extension.

The point is forcefully demonstrated by a passage in Philemon Holland's translation of Plutarch's *Moralia*. In the table of contents for "The Opinions of Philosophers," Holland provides this title for chapter 10 in book 1: "Of the Forme called *Idea*."[17] The chapter itself then runs in toto as follows:

Chap. X.
Of *Idea*.

Idea is a bodilesse substance [literally, "that which underlies"], which of it selfe hath no subsistence, but giveth figure and forme unto shapelesse matters, and becommeth the very cause that bringeth them into shew and evidence.

SOCRATES and PLATO suppose, that these *ideae* bee substances separate and distinct from Matter, howbeit, subsisting in the thoughts and imaginations of God, that is to say, of Minde and Understanding.

ARISTOTLE admitteth verily these formes and *Ideae*, howebeit, not separate from matter, as being the patterns of all that which God hath made.

The STOICKS, such as were the scholars of *Zeno*, have delivered, that our thoughts and conceits were the *Ideae*.

17. *Morals*, 802. For the expression of this doctrine by Augustine, see Russell A. Peck, "Number as Cosmic Language," in *By Things Seen: Reference and Recognition in Medieval Thought*, ed. David L. Jeffrey (Ottawa: University of Ottawa Press, 1979), 47. For an expression of it in the Renaissance (actually a Latin redaction of the passage in Plutarch), see the chapter "De idea, seu forma" in Valla (kk4). Agrippa made it current throughout the Renaissance: "*Platonists* say that all inferiour bodies are exemplified by the superiour *Idea's*. Now they define an *Idea* to be a form, above bodies, souls, minds, and to be one, simple, pure, immutable, indivisible, incorporeal, and eternall . . ." (26; see also 171). For the causal process by which this "form" produces effects, see Agrippa, 30–31. For application of this doctrine in practical instructions for sketching, see Peacham, C2–C4.

Here in brief compass we see the word *idea* transmute from a supernal form that nonetheless may be imposed upon matter, through an Aristotelian version where it indeed becomes material, to its present-day meaning of merely a subjective thought. In the platonist discourse that I am delineating, however, an idea or form remained an unalterable and immaterial design ultimately lodged in the mind of deity.

As a result, Greek *idea* covers mathematical forms such as the four-part tetrad—but also, the seven-part week of the heptaemeron, the eight-part diapason in music, and the twelve-part calendar. The term covers as well a quasi-mathematical concept such as beauty, which is determined by its proportion (the relation between part and whole) and by its harmony (the relations between part and part). *Idea* covers also such concepts as justice and friendship, which to us seem divorced from mathematics but which to platonists *must* derive from number since they, like beauty, are ideas (forms) and therefore should submit to mathematical analysis. Justice is said to be four-square, equal on all sides; and friendship is "one for all and all for one." When taken to extremes, this is the sort of wackiness that left platonism vulnerable to attack, and seventeenth-century empiricists marginalized platonism, forcing it into magic and mysticism. But the privileging of formal properties follows logically from the cosmological premises expressed in the *Timaeus,* and it explains the notice reportedly placed over the door of Plato's Academy forbidding entrance to anyone not trained in mathematics.

The purpose of this tortuous excursion into platonist cosmology has been to show that mathematical form and philosophical concept are not incompatible, as in our present-day hylocentric culture, but rather are both implied in the single Greek word *idea*. It is also clear that this mode of thought would result in a culture characterized by logocentrism. The term "logocentrism" designates a culture centered in language, a reasonable observation about the Renaissance humanists; but it implies much more than that. The Greek *logos* does not mean the uttered word, but rather the idea that the uttered word signifies. To use Saussurian terminology, the *logos* is the signified, not the signifier. In the popular gospel according to Saint John, Christ appears to humankind as the *logos,* and of course he brings a message of uttered words. But what counts is the meaning of his message, the doctrine, the *logos*. That, rather than its verbalization, is what existed in the beginning.

And this *logos* also shades into numerical forms. Although today the Greek term is most usually translated simply as "word," the primary meaning of *logos* is "plan," an arrangement, a *schema*. In Latin it was regularly translated as *ratio*, where it stands behind the mathematical term "ratio," but where of course it also means "reason."[18] *Ratio* in Latin, like *idea* in Greek, embraces both mathematical form and philosophical concept, consonant with a logocentric culture.

So logocentrism implies that a culture is language-centered, but only because language expresses ideas. The culture places authority in forms, in the potential for relationships. All things, in fact, are interrelated in a vast network determined by the numbers/forms/ideas residing in the mind of deity. And in our cultural history as long as Christ is conceived as the *logos*, logocentrism remains a viable force. At the end of the sixteenth century in England, despite the disruptions and contradictions that deconstructionists can so readily discover, it remained a central determinant in the culture.

Given the dominance of logocentrism at the time, is it appropriate to analyze Renaissance works by applying the conclusions of deconstruction, which dictates an ontology opposed to logocentrism? As we have just seen, logocentrism posits an objective reality identified as an unalterable, immaterial realm of absolute being and described as a nonpalpable system of numbers/forms/ideas in the mind of deity. In opposition, poststructuralist thought pushes us beyond skepticism and relativism, arriving at a subjectivism that annihilates all else.

Derridean deconstruction not only rules out the possibility of our knowing an objective reality (if it existed), but even precludes the possibility that it might exist. According to rigorous poststructuralists, phenomena must be relative to the percipient alone, since all anterior conditions are dismissed. Origin or authority of any sort is denied, and the linkage of cause-effect is severed. In the absence of all other referents, *reality* must be relative to the percipient. There can be no objective reality. The very truth that art is supposed to lead us to in a logocentric culture is denied an existence in a poststructuralist environment. So is it not futile to deconstruct

18. The range of L. *ratio*—covering the modern meanings of both "reason" and "mathematical ratio"—is exemplified by Bede: "It should be noted that all art operates by virtue of *ratio*. Music also consists in and is contained in the *ratio* of numbers" (Notandum est, quod omnis ars in ratione continetur. Musica quoque in ratione numerorum consistit atque versatur) ("Musica theorica," in *Opera*, 8 vols. [Basle, 1563], 1.403). Throughout his "De musica" Augustine uses *ratio* in this dual sense ("On Music," trans. Robert C. Taliaferro, in *Writings of St. Augustine*, Fathers of the Church, 6 vols. [Washington, D.C.: Catholic University of America Press, 1947], 2.153–379).

the texts of Dante or Petrarch or Spenser or Milton? Are not the conclusions foregone, predetermined by the methodologies themselves? Is it not just as pointless as analyzing Pound's *Cantos* solely in terms of the numbers and measures of the verse, where of course we would find only the logocentric imperatives at work?

Let us begin our answer by recapitulating Derrida's attack on logocentrism. He is right in his description of logocentrism, although he guarantees his conclusions by analyzing it in terms of Saussure's negative view of the linguistic sign. By any account, though, logocentrism is indeed grounded in platonist discourse that extols an originary power and sees the things of this world as derivatives of a supernal force.

For a concise definition of logocentrism as Derrida conceives it, for his catenation of writing and speech and the divine source, we can take this passage from *Of Grammatology*, which purportedly digests Aristotle:

> The voice, producer of *the first symbols*, has a relationship of essential and immediate proximity with the mind. Producer of the first signifier, it is not just a simple signifier among others. It signifies "mental experiences" which themselves reflect or mirror things by natural resemblance. Between being and mind, things and feelings, there would be a relationship of translation or natural signification: between mind and logos [i.e., the divine originary power], a relationship of conventional symbolization. And the *first* convention, which would relate immediately to the order of natural and universal signification, would be produced as spoken language. Written language would establish the conventions, interlinking other conventions with them. (11)

When Derrida attacks logocentrism, then, what he denies is an "order of natural and universal signification." But he goes further than denying a spontaneous or divinely ordained system of language. At basis he calls into question the proposition that human beings share certain psychic states by virtue of their encounter with reality—what he calls "'mental experiences' which themselves reflect or mirror things by natural resemblance." And not only is the proposition unlikely. According to Derrida, it is not even possible. There is no objective reality, no *logos*, to act as a signified motivating signifiers. There is no transcendental signified.

It is important to pause and take note of what is at stake here. At issue is the humanist assumption that humankind shares a common condition expressed in common experience and preserved in a common heritage. Small wonder the dispute has been so passionately joined. Just as the imposition of a male narrator compromises and discomforts the female reader, so we as academics (male and female) become disenfranchised when we are denied those values and institutions that have fashioned us. We are asked to discredit "the great epoch covered by the history of metaphysics, and . . . the narrower epoch of Christian creationism and infinitism when these appropriate the resources of Greek conceptuality" (13). Must we actually renounce "the resources of Greek conceptuality" (a.k.a. the Western tradition)? It may be salutary that we do so, but we should be apprised of the costs and the consequences. Does that include logic? And we may rightly ask, What is left?

We should also note an insidious inconsistency in Derrida's argument that may well give us pause. He remarks the "totality" of the logocentric culture during this long era, and on the following page proposes that "the sign and divinity have the same place and time of birth" (14), equating the power of the linguistic sign with the originary authority of the *logos*. Derrida totalizes the premodern period as the Christian era. But at the same time he characterizes that Christian culture by an opposition within its theory of language: "To this epoch belongs the difference between signified and signifier, or at least the strange separation of their 'parallelism,' and the exteriority, however extenuated, of the one to the other." On the one hand, the *logos* rigorously controls language, being contemporaneous with it; but on the other, language conceals a rift between signified and signifier. What has been presented as unified in order to decry its hegemony is subsequently shown all along to have been essentially divided.

Such a characterization of our premodern heritage, however, is inaccurate and unsustainable. What should be emphasized in earlier periods is the interdependence of signifier and signified, not their alterity. Rather than separating signifier from signified, as Derrida would have it, the Christian era until the seventeenth century readily adopted the account in Genesis of how language originated. Adam named the creatures, thereby inscribing a book of nature that makes knowable to mere mortals the universal scheme and insuring a direct exchange between the divine will and human experience.[19] Secure within these parameters, the signified and signifier—though distinguishable, like sacred and profane, or soul and body—enjoy an inviolable bond and a mutually respectful complementarity.[20] Certainly,

19. See my *Sidney and Spenser,* 114–25.
20. In Plato's *Cratylus* Hermogenes argues that a vocabulary is culturally determined: words

as in the *Phaedrus* (268A–275E), it was recognized that language can be put to nefarious uses; but such an abuse of language is "bastard" speech (276A), as Plato says, unnatural, to be deplored and avoided. The thrust of Plato's argument in the *Phaedrus* supports the integrity of language.

Furthermore, to confirm the bond between signified and signifier, as the New Testament was read in the Renaissance, God had sent his only son as the Word to exemplify in terms of language the immediate interaction between—to use the platonic terms recalled by Derrida—the sensible and the intelligible. Derrida seizes upon Saussure's sometime privileging of the signifier at the expense of the signified to annihilate the intelligible, to disempower the *logos*. But that is a poststructuralist, retrospective critique of linguistic practice, and the disjunction between signified and signifier that sanctions it cannot be found in the Cratylian-Hebraic theory of language that by Derrida's account prevailed during the Christian era.

Derrida's argument, of course, as intended, strikes at the very purpose of the humanistic program, which was to see humankind created in the image of God and consequently sharing certain universal and timeless qualities. According to the humanists, who drew upon both classical and biblical authority for their views, speech is a divine gift, a sacred power breathed into Adam by God as the culminating act of creation. Derrida is right in pointing out that honoring the spoken language, as humanism does, places humankind in juxtaposition with the *logos*, the deity. Speech permits humankind to participate in right reason, and to understand and express it in terms comprehensible to mortals. Dante explains speech in exactly these terms and identifies it as the quintessential human act.[21] To quote an aphorism that Sidney found in Cicero, "*Oratio* [is] next to *ratio*, speech next to reason," and Sidney proceeds to exalt it as a "blessing" and "the greatest gift bestowed upon mortality" (100.26–28).

When Derrida attacks logocentrism, therefore, he repudiates these humanistic tenets. He may choose not to accept them himself, as may we.

---

acquire meanings as a social convention to allow the exchange of thoughts among a community of speakers. But Hermogenes does not suggest any disjunction between signified and signifier. The social convention is as strong an imperative as Cratylus' or Adam's divine authority when it comes to insuring the usability of language in a culture. Saussure, I believe, in the final analysis would have agreed with Hermogenes on this point, being himself more a structuralist than a poststructuralist.

For the major shift in the Cratylian-Hebraic theory of language, see Margreta de Grazia, "The Secularization of Language in the Seventeenth Century," *Journal of the History of Ideas* 41 (1980): 319–29.

21. *Dante in Hell: The* De Vulgari Eloquentia [2.8–3.3], trans. Warman Welliver (Ravenna: Longo, 1981), 47.

But it is folly to disregard their former force. These fundamental beliefs were commonly held throughout the Renaissance. They are professed by Dante, and they sustain Milton. Derrida dubs his argument "anti-theological," and once more he is right. It would have been heretical in Elizabethan England—as well as treasonous, since it undermines the divine right by which princes ruled. I am aware of no evidence to suggest that such thinking was commonplace at the time, and to read texts of the period as though it were therefore seems to me perverse.

Moreover, to insist that such thinking, though not evident, is nonetheless concealed in texts because it had been marginalized by an oppressive authority seems to me a desperate maneuver and puts the burden of proof upon those who make such claims. Anecdotal accounts of such suppression here or there, being merely texts composed by an interested party and open to interpretation, will not suffice. More seriously, they may be anomalous. I want evidence inscribed in the society at large, because my reading of the culture suggests just the opposite. Humanistic doctrine insisted upon the sanctity of the individual as a quasi-divine creature and denounced his or her brutalization. Prospero is himself diminished by the bestial state in which we find—and leave—Caliban. While as a matter of record I recognize that religion was often used in the service of empire—appropriation of the Americas is an appalling case in point—such a reading of history is not the entire story, or even the most important part of it. Humanism institutionally committed to oppression could not have eventuated in our nation: it would be incapable of producing either the individuals whom we know as our founders (women as well as men), our body of laws exemplified in the Constitution and the Bill of Rights, or the majority opinion that established and has maintained those laws. Incidents of oppression, lamentably numerous, represent a perversion of the culture—just as insider trading, although instances of it occur, represents a violation of the principle of free and open markets. We must not take the anomaly as the institutionalized norm. Such a biased reading of any culture—or any text—simply reproduces the assumptions of the interpreter and is bound to get it wrong.

But, again, let me suggest a way to take into account the competing discourses that filled the epistemological space that I call the Renaissance without excluding or exaggerating any of them. The difficulty with deconstruction is its absolute iconoclasm. In its headlong determination to break with tradition, it renounces all predecessors, thereby becoming unbearably exclusive and as a matter of principle refusing to recognize any alternative. Those who fight the academic wars by presuming to know what is politically correct take no prisoners.

I shall approach my goal through architecture, an art that we have not yet considered, and I shall begin with the logocentric imperatives that Renaissance architecture manifests. The orthodox aesthetic placed music at the center of any taxonomy for the arts because of its mathematical basis, because of its *ratio*. And we have seen how poetry assimilated to music by virtue of its measures, its shared formal properties. Architecture also exhibited formal properties expressed through the measurements of its buildings, so it also assimilated to music. Indeed, during the late Middle Ages architecture had been music's closest sibling among the various arts, because both readily adapted to the pious exercise of making palpable the beauty and meaning of God's intention for his creation.[22]

The architect, like a Timaean maker, begins with a design in his mind, and from this *logos* or *ratio* he produces an extended structure. Like Socrates versifying Aesop, the architect imposes form upon his inchoate materials. His building, of course, repeats in its dimensions the proportions and harmony of the cosmos.[23] In floor-plan or in facade—or perhaps in both, as well as in smaller features—it displays the beauty that resides in numerical relationships. Figure 1 from a redaction of Vitruvius exhibits on the right the proportion between an Ionic column (eight units in diameter) and its base (eleven units wide at its bottom), as well as on the left the numerical proportions that literally inform the base itself.[24] By its formal properties the architect's construction confirmed the logocentric imperatives of the culture, and therefore found its natural place in service to the Church.

These conservative principles were set out for the Renaissance by Leon Battista Alberti in his influential treatise *De re aedificatoria libri decem*,[25] which

22. The classic study of this tradition is Otto Georg von Simson, *The Gothic Cathedral: Origins of Gothic Architecture and the Medieval Concept of Order*, 2d ed., Bollingen Series 48 (New York: Pantheon Books, 1962). The identification of music and architecture persists in our own century, though reinterpreted in empiricist terms: "In a sense architecture is a sort of solidified music. A building is like a stone symphony whose parts coexist in space instead of succeeding one another in time" (Etienne Gilson, *Painting and Reality* [1957], Bollingen Series 35, 2d printing [Princeton: Princeton University Press, 1968], 282).

23. The classic study of this tradition is Rudolf Wittkower, *Architectural Principles in the Age of Humanism* (New York: Random House, 1965). For a review of how proportion in architecture has been dealt with since Wittkower's book, and for an instance where it obtains, see Catherine Wilkinson, "Proportion in Practice: Juan de Herrera's Design for the Façade of the Basilica of the Escorial," *Art Bulletin* 67 (1985): 229–42.

24. Note that in his title Sagredo uses *ratio* in the sense of both "reason" and "ratio."

25. Completed in 1452 and first published (in Latin) at Florence in 1485 by Angelo

combined a new technology with a novel sense of classicism grounded in mathematics. It was summarized in principle by John Dee in his "Mathematicall praeface" to Euclid, where Dee concludes flatteringly, "We thanke you Master *Baptist*, that you have so aptly brought your Arte . . . to have some Mathematicall perfection: by certaine order, number, forme, figure, and *Symmetrie* mentall: all naturall & sensible stuffe set apart" (d4). Alberti, in fact, remained a seminal authority, and the diplomat-aesthete Sir Henry

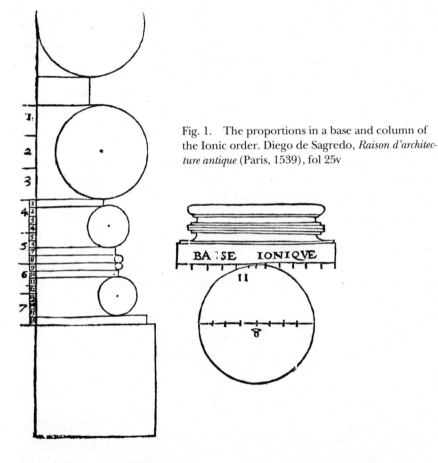

Fig. 1.   The proportions in a base and column of the Ionic order. Diego de Sagredo, *Raison d'architecture antique* (Paris, 1539), fol 25v

Poliziano, who dedicated his volume to Lorenzo de Medici. It is handily accessible as *Ten Books on Architecture*, trans. James Leoni [1726], ed. Joseph Rykwert (London: Alec Tiranti, 1955), although the translation is somewhat free. The benchmark for the second half of the sixteenth century was an illustrated translation in Italian by Cosimo Bartoli, *L'Architettura* (Florence, 1550).

Wotton, benefiting from two decades of travel in Italy, was still quoting him with approval in 1624.[26]

The residual logocentrism of architecture is well exemplified by Wotton's own treatise on the art. Quite early in his presentation Wotton distinguishes between the "Superintendent," who oversees the actual construction of the building, and the "*Architect*, whose glory doth more consist, in the Designement and *Idea* of the whole *Worke.*" Wotton continues to delineate the latter's role: "His truest ambition should be to make the *Forme*, which is the nobler Part (as it were) triumph over the *Matter*" (11–12). By way of an example to be emulated, Wotton then points to "the Church of *Santa Giustina* in *Padoua*: In truth a sound piece of good Art, where the *Materials* being but ordinarie stone, without any garnishment of sculpture, doe yet ravish the Beholder, (and hee knows not how) by a secret *Harmony* in the *Proportion*."[27] Wotton is careful to express the proper sentiments and sound the necessary buzz-words. Especially pertinent to our concerns is his use of the platonist term "idea," its equation with "form," and their distinction from "matter." We should note also the rhetoric of the church in Padua with its effect upon the percipient deriving from its proportion, its inner form, rather than from any surface phenomena such as sculpture. Outer "garnishment," in fact, is scorned as incidental and dispensable decoration.

The logocentric imperatives in architecture inherited from the Middle Ages were reinforced and specified by the resurrection of Vitruvius, a Roman authority whose recently recovered manuscript was known to Alberti. Vitruvius' *De architectura libri decem* became the vade mecum of architects and the source of a neoclassical style that held sway for centuries.[28] From

26. *The elements of architecture* (London, 1624), 53–54. Wotton cites Alberti on the desirability for symmetry in windows and doors (cf. *De re aedificatoria*, 1.13).

27. To this day, Santa Giustina lacks a facade, and hence "any garnishment of sculpture." What Wotton responded to was the symmetry of the impressive interior.

28. After an *editio princeps* at Rome in 1486, Vitruvius was republished with inordinate frequency throughout the Renaissance in a variety of languages; see Bodo Ebhardt, *Vitruvius: The "Ten Books of Architecture" of Vitruvius and Their Editors Since the Fifteenth Century* (Ossining, N.Y.: William Salloch, 1962). The first illustrated edition was prepared by Fra Giovanni Giocondo and printed at Venice in 1511. The benchmark text, however, was an Italian translation edited and illustrated by Cesare Cesariano, *De architectura libri dece* (Como, 1521). Even more ambitious was the Italian translation with illustrations after designs by Palladio and with commentary by Daniello Barbaro, *I dieci libri dell'architettura* (Venice, 1556). No treatise was more handsomely printed in a succession of stunning editions, with both commentary and illustrations proliferating. And of course there were spin-offs: Vignola, Sagredo, Serlio, Barbaro, Delorme, Palladio (see Peter A. Wick, ed., *Sixteenth-Century Architectural Books from Italy and France* [Cambridge, Mass.: Harvard College Library, 1971]). See also Lucia Ciapponi, "Il 'De Architectura' di Vitruvio nel primo Umanesimo," *Italia medioevale e umanistica* 3 (1960): 59–99.

the beginning of his treatise Vitruvius insists upon the conceptual and semantic components in an edifice, and he talks about it in terms acceptable to a Saussurian linguist:

> In all matters, but especially in architecture, two elements are present: what is signified (quod significatur) and what does the signifying (quod significat). The matter (res) put forward to be signified is what is being spoken of; that which does the signifying is a statement (demonstratio) of the signified set forth according to the laws that govern the expression of meaning (rationibus doctrinarum explicata). So it is clear that anyone who follows the discipline of architecture must be competent to deal with both elements.[29]

There follows a directive about the education of the architect:

> He should be well-read, skilled in the use of drafting instruments, knowledgeable about geometry; and he must be familiar with a large number of histories, diligently acquainted with the major philosophers, informed about music, not ignorant about medicine, familiar with the opinions of those who interpret the laws, and cognizant of astronomy and of the observed movements of the heavens.[30]

Vitruvius demands a broad-based education for the architect (cf. 1.1.12), rather like Quintilian's curriculum for the orator. Not surprisingly, Dee observes: "Take his boke in your hand, and slightly loke thorough it, you would say straight way: This is *Geometrie, Arithmetike, Musike, Anthropographie, Hydragogie, Horometrie. &c.* and (to conclude) the Storehouse of all workmanship" (d4). With particular urgency Vitruvius explains why the architect must be knowledgeable in the ratios of music (1.1.8–9; cf. 5.3.7–8).

For a long time, numbers encoded in the dimensions of buildings had been used to express theological meanings.[31] But Vitruvius offers a different system of numerical signification, a system dependent upon mathe-

---

29. 1.1.3 (my translation, from the Loeb Classical Library). Dee also translates this passage (d3).

30. John Shute in essence repeats this passage (*The first and chief groundes of architecture* [London, 1563], B2v–B3v), as does Dee (d3–d3v).

31. See Elizabeth Read Sunderland, "Symbolic Numbers and Romanesque Church Plans," *Journal of the Society of Architectural Historians* 18 (1959): 94–103.

matical relationships rather than the simple semiotics of symbolic numbers. He emphasizes the importance of just proportion in a building
(3.1.1–9). Beauty, in fact, depends upon symmetry, the harmonious arrangement of parts within a total design—in his words, "the appropriate consent arising out of the details of the work itself" (1.2.4). Furthermore, the
proportions that insure beauty have their prototype in the human body,
which in turn is a natural composite of parts arranged perfectly to accord
with the intervals of the Pythagorean tuning system (3.1.2–9).[32] Christian
humanists had no difficulty conflating this notion of human symmetry
with the ancient notion that the human body is a microcosm—as they saw
it, God's masterwork created on the last day of the hexaemeron.[33] Because
of this assimilation of architectural beauty to the fairest of God's creatures
as well as because of the comparison of architecture and music, theorists
such as Albrecht Dürer[34] happily adopted Vitruvius as confirmation of the
orthodox aesthetic (Figs. 2 and 3).[35]

But while Vitruvius, tactfully deployed, confirmed in principle the logocentric culture, when put into practice he generated possibilities that subverted it—or, at least, provided the venue for alternatives. Early in his treatise, as one of the essential elements in architecture, Vitruvius lists
"arrangement" (*dispositio*), which he defines as "the apt bringing together

32. See Erwin Panofsky, "The History of the Theory of Human Proportions as a Reflection
of the History of Styles," in *Meaning in the Visual Arts* (Garden City, N.Y.: Doubleday/Anchor,
1955), 55–107.

33. Dee defines a science, "Anthropographie," which he describes as follows: "the description of the Number, Measure, Waight, figure, Situation, and colour of every diverse thing,
conteyned in the perfect body of MAN" (c4). Cf. Agrippa, 263ff.; and Sagredo, fols. 6–7v.

34. See Dürer, *De symmetria partium in rectis formis humanorum corporum, libri in Latinum conversi*, trans. Joachim Camerarius (Nuremberg, 1532) [Books 1 and 2]; and *De varietate figurarum
et flexuris partium ac gestibus imaginum, libri duo* (Nuremberg, 1534) [Books 3 and 4]. For a
handsome translation into French, see *Les quatre livres . . . de la proportion des parties & pourtraicts des corps humains*, trans. Loys Meigret (Paris, 1557). Dee cites Dürer's text (c4).

35. Leonardo da Vinci manipulated this tradition to produce one of the most familiar
icons of the Renaissance, a male figure inscribed within both a circle and a square; see
Charles Carman, "Leonardo's 'Vitruvian Man': A Renaissance Microcosm," forthcoming.
The motif was popularized by Agrippa (263ff.); for its explication, see Sagredo, fol. 8. Spenser
also appropriates this tradition in the notorious "numerological" stanza in book 2 of *The
Faerie Queene* (9.22), where he describes the human body in geometrical terms as a composite of circle, square, and triangle. The image of the human body as a castle or temple
was also commonplace; cf. Thomas Elyot, *The castel of helth* (London, 1534); and Francesco
Sansovino, *L'Edificio del corpo humano* (Venice, 1550). In a distinctly Vitruvian vein, there is
a curious essay on feminine beauty based upon proportions in the human body and offering an inventory of components comprising the lady (including her mind), rather in the
manner of a sonneteer's blazon: Agnolo Firenzuola, "Dialogo . . . delle belleze delle donne,"
in *Prose* (Florence, 1548), fols. 61–89.

of particulars and the elegant effect of this composition resulting in a distinct character for the building" (1.2.2).[36] Vitruvius then delineates three different sorts of arrangement, which, in his words, "the Greeks call *ideae*"; and he identifies each: (1) *ichnographia*, consisting of the floor-plan for the

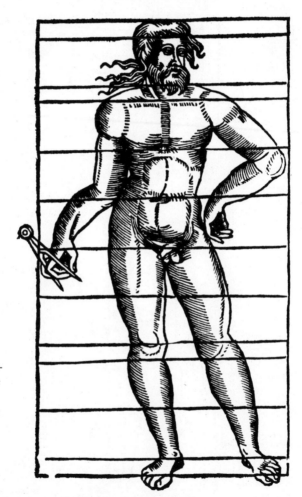

Fig. 2. Architectural proportions derived from the human figure. Diego de Sagredo, *Raison d'architecture antique* (Paris, 1539), fol. 6v

36. This concept of "arrangement" as a criterion for artistic excellence drew support also from Aristotle: "A beautiful thing, either a living creature or any structure made of parts, must have not only an orderly arrangement of these parts, but a size which is not accidental—for beauty lies in size and arrangement" (*Poetics*, 1450b34–36; cf. *Metaphysics*, 1078a36). Aristotle then applies this criterion to the plot in drama: "Just as in the other mimetic arts a single (unified) imitation is of a single object, so also the plot, since it is an imitation of

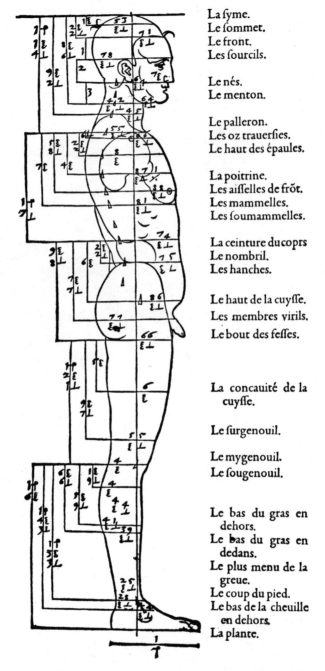

La ſyme.
Le ſommet.
Le front.
Les ſourcils.

Le nés.
Le menton.

Le palleron.
Les oz trauerſies.
Le haut des épaules.

La poitrine.
Les aiſſelles de frõt.
Les mammelles.
Les ſoumammelles.

La ceinture ducoprs
Le nombril.
Les hanches.

Le haut de la cuyſſe.
Les membres virils.
Le bout des feſſes.

La concauité de la
cuyſſe.

Le ſurgenouil.

Le mygenouil.
Le ſougenouil.

Le bas du gras en
dehors.
Le bas du gras en
dedans.
Le plus menu de la
greue.
Le coup du pied.
Le bas de la cheuille
en dehors.
La plante.

Fig. 3.   The proper proportions for drawing a mature man. Albrecht Dürer, *Les quatre livres . . . de la proportion des parties & pourtraicts des corps humains,* trans. Loys Meigret (Paris, 1557), fol. 36v

building; (2) *orthographia,* consisting of the frontal elevation for the building; and (3) *scaenographia,* consisting of a sketch drawn in perspective and revealing the building in three dimensions. Figure 4 from Fra Giocondo's edition of Vitruvius illustrates the passage.

Notably here, the same building is depicted from three distinct points of view: (1) the ichnographic, which reveals the basic inner-form seen from above, a privileged vantage point unavailable to earthbound mortals, perhaps *sub specie aeternitatis;* (2) the orthographic, which expands the ichnographic version from a plane surface into a volume, thereby projecting the building into the realm of space and time; and (3) the scaenographic, which recognizes that the building exists as a mutable object and that its perceived shape changes relative to the position of the percipient. The same building, then, can be described in three quite different ways, can be represented accurately and truthfully by three quite different versions. The same artifact submits to three variant interpretations, each of which is valid. The same "text" produces three readings, and all carry truth-value. So Vitruvius licenses pluralism.

At the same time, though, while each version is independent of the others in its ability to represent the building, they are complementary. And all three are necessary to the full representation of it—to a representation adequate for the architect to proceed with construction. Certainly the floor-plan and the frontal elevation are essential. But also the three-dimensional drawing is required, because it alone reveals the relationship between the facade and the sides, which determines the roofline.[37] Moreover, as Vitruvius emphasizes, all three versions have a common origin: the mind of the artificer. Vitruvius states pointedly, "They are born in the *cogitatio* and *inventio* of the architect." So Vitruvius respects the seminal importance of the human mind, and he recognizes the intercourse through *ratio* between the *mens poetae* and the *logos.*

Despite this inherent logocentrism, however, Vitruvius does legitimize at least three distinct versions of any artifact. Although preserving an immutable essence for the artifact secure in its ichnographic form devised by the artificer and modeled on a perfect form in the mind of deity, Vitruvius assigns truth-value also to a version that exists in the mutable

---

an action, should be an imitation of an action that is unified, and a whole as well, and the constituent events of the plot should be so put together that if one of them is placed elsewhere or removed, the whole is disjointed and dislocated" (1451a30–34).

37. See Michael Kubovy, *The Psychology of Perspective and Renaissance Art* (Cambridge: Cambridge University Press, 1986), 28–30.

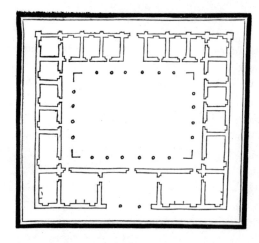

Fig. 4. The three modes of representing a building according to Vitruvius: (a) the ichnographic, (b) the orthographic, and (c) the scaenographic. Vitruvius, [*De architectura libri decem*], ed. Fra Giovanni Giocondo (Venice, 1511), fols. 4–4v

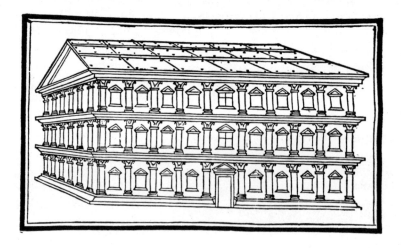

realm of time and space, and to yet another version that changes relative to a perceiving subject. This theory of art is still logocentric, and therefore no threat to the orthodox culture; but it also accommodates the ephemerality of our world and the relativism of human impressions. In consequence, while remaining acceptable to the logocentrists, Vitruvius also submitted to adaptation by those who wished to implement the hylocentric imperatives emerging at the time. He allowed even devout Christians to construct buildings whose appeal was directed primarily to the senses rather than the soul.

Or during this period we are calling the Renaissance, perhaps, Vitruvius allowed the construction of buildings that simultaneously appealed to both senses and soul, thereby satisfying both hylocentric and logocentric expectations. Renaissance buildings address at once both the eye and the reason. And this ambiguous potential is made possible by that very word *ratio* and the diverse ontological systems it activates. *Ratio* is mathematical proportion visible to the eye, as well as ideal form unalterably preserved in the *logos*. *Ratio* makes knowable the otherwise inaccessible subtext of form.

As an example of how profitably the sort of pluralism condoned by Vitruvius can be applied to a literary text, we may take the February eclogue in *The Shepheardes Calender*. This second month in Spenser's calendrical arrangement comes as winter ends and spring begins. It consists of a débat engaging two denizens of a blasted Arcadia, one young and the other old, and punctuated by a lengthy fable about the oak and the brier. Cuddie, a "Heardsmans boye" (as E. K. calls him), complains about the cold and economic deprivation, while "an olde Shepheard," Thenot, counsels patience as the only means of overcoming adversity.

The divided form of the débat provides the ground plan for the poem and serves as its ichnographic representation. There is a basic confrontation between contraries, manifested variously as youth and old age, exuberance and caution, spring and winter. The form is the familiar binary system that we shall consider more fully in chapter 4. Furthermore, the two disputants are not only opposed, but also ranked in a hierarchy. Elderly Thenot has the advantage of experience and is privileged to tell the fable; the fable itself demonstrates the advisability of restraint rather than brash activism; winter precedes spring and makes way for it.

The hermeneutic question hinges upon the stability of this hierarchy. Is it confirmed by the text? Overturned? Merely challenged, and thereby energized? The motif and the narrative strategy are the same as those employed by Shakespeare in the songs of the cuckoo and the owl concluding *Love's Labor's Lost,* although there the order of reading is reversed—that is, the spring song precedes the winter song. Does the inexorable progress of the seasons in actual time determine the outcome of the hermeneutic question in these poems? As E. K. says in the argument, "The matter very well accordeth with the season of the moneth, the yeare now drouping, and as it were, drawing to his last age." But does winter prevail, so that Thenot subdues his youthful adversary? Is the eclogue conservative and prescriptive, to the discredit of Cuddie? E. K. opts for this sort of reading in the first line of the argument—but, of course, we need not concur with E. K.

The conflict between seasoned age and upstart youth is dramatized in the Aesopic fable of the oak and brier recounted by Thenot, and through this narrative the basic form of the eclogue is extended into time and space, providing an orthographic version of the construction. We see the schematized ichnographic débat expand into the third dimension with increased palpability. As E. K. notes in the argument, "The olde man telleth a tale of the Oake and the Bryer, so lively and so feelingly, as if the thing were set forth in some Picture before our eyes, more plainly could not appeare." In addition, E. K. makes a transfer from the macrocosm to the microcosm: "As in this time of yeare, so then in our bodies there is a dry and withering age"; and he suggests a moral reading of the fable, applying it to human affairs. So in this sense also the schematized version of the débat is given orthographic extension by noting its efficacy as a moral imperative in everyday events. Some scholars—under the tutelage of E. K., who opines, "This Æglogue is . . . morall and generall"—have arrived at such a worldly reading.[38]

Although E. K. warns against the historical interpretation of the eclogue, saying that it is "generall" rather than "bent to any secrete or particular purpose," the fable especially evokes speculation about who the oak and the brier and the husbandman might really be. And this speculation particularizes the moralism as a pointed political report, thereby providing a scaenographic version of the poem. The multidimensional construction in all its aspects heaves into view. This representation is relative to the readers, of course, because it depends upon the information available to them. Different readers have different data to apply and consequently arrive at different conclusions about the personal references.

38. For example, W. L. Renwick, ed., *The Shepherd's Calendar by Edmund Spenser* (London: Scholartis Press, 1930), 182.

Such a perspective view of the construction allows the poem its fullest extension, reaching unto even the most minute of details. Spenser's contemporaries, naturally, would have identified the characters in the fable according to what each knew, not always agreeing upon the *clef*. But most, I think, would have assumed that actual political figures had been intended in a specific set of circumstances. Such an inference is warranted by topical hints, both political and theological.[39] Several scholars in our century have argued for various disclosures, agreeing on little, though, except the identification of the husbandman as Queen Elizabeth.[40]

Despite a number of proposals, however, no consensus has been reached. Are all equally valid? Since this is "history" as fictive narrative, as a "text" whose meaning is relative to the reader, the answer is yes. But note also that this pluralism recognizes the first version, the ground plan of the débat, as authoritative. The poem in its thrust seems moral and conservative: cautious age outargues heedless youth. It is logocentric, although admitting diversity in the multiple representations of its essence. While enlarging the discourse, Spenser does not violate the orthodox imperatives of his culture. Thenot, for example, introduces his fable by endowing it with the authority of Chaucer and calling it "a tale of truth" (91–93).

Even so, the skeptical Cuddie, who has the final word, counters by using the term "novells" to describe Chaucer's stories (95)—and by implication, Thenot's. These "tales" are no more than Italian fictions, *novelle*. And eventually he interrupts Thenot's narrative with an outburst of impatience: "Here is a long tale, and little worth" (240). The fable, says Cuddie, despite its length and its verse, lacks truth-value. By this pronouncement, does Cuddie discredit the fable? Or, does this line expose Cuddie's callow folly? What does the text "mean" here? One reading, or the other? Or both?

During the Renaissance, Vitruvius (and others) licensed pluralism in the presentation and interpretation of artifacts. But for pluralism to prevail, the culture itself in its larger practices must have been congenial to it. So what were the dynamics of the general culture? In chapter 1 we spatialized the Renaissance in order to remove it from temporal flow and to have all its phenomena simultaneously present. Now to this synchronic analysis we

39. For example, the reference to "a mayden Queene" (132) and the sacred mysteries associated with the oak (207–10).

40. See Edmund Spenser, *The Works: A Variorum Edition*, ed. Edwin Greenlaw et al., 11 vols. (Baltimore: Johns Hopkins University Press, 1932–57), 7.254, 261–62, 264–65; and Paul E. McLane, *Spenser's* Shepheardes Calender: *A Study in Elizabethan Allegory* (Notre Dame, Ind.: University of Notre Dame Press, 1961), 61–76.

need to add a diachronic dimension. How did the conception of reality change in the course of the Renaissance?

Because to a large extent we are fashioned by the culture that prevails in our own time, we need to clarify the term "reality." Today we are likely to locate reality among the items of physical nature because for the last several centuries our culture has assumed that matter is what is ultimately real. We have elaborate theories about atoms and molecules and quarks that serve as the basis for our knowledge and the grounds for making practical decisions. We live in a materialist culture: reality consists of matter and its effects. In an earlier culture, however, the things of this world were viewed as evanescent and conducive to sinful pleasure, deserving of contempt; and ultimate reality resided with a transcendent deity. Knowledge came from meditation upon his attributes. All creatures flowed from God and were subject to his laws rather than the laws of an autonomous nature, and an elaborate doctrine was developed to help us live in accordance with his will.

During the course of the period I call the Renaissance, then, there was a major shift in the dominant ontology. The pious view that reality is vested in an eternal deity was challenged by a growing group of secularists who assigned to matter an objective existence. The logocentric culture grounded in unalterable Platonic essences or immutable attributes of God was confronted and overcome by a hylocentric culture grounded in the perceptible phenomena of natural objects. This transition has been described variously as the Age of Faith giving way to the Enlightenment, as the Copernican revolution, as the introduction of scientific method, or as the triumph of empiricism.[41] To avoid Hegelian assumptions about the inexorable progress of human affairs, I prefer to think of this ontological shift more neutrally as simply a relocation of reality. That which constitutes reality, the basis of knowledge and the ultimate referent for the assignment of meaning, was redefined from a transcendental and all-encompassing *logos* to a perceptible nature that is diverse and transient.

---

41. A book whose implied thesis recounts this triumph of empiricism is the collection of essays edited by Brian Vickers, *Occult and Scientific Mentalities in the Renaissance* (Cambridge: Cambridge University Press, 1984). See esp. the Introduction (1–55), where Vickers distinguishes between the occult and the nonoccult (i.e., empirical) sciences, and suggests that the occult did not prepare for and lead into the nonoccult—as, for example, Frances Yates had proposed. Rather, Vickers argues, science in the modern sense already existed in the late Renaissance as an autonomous enterprise based upon premises different from those of the magical sciences and oriented toward different goals. I might add that this ambiguity has long been recognized in Johann Kepler, essentially a man of science, and in Sir Thomas Browne, essentially a man of letters.

Considerable anxiety accompanied this relocation of reality and the bifurcated efforts to accommodate it, particularly in sixteenth-century England. As a case in point, we can detect the nervousness and disapproval it induced in Pierre de La Primaudaye (b. 1545), the protestant encyclopedist whom like-minded Englishmen reverentially transported across the Channel.

In the preface to *The French academie,* first printed in France in 1577, La Primaudaye voices the traditional justification for observation of the physical world and draws upon the authority of Aristotle's *De mundo* to substantiate it: "This treatise . . . [is] wholly occupied in these two principall points: namely, in the description of the universall frame of the world, and in the declaration of the nature of God the workemaister thereof."[42] According to La Primaudaye, his purpose is to describe our universe and disclose the essential qualities of its creator. We use our senses to detect the presence of deity in the world around us. We read the book of nature in order to discern the underlying signifieds, the attributes of God. As La Primaudaye states in the preface to *The third volume of the French academie,* the "beginning and principall scope" of his study is "to know God and his providence, to the end to glorifie him."[43] This motive for scientific investigation is encouraged by Psalm 19: "The heavens declare the glory of God, and the firmament sheweth His handiwork." In this vein, La Primaudaye continues in the first volume of *The French academie*:

> For what can be more certaine than the ordinarie course of the Sunne, Moone, & Starres, which have continued in their appointed race from time to time, and from one age unto another? What greater certaintie than that which to our comfort appeereth in the mutuall turnes and returnes of times and seasons, of Sommer and Winter, Spring and Autumne, day & night? (A4)[44]

La Primaudaye and his contemporaries found solace in this providential scheme, in this "course of kind," to use an Elizabethan phrase—in this "constant continuance of the irrevocable order appointed by God in this

---

42. Trans. Thomas Bowes (London, 1586), A4.

43. Trans. R. Dolman (London, 1601), A8v. Cf. "The preface to the reader" in Robert Recorde, *The castle of knowledge* (London, 1556), a4–a7v; and the chapter "Of the Woorkes of God" in Thomas Palfreyman, *The treatise of heavenly philosophie* (London, 1578), 67ff.

44. See also *Third volume of French academie,* 160–61, where La Primaudaye expounds the marginalium, "Testimonie of the providence of God in the harmonie of the seasons of the yeere."

whole frame," to use the words of La Primaudaye (cf. Fig. 5). In Spenser's "Cantos of Mutabilitie," the predictability of the natural order provides the argument that Nature finally advances to put down the upstart Change (*Faerie Queene* 7.7.58). The very orderliness of change and the multeity that comprises the cosmos is proof of God's benevolence toward humankind, as La Primaudaye goes on to say:

> If we looke either to the variable motions of the Spheres in the ethereall region, or to the contrary qualities of the elements in the aerie and lower part of the world, or to the varietie of foules, fishes, beasts, plants, graine, stones, mettals, &c. and consider withall what a sweete harmonie ariseth from all these, as it were from a well tuned instrument that hath strings of all sorts, or like to a lively picture that hath all kinds of colours mingled in it, or to a well ordered citie compounded of sundry occupations, callings, & conditions, of poore and rich, yoong and old, bond and free, we may see if we have but halfe an eie, and feele if we be blind, that in this rare peece of worke and frame of the world, there is most excellent conveiance without confusion, great varietie concurring in unitie, and diversitie of all kinds without disorder.

And we must remember that La Primaudaye is no superstitious papist, but a militant protestant. Nonetheless, his chief concern is not the persistence of orthodoxy, but rather the challenge of radicalism that prescribes a novel ontology based upon the observation of natural objects. In a later chapter, beside an ominous marginalium—"How we must behave our selves in searching out the secrets of God"—he warns:

> Naturall philosophie consisteth chiefly in the Mathematiks, which are divided into many parts and particular sciences, of which the most of them seeme to manie not greatly necessarie, as that which intreateth of the nature of the heavens, of the sunne, of the moone, of their motions, measures, & of the naturall causes of things so curiously, that in the end they strive to finde out another beginning of all things than God: whereby at length they remain deceived and confounded in their knowlege. (41)

Already La Primaudaye is fearful that the originary authority of the *logos* will be impugned. The new scientists will read the book of nature not to

Fig. 5. A philosopher observing the orderly movements of the heavens dominated by the Sun and Moon in the top corners, but including also the wandering stars (planets), the twelve signs of the zodiac, and the sphere of fixed stars. Below is the elemental region, comprising the realms of fire, air, water, and earth, upon which the philosopher stands with a wind-rose(?) to the left and an armillary sphere to the right. The bound volume in his right hand is a metonym for the book of nature he is reading, with particular attention to the passage of time. Giovanni Campano, *Tetragonismus idest circuli quadratura* et al., ed. Luca Gaurico (Venice, 1503), title page

perceive therein the attributes of deity in order to accord with God's will, but rather to disclose physical laws in order to manipulate what now appears within human control. The definition of nature has changed from the invisible scheme that underlies and maintains our universe[45] to the aggre-

45. Elsewhere, in answer to the marginalium "What Nature is," after a long discussion La Primaudaye concludes: "Nature is nothing els but the order and continuance of the

gate of perceptible phenomena that we can investigate with our measuring instruments. The Greek φύσις is now modern physics.

These sentiments of La Primaudaye appear also in the works of Lambert Daneau (1530–95), an active Calvinist who similarly had an admiring audience in England. The title page of *The wonderfull woorkmanship of the world,* as translated by Thomas Twynne, clearly sets forth the intention of Daneau's treatise: "wherin is conteined an excellent discourse of Christian naturall Philosophie, concernyng the fourme, knowledge, and use of all thinges created: specially gathered out of the Fountaines of holy Scripture."[46] In addition to looking in the book of nature, the scrupulous reader could of course find the *logos* also in the sacred writings. Twynne's dedicatory epistle addressed to Sir Francis Walsingham clearly stakes out this devout position.

Daneau's treatise opens with the Student's question: "What is natural Philosophie?" And, like La Primaudaye, the Master answers in accord with Christian doctrine: "It is the true knowledge or discourse concerning the Creation and distinction of all this whole worlde with the partes therof, of the causes by which it was so wrought, and likewise of the effectes whiche followe thereon, apperteinyng to the praise of God the Creatour" (fol. 1). Shortly, however, the Master modifies this orthodox position. He recognizes an objective nature and makes allowance for the empirical observation of the natural world:

> For as muche as this woorde, *Nature,* in the common use of the Greeke tongue, is, for the moste parte, applied to suche thynges as doe consiste, not of essence onely, of which sorte GOD is, but are compounded with certein accidentes adjoined, suche as are all the thynges that wee beholde with our eyes, and whereof this visible worlde consisteth: that knowledge seemeth moste properly to bee termed naturall Philosophie, whiche is busied in the handlyng of the mixt, compounded, and materiall thinges, that it maie bee distinguished from Divinitie. Wherefore, Naturall Philosophie, saie thei, is the knowledge of Materiall and Instrumentall beginnynges. (fols. 1v–2).

Daneau acknowledges a physics distinct from (if not independent of) divin-

---

woorkes of God" (*The second part of the French academie,* trans. Thomas Bowes [London, 1594], 424–26).

46. (London, 1578), translating Daneau's *Physicà Christiana* (Geneva, 1576).

ity, and natural philosophy now consists of openly investigating it. But those natural philosophers who forget their ulterior motive of praising God are launched upon a fruitless and dangerous project: "Thei make the cause of the thyng, of that whiche thei call the thyng it self"—that is, they mistake observable laws in nature to be essences, and thereby they fail to penetrate to the true *logos*. So Daneau chastises such errant fools:

> Whereby it commeth to passe, that this moste excellent knowledge, among them is full of vaine ostentation of the minde, of strife, and of contention: as for the glorie of God, it neither setteth it forth, neither once toucheth it, so that verie many of those Natural Philosophers, dooe at the length become indeede, verie naturalles, that is too saie, fleshely men, and Athiestes. (fol. 11)

In the view of Daneau and his ilk, damnation will certainly follow such worldly materialism.

This division between divinity and nature, which eventually developed into a full-blown schism between theology and science, took hold in Elizabethan England and manifested itself in all its cultural institutions. We can see it in every confrontation between the logocentric and the hylocentric that I have used as a criterion for defining the Renaissance. Nowhere, though, is this division (and the need to accommodate it) more evident than in the poetics of the period. In his landmark treatise *The Defence of Poesie*, Sidney sensed that in his day reality was undergoing a rapid relocation, so he called upon the authority of Aristotle's *Poetics* to deal with the ontological crisis. This is the occasion for his renunciation of versing and rhyming, and at the same time for his radical redefinition of poetry as an art of imitation in the Aristotelian mode. A mimetic poem, though, is not a direct replication of nature, itself to be perceived by the senses alone. Rather, through its plot, the mimetic poem rises above the particulars of actual occurrence and represents instead what might be or should be according to probability or necessity. It represents the universal. Thereby, since an Aristotelian universal approaches the absoluteness of a Platonic idea, the poem eludes the partiality of the individual instance and achieves a normalcy that is generally applicable. Thereby the poet, despite the fictiveness of his narrative, endows it with truth-value.[47]

But what about the readers? Faced with a text representing a universal

47. See my *Sidney and Spenser*, esp. 237–54.

necessarily expressed in a particular narrative, how are they to respond? Well, readers may go in either of two diverging directions. They may pursue the universal, in which case they will likely arrive at an abstraction, an idea, a truism. This is the logocentric approach. Or readers may further particularize the particular, in which case they identify more and more details in terms of the experiential world. This is the hylocentric approach. To again pose the question at the end of the last section, do readers accord with Thenot and imply a moral reading for the February eclogue, or do they side with Cuddie and deny the old man's moralisms as impractical? Of course, if a choice must be made, it depends upon the mind-set of the individual reader. If he or she is conservative, the audience targeted by La Primaudaye and Daneau, the reader will no doubt maintain the hierarchy to the advantage of Thenot. If the reader is radical, though, he or she will invert the traditional hierarchy and arrange it so that Cuddie prevails. There is truth-value in both readings.

Still, how about us postmoderns, the sophisticated readers who see both possibilities? The all-knowing reader? The informed reader? To be honest, there is no such creature. That convenient myth has been exploded. But how about the reader without constraints, the libertine who has the freedom to go wherever personal proclivities may lead? Again, this is a license without substance, because such a reading merely reproduces the assumptions that guide it. At most, a sensitized and engaged reader shuttles among a range of likely interpretations.[48]

---

48. For a systematic critique of reader-response theory, see Ellis, 115–29.

3   The Origin of the Sonnet
Form as Optimism

I would exhorte you also to beware of rime without reason.
—*George Gascoigne*[1]

he fourteen-line sonnet—or, more properly, the quatorzain[2]—was unknown in the ancient world. Certain
lyric forms, such as the ode and the elegy, were common and persisted
throughout the medieval period in both secular and theological modes.

1. "Certayne Notes of Instruction Concerning the Making of Verse or Ryme in English"
[1575], in *Elizabethan Critical Essays,* ed. G. Gregory Smith, 2 vols. (London: Oxford University
Press, 1904), 1.51. Note the affinity between "rime" and "reason." "Rime" derives from Gr.
arithmos, number. When spelled "rhyme," the word more obviously equates with "rhythm,"
which also derives from the same Greek word. "Reason," as we have seen, is the usual translation of L. *ratio,* which like "rhythm" involves the relationship between two mathematical
entities. The phrase "rime and reason," then, is one of those pairs of alliterative synonyms
so dear to English-speakers: e.g., "might and main," "time and tide," "rant and rave"—and,
indeed, "songs and sonnets." Harington plays upon the affinity between rhyme and reason
when, translating some Latin verse, he comments: "Because I count it without reason, I will
English without rime" (201.4–5).
    John W. Draper traces the use of rhyme in the West back to *De judicio domini* (c. 200 A.D.)
attributed to Tertullian; and beyond that, to the cult of Mithras in Persia ("The Origin of
Rhyme," *Revue de littérature comparée* 31 [1975]: 74–85).
    2. Gascoigne inaugurated the term "sonnet" to indicate a poem specifically of fourteen
lines. As he observes, the term had been commonly used to denote any love lyric: "Some

But the peculiar arrangement of octave and sestet that characterizes the quatorzain was not a classical form. It appeared quite suddenly about 1220 at the court of Frederick II in Sicily, apparently the work of a single poet, Giacomo da Lentini; and it quickly established itself as a major literary fashion. What cultural imperatives called it into existence?

Frederick II of Hohenstaufen (1194–1250),[3] Holy Roman emperor from 1220 to 1250, maintained a brilliant if peripatetic court, most notably in Sicily. He patronized a vigorous coterie of philosophers, mathematicians, natural scientists, and men of letters from all centers of learning in the East as well as West. He encouraged the study of cosmology as that discipline had come down from the ancient world in the texts of Ptolemy and kept at court two prominent astrologers, Michael Scot and Theodore of Antioch. In addition, as Van Cleve notes, "His insatiable intellectual curiosity carried him also into the world of pure mathematics," thereby acquainting him with Leonardo Fibonacci of Pisa, "the foremost mathematician of his era" (310). Most germane to our interests, of course, is Frederick's support of translators and poets. Frederick and his courtiers themselves wrote verse and generously patronized others who did likewise.

Although in many ways conditioned by lyric practice in Provence, northern France, and Germany,[4] this *scuola siciliana* is seen by most historians of literature as the beginning of Italy's national literary tradition. And foremost among the literati at Frederick's court, along with Piero della Vigna,[5]

---

thinke that all Poemes (being short) may be called Sonets, as in deede it is a diminutive worde derived of *Sonare*, but yet I can beste allowe to call those Sonnets whiche are of fouretene lynes, every line conteyning tenne syllables" (1.55). And he continues to describe the so-called English sonnet of three quatrains with alternating rhymes plus a concluding couplet: "The firste twelve [lines] do ryme in staves of foure lines by crosse meetre, and the last two ryming togither do conclude the whole."

3. Frederick has been popular with biographers. The two who give the most detailed information about his intellectual interests are Ernst Kantorowicz, *Frederick II 1194–1250* [1931], trans. E. O. Lorimer, rev. ed. (New York: Frederick Ungar, 1957), esp. 132–35, 157–58, 293–368; and Thomas Curtis Van Cleve, *The Emperor Frederick II of Hohenstaufen: Immutator Mundi* (Oxford: Clarendon, 1972), esp. 299–318, 333–46. See also Charles Homer Haskins, *Studies in the History of Mediaeval Science* (Cambridge: Harvard University Press, 1924), 242–69. More recently, David Abulafia has demythologized Frederick, particularly as precursor of the Renaissance (*Frederick II: A Medieval Emperor* [London: Allen Lane/Penguin, 1988], esp. chap. 8).

4. For a summary of earlier influences upon the Sicilian school, see Van Cleve, 326–28; and Christopher Kleinhenz, *The Early Italian Sonnet: The First Century (1220–1321)* (Lecce: Milella, 1986), 10–14.

5. On Piero della Vigna, see Jean Louis Alphonse Huillard-Bréholles, *Vie et correspondance de Pierre de la Vigne* [1865] (Reinheim: Scientia Verlag Aalen, 1966); and Kantorowicz, 298–305.

was Giacomo da Lentini (fl. 1220–40),[6] by profession a notary entrusted with the drafting and implementation of imperial documents. While identification of the first poet to write a quatorzain is neither certain nor of paramount importance, the innovation is commonly attributed to Giacomo,[7] whom Dante singles out as a forerunner of *il dolce stil nuovo* (*Purgatorio*, 24.56). As Kleinhenz asserts, "The invention of the sonnet by Giacomo da Lentini at the imperial court was perhaps the single most important event in the history of early Italian literature" (223).

So it was Giacomo, seemingly, who first devised the characteristic form of the quatorzain, comprising an octave followed by a clearly distinguished sestet. Although it is impossible to ascertain the chronological order of the twenty-five or so extant quatorzains by Giacomo, even if it were desirable, we can take the following example as a prototype:

Io m'aggio posto in core a Dio servire,	a
com'io potesse gire in paradiso,	b
al santo loco, c'aggio audito dire,	a
o' si mantien sollazzo, gioco e riso.	b
Sanza mia donna non vi voria gire,	a
quella c'à blonda testa e claro viso,	b
che sanza lei non poteria gaudere,	a
estando da la mia donna diviso.	b
Ma no lo dico a tale intendimento,	c
perch'io pecato ci volesse fare;	d
se non veder lo suo bel portamento	c
e lo bel viso e 'l morbido sguardare:	d
che'l mi teria in gran consolamento,	c
veggendo la mia donna in ghiora stare.[8]	d

6. The standard edition of Giacomo has been prepared by Roberto Antonelli (*Poesie* [Rome: Bulzoni, 1979]); but see also Ernest F. Langley, ed., *The Poetry of Giacomo da Lentino* (Cambridge: Harvard University Press, 1915). For a summary of the sparse biographical information about Giacomo, see Langley, xiii–xxi; Antonelli, xi–xii; and Frede Jensen, ed. and trans., *The Poetry of the Sicilian School*, Garland Library of Medieval Literature, ser. A, 22 (New York: Garland, 1986), xxv–xxvi. For a reconstruction of the interaction between Giacomo and Frederick II, see Paul Oppenheimer, *The Birth of the Modern Mind: Self, Consciousness, and the Invention of the Sonnet* (New York: Oxford University Press, 1989), 13–25.

7. See Ernest Hatch Wilkins, "The Invention of the Sonnet," in *The Invention of the Sonnet and Other Studies in Italian Literature* (Rome: Edizioni di Storia e Letteratura, 1959), 17; Kleinhenz, 10, 23, 37; Paul Oppenheimer, "The Origin of the Sonnet," *Comparative Literature* 34 (1982): 289–304; and Pierre Blanc, "Sonnet des origines, origine du sonnet: Giacomo da Lentini," in *Le sonnet à la Renaissance: Des origines au XVIIe siècle*, ed. Yvonne Bellenger (Paris: Aux Amateurs de Livres, 1988), 9–18.

8. Antonelli, 316.

I have set my heart on serving God,
so that I may go to Paradise,
to the holy place I have heard people speak about,
where pleasure, joy and merriment never cease.

Without my lady, I would not want to go there,
the one who has blond hair and a shining brow,
for without her, I could not have any joy,
being separated from my lady.

But I am not saying this with the intention
that I might want to commit a sin there;
but only in order to see her dignified bearing

and the beautiful face and the sweet gaze,
for I would consider it a great consolation,
beholding my lady standing in glory.[9]

In the Italian text of this sonnet there are fourteen lines of hendecasyllabic verse. In both versions printed here the *volta* at line 9 is clearly evident, signaled by the word *Ma* (but) and dividing the text into an octave and a sestet.[10] The eight lines of the octave rhyme *a b a b a b a b;* the six lines of the sestet rhyme *c d c d c d.*[11]

9. Jensen, 39. For "a literal translation" of this quatorzain, and an examination of the verbal system that such an exercise entails, see Edgar C. Knowlton, Jr., "Jacopo da Lentini's Sonnet 'Of His Lady in Heaven,'" *Allegorica* 6.2 (1981): 95–101.

10. The sestina is the only other literary form with such narrowly prescribed metrics (the *canzone* and *ballata*, for example, occur in a variety of stanzas). François Jost comments upon the remarkable persistence of this requirement for the quatorzain ("Les genres passent, le sonnet demeure"), and then offers useful analyses of how later sonneteers—e.g., Petrarch, Wyatt, Ronsard, Spenser, Shakespeare—modified the arrangement of octave and sestet ("Le sonnet: Sens d'une structure," in *Le sonnet à la Renaissance*, 57–65). For an early study of the quatorzain form, see Leandro Biadene, "Morfologia del Sonetto nei sec. XIII e XIV," *Studi di Filologia Romanza* 4 (1889): 1–234. For the modern, familiar explanation of the relation between octave and sestet, see Paul Fussell, Jr., *Poetic Meter and Poetic Form* (New York: Random House, 1965), 119–33.

11. Of the twenty-five quatorzains attributed to Giacomo with reasonable assurance, all have an octave rhyming *a b a b a b a b.* The rhyme scheme of the sestet, however, varies: fourteen have a sestet rhyming *c d e c d e,* nine have a sestet rhyming *c d c d c d,* one has a sestet rhyming *a c d a c d,* and another has a sestet rhyming *a a b a a b* (Kleinhenz, 37). As Wilkins says, however, "The fact that the scheme CDECDE occurs in more of the . . . sonnets than does the scheme CDCDCD does not constitute a proof, or even an indication, of priority: as far as these data are concerned, the original rhyme-scheme of the sestet might have been either CDECDE or CDCDCD" (18; cf. 21–22). I opt to take *c d c d c d* as the prototype because it continues the pattern of distichs in the octave, although this rhyme scheme is not essential to my argument.

What I want to focus upon first is the arrangement of this octave and sestet, and the significance of the proportion 8/6.[12] When reduced to its lowest ratio, this proportion becomes the relationship between 4 and 3, actually the operative mathematical relationship in this particular verse form and the prototype for proportionality.[13] The prominence of the ratio

---

In the sixteenth century the most detailed description of the quatorzain is provided by Antonio Minturno, who divides the octave into two quatrains and the sestet into two tercets (*L'Arte poetica* [Venice, 1564], 243–45). But by then, of course, printed texts of Petrarch had become the norm.

12. "Proportion" was commonly recognized as a technical term designating a special relationship between two numbers. Writing with Vitruvius in mind, Giovanni Paolo Lomazzo—the influential theorist of painting, sculpture, and architecture in the late sixteenth century—noted its importance and prevalence:

> Neither yet is this proportion proper unto painting alone, but extendeth it selfe, even unto all other arts; insomuch as it is drawne from mans body, which as the painter chiefely proposeth to himselfe (as *Vitruvius* noteth) so doth the *Architect* much imitate it, in the conveiance of his buildings, and without which, neither the carver [sculptor], nor any handicrafts man, can performe any laudable worke: because it was the first patterne of all Artificiall thinges; so that there is no arte, but is some way beholding to Proportion.
> (*The artes of curious paintinge, carvinge & buildinge*, trans. Richard Haydocke [Oxford, 1598], 26)

Proportion, like the idea of cosmos, was in the heavenly maker's mind at the time of creation: "It was the first patterne of all Artificiall thinges." For an informative little treatise arguing that proportion is found in everything, based primarily on Michelangelo, see Vincenzio Danti, *Il primo libro del trattato delle perfette proporzioni di tutte le cose che imitare, e ritrarre si possano con l'arte del disegno* (Florence, 1567).

"Proportion" and its grounding in music received special attention in almost every textbook of arithmetic or geometry. Luca Pacioli, friend of Leonardo da Vinci, gave it prominent treatment in his *Summa de arithmetica, geometria, proportioni & proportionalita* (Venice, 1494), esp. 82. In his *Divina proportione* (Venice, 1509), Pacioli proposed rules of proportion for all the arts. For a particularly full treatment of proportionality, see an anonymous "Rudimenta musicae figuratae" appended to Gregor Reisch, *Margarita philosophica*, ed. Oronce Finé (Basle, 1583), 1161–99; or Thomas Hylles, *The arte of vulgar arithmeticke* (London, 1600), 2d book, fol. 83ff. See also Michael Baxandall, *Painting and Experience in Fifteenth Century Italy* [1972] (Oxford: Oxford University Press, 1983), 94–102.

The "Rudimenta musicae figuratae" offers a standard definition: Proportio est duorum numerorum inaequalitas (1180; Proportion consists in the inequality between two numbers).

13. Robert Recorde, who provided the best mathematical textbooks for Elizabethan England, used the proportion 4/3 as his exemplary case: "Any .2. nombers maie have comparison & *proportion* together, although thei be *incommensurable*. As .3. and .4. are *incommensurable*, and yet are thei in a *proportion* together"; and he continues: "If the greater comprehende the lesser, and his thirde parte, then is that named S*esquitertia* proportion. As in these. 4. to .3: 8. to .6: 12. to .9: 16. to .12: 20. to .15" (*The whetstone of witte* [London, 1557], B1–B2).

4/3 becomes even more assertive when we look at the arrangement of Giacomo's sonnet as it appears in the earliest (and only premodern) version that we have, a manuscript text in Vaticano Latino 3793 dating from the late thirteenth century:[14]

Iomagio posto jncore adio servire. comio potesse gire jmparadiso. b
  alsanto loco cagio audito dire oue simantiene sollazo gioco eriso.   b
  sanza lamia donna nonui voria gire. quella ca lablondda testa
                                  elclaro viso.   b
  chesanza lei nomporzeria gaudera. estando dalamia don(n)a diviso.   b

Manolodico atale jntendimento. perchio pecato ciuellesse fare.   d
  seno(n)vedere losuo bello porttamento. Elobello viso
                          elmorbido squardare.   d
  chelomi teria jngrande comsolame(n)to. vegiendo lamia
                        don(n)a jnghiora stare.   d[15]

A convenient locus for such thinking occurs in Martianus Capella, who begins an extended passage on numbers with the observation: "These two numbers (three and four) are marked by a harmonious relationship with each other" ("The Marriage of Philology and Mercury" [103–8], trans. William Harris Stahl and Richard Johnson, in *Martianus Capella and the Seven Liberal Arts*, 2 vols. [New York: Columbia University Press, 1971–77], 2.36). Martianus continues by noting "the threefold harmonies in music" generated by these two numbers:

> For the ratio three to four is called the epitritus in arithmetical calculation, and it is named the fourth [diatesseron] by musicians. Within it lies the ratio three to two, which is a hemiolius, and these two numbers produce the secondary concord called a fifth [diapente]. The third harmony is called the octave [diapason] by musicians and is produced by a double ratio that is in the proportion of one to two. (2.37)

For a chapter on the consonances of the diatesseron involving four and three, see Valla, g8v.

The eight notes of the diapason according to the Pythagorean tuning system were produced by manipulating the two sesquitertial proportions 12/9 and 8/6 (see my *Touches of Harmony*, 95–97). In Raphael's celebrated fresco in the Vatican known as *The School of Athens*, the lower left corner is dominated by a heroic figure of Pythagoras, while a disciple holds a slate diagraming how the diapente and the diatesseron as well as the diapason derive from the numbers six, eight, nine, and twelve. This musical lore was commonplace.

14. This ms. is privileged by every editor of the *scuola siciliana* not only because it is the earliest extant, but also because it provides the most nearly complete text of Giacomo's canon; see Antonelli, xxviii–xxxi, xlviii–xlix. It has been published as *Il libro de varie romanze volgare: Cod. Vat. 3793*, ed. Francesco Egidi et al., Documenti di storia letteraria (Rome: Società filologica Romana, 1908).

15. Antonelli, 317; cf. Egidi, 327.

In this version, a manuscript within a half-century of Giacomo himself and the only authoritative text, there are seven lines of double hendecasyllabic verse. The *a* rhymes are internalized in the first four lines, and the *c* rhymes are internalized in the last three lines. We may schematize the result as follows:

a	b
a	b
a	b
a	b
c	d
c	d
c	d

In what we must take as the original arrangement of Giacomo's verse form, the octave and sestet of the modern version are collapsed into a quatrain and tercet, and the numbers four and three are obtruded by the four *b* rhymes and the three *d* rhymes, respectively.

This arrangement of seven double hendecasyllabic lines was preferred also by Petrarch for his quatorzains. In Vaticano Latino 3195, which is the most authoritative manuscript of the *Canzoniere* because it contains Petrarch's final revision of the 366 items and is largely in Petrarch's autograph, the 317 quatorzains are all inscribed as seven double hendecasyllabic lines.[16] Drawing upon the evidence for Giacomo's practice in Vaticano Latino 3793 and for Petrarch's practice in Vaticano Latino 3195, then, the two preeminent manuscripts for the earliest history of the sonnet, we must conclude that the seven-line version represents its earliest form.

16. H. Wayne Storey is preparing a methodical study of what he calls "the visual poetics" in all the early manuscripts of Petrarch's poems. He observes:

> Both Petrarch's life-long draft copy (Vat. Lat. 3196) and his final copy (Vat. Lat. 3195) reveal a consistent application of scribal forms for the *Canzoniere's* various lyric genres. . . . For example, his own written format for the sonnet abandoned earlier Italian scribes' prosaic arrangements to present the fourteen verses in two symmetrical columns of seven lines of twenty-two syllables with a measured space between the two columns.
> (from the prospectus for a book entitled *Margins to the Middle: The Written Shape of Medieval Italian Lyric Poetry*, quoted by permission)

By clarifying the nonverbal signs in Petrarch's presentation, Storey will radically revise our reading not only of the sonnets in the *Canzoniere*, but also of the other verse forms.

Because Petrarch sophisticated the rather simple pattern of Giacomo's rhymes, however, the rhyme scheme of Petrarch's seven-line version does not conform to that of Giacomo's prototype diagramed above. But fours and threes are still prominent in Petrarch's modification. Although the sestet in Petrarch's quatorzains varies in rhyme, the most frequent arrangement is as follows:

a	b
b	a
a	b
b	a
c	d
e	c
d	e

This rhyme scheme displays some of the same fascination with permutations that we observe more rigorously pursued in the sestina.[17]

So what do we make of these salient numbers four and three in the quatorzain's form, and of their arrangement into a proportion 4/3? Here I propose we resort to the commonest symbolism of the Pythagorean-platonic tradition, even as it had been Christianized. Four is the mundane number—the number of the four basic qualities (hot, cold, moist, dry), of the four elements that comprise the macrocosm, of the four humours that comprise the microcosm, of the four seasons that comprise the annual unit of time, of the four ages that comprise the full human life, of the cardinal winds that comprise the wind-rose, and so on. In short, four is the number of the tetrad, the form that underlies all the systems that make up our natural universe (see pages 41–43 above). We can interpret the number four as not only pertaining to, but also confined to, the realm we know from our daily lives. Four signifies this world.

To interpret the number three, we need merely recall that in the platonic-Christian tradition it is the sacred number, the number of the Trinity. Three signifies the deity. Furthermore, it implies the mystery of three-in-one, the miracle of multeity subsumed in the holy One.[18] In the terza rima and tripartite division of the *Divina commedia,* Dante exemplifies how a

17. See Margaret Spanos, "The Sestina: An Exploration of the Dynamics of Poetic Structure," *Speculum* 53 (1978): 553–57; and Marianne Shapiro, *Hieroglyph of Time: The Petrarchan Sestina* (Minneapolis: University of Minnesota Press, 1980).

18. "Was not Nomber, thinke you, wonderfullie honoured, when noe name was thought

devout poet can use this number in the construction of a monumental edifice with pointed theological import.

Now, I believe, the significance of the proportion 4/3 becomes evident: four represents this world, while three represents divinity. Moreover, the sum of these integers, seven, represents the entire range of human experience from lowest to highest. Of course, seven has been assigned special meaning in most systems of number symbolism, but the one operative here is defined by Agrippa: "The *Pythagorians* call it the Vehiculum of mans life . . . for the body consists of four Elements, and is endowed with four qualities. Also the number three respects the soul"; and Agrippa concludes: "The number seaven therefore, because it consists of three, and four, joyns the soul to the body" (193). The proportion 4/3, then, encapsulates the relation of body to soul, reflecting the relation between the mundane and celestial in the macrocosm. And as readers proceed through the sonnet, passing from quatrain to tercet (or from octave to sestet in the fourteen-line scheme), they proceed from this world toward heaven.

The pattern is described more systematically by Augustine, who delineates seven "degrees" of the soul, "expounding the soul's power in the body, its power in itself, its power before God."[19] The final stage results in the soul's perfection: "At length, in the vision and contemplation of truth, we come to the seventh and last step, not really a step, but a dwelling place to which the previous steps have brought us"; and Augustine dissolves into rapturous silence: "What shall I say are the delights, what the enjoyment, of the supreme and true God; what breath of undisturbed peace and eternity" (142; cf. 147). At the static stage of beatitude, the soul reaches beyond the efficacy of signifiers.

So the sonnet carries its readers along this trajectory toward blessedness, and after completing its seven-part form they eventually arrive in the presence of the deity, like Dante at the end of the *Paradiso* and Spenser at the end of *Fowre Hymnes*. Or like the worshiper in a church, who enters the main portal, traverses the nave (the "ship" that symbolizes the voyage of our life), reaches the holy point of the crossing where the altar stands, and peers forward into the inner sanctum of the choir.[20] The form represented

moare meter for God, then the name of Nomber? I meane .1. and .3. the name of the Trinitie" (Recorde, *Whetstone*, b2).

19. "The Magnitude of the Soul (De quantitate animae)," trans. John J. McMahon, S.J., in *The Immortality of the Soul* et al., trans. Ludwig Schopp (New York: Fathers of the Church, 1947), 136. On the number seven, see also *De civitate Dei*, 11.31.

20. The architectural comparison may be demonstrated precisely by devising a church according to the principles described by Sunderland. We could have a church with a nave

by the proportion 4/3 leads inexorably toward heaven, toward arrival in the presence of God, toward salvation. To corroborate this interpretation of the number symbolism, recall that seven is the number of the heptae-meron, which culminates in the sabbath.[21]

Finally, note that the form alone makes this statement, quite apart from the semantics of the verbal system. Regardless of what the language of the sonnet might say, its form guarantees redemption and proves the force-fulness of providence. The form of the quatorzain is unmitigatedly opti-mistic.[22]

In this sonnet by Giacomo da Lentini, the form and the verbal system mutu-ally confirm one another. The optimism inherent in the form coincides

---

comprising four bays, and with both transepts, the crossing, and the choir comprising one bay each (Fig. 6). A visitor entering the west door would experience the number four in the nave, the number three in the crossing, and finally the number one. The total number of bays, incidentally, equals eight, the number of baptism—that is, the number indicating the start of a Christian life.

In the Old Testament several passages contain such measurements to suggest symbolic form, most notably Noah's construction of the ark (Genesis 8), Moses' construction of the tabernacle (Exodus 25–40), and Solomon's construction of the temple (Ezekiel 40–45). On the symbolism of Noah's ark, see Augustine, *De civitate Dei*, 15.26; on its size and shape, see Don Cameron Allen, *The Legend of Noah: Renaissance Rationalism in Art, Science, and Letters* (Urbana: University of Illinois Press, 1949), 71–72, 78–80.

On the move away from this theory of architectural form during the sixteenth century, see James S. Ackerman, *The Architecture of Michelangelo,* Studies in Architecture 4, 2 vols. (London: Zwemmer, 1961), 1.1–7.

21. I have found no early writer on the sonnet who explicitly confirms my interpretation of the relationship between octave and sestet. Similarly, there is no contemporary treatise explaining the rationale for the geometrical tracery in stained-glass windows. But the significance of the proportion 4/3 was so evident in the culture that no one bothered to make it overt. Writing on early music, Hughes comments, "In the thirteenth century there was constant musical expression of the union between divine and earthly," and he proceeds to give examples depending largely upon manipulation of "the divine 3" and "the earthly 4" (8.590–91). Literary composition based upon number symbolism, of course, had been commonplace throughout the medieval period; for an annotated bibliography of modern scholarship, see Patrick S. Diehl, *The Medieval European Religious Lyric: An Ars Poetica* (Berkeley: University of California Press, 1985), 297n201.

22. Kleinhenz in his reading of Giacomo's sonnet does not resort to numerical analysis of the sort that I have used. Nonetheless, relying upon analysis of the language alone, he arrives at an interpretation that reinforces mine:

> The poet does not really expect to enjoy carnal pleasure with his lady in Heaven, but only to gaze upon her corporeal perfection. However, given that this cel-ebration of earthly beauty will occur in Paradise, in the presence of the Eternal Glory, we sense in the poet's attitude of worshipful adoration the beginnings

with the optimism of the speaker's expressed hope of beholding his lady beatified.[23] The significance of the mathematical construction produced by distribution of the lines as they are arranged by the rhyme scheme is reiterated by the language of the poem. The formal properties and the words say the same thing. Verbal and nonverbal signs coalesce.

Later poets, however, recognized that the formal properties of the sonnet and its actual language constitute two different systems; and while they can be coordinated—harmonized and synchronized—they may also be differentiated and opposed. So later sonneteers learned to play off one system against the other.[24] The subtext of form becomes a counterpoint to

of that upward movement in love, that transfiguration of the lady into the transcendental being, the true "donna angelicata" through whom the poet-lover may rise to the Divine. (42)

And he continues: "In these fourteen lines an immense distance, both spatial and ideological, has been traversed: from the poet's declaration of his humble desire to serve God on earth to win salvation in Heaven to his hoped-for eternal sojourn in Paradise."

Oppenheimer, like me, calls upon Pythagorean-platonic number theory to assign significance to the arrangement of octave and sestet in the quatorzain ("Origin of Sonnet," 302–4). While his hunch is right, though, his pursuit of it takes him wide of the mark. Naturally, he notes the proportion of eight to six, and then he wants to complete the harmonic proportion (6 : 8 : 12) by finding somewhere the number twelve. He does so by claiming that the last two lines of Giacomo's quatorzains act as a conclusion and break away from the rest: "These seem always, and despite appearances and rhyme scheme, to stand off by themselves, and so in a sense to leave the previous twelve lines as a rhetorically and numerically separate unit within the poem" (303). This observation seems dubious to me, but—voilà! Oppenheimer comes up with a twelve. On the harmonic proportion, see my *Touches of Harmony*, 90–95. What significance the presence of the harmonic proportion would have—in contrast, say, to the arithmetical or the geometrical proportion—is not clear in Oppenheimer's presentation.

An analysis of the quatorzain's structure more compatible with mine has been offered by Wilhelm Pötters ("La natura e l'origine del sonetto: Una nuova teoria," in *Miscellanea di studi in onore di Vittore Branca*, 5 vols. [Florence: Olschki, 1983], 1.71–78). Pötters observes that in Vaticano Latino 3195, a ms. of the *Canzoniere* in considerable part by Petrarch's own hand, the sonnets appear not as fourteen hendecasyllabic lines, but rather in seven double hendecasyllabic lines—that is, in the same arrangement as Giacomo's quatorzain in Vaticano Latino 3793 (see pages 73–76 above). The result is seven lines, each containing twenty-two syllables, the preferred disposition of the quatorzain in early mss. as confirmed by Petrarch's example. Pötters then notes that the proportion 22/7 is the quantity we indicate by *pi*, the mathematical sign representing the relation between the circumference of a circle and its diameter, and he concludes that the quatorzain is a metrical version of a circle. Like me, Pötters argues that the quatorzain comprising octave and sestet was a genuinely novel construction rather than an adaptation of existing stanza forms, as previous scholars have proposed.

23. Love is the common theme of Giacomo's quatorzains. All but one deal with love of the lady, and the exception addresses the theme of friendship, another sort of love.

24. Jensen notes this "movement away from unity" (75–76, 223–24).

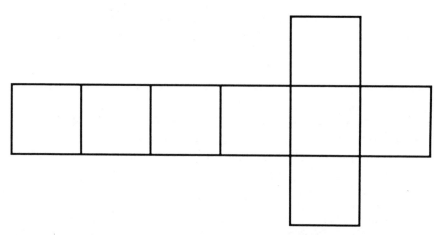

Fig. 6.   The floor plan of a church constructed like a quatorzain

what the words themselves might say. Although the form of the sonnet remains unrelentingly optimistic, promising salvation after the divagations and tribulations of this world, the language of the sonnet might very well express doubt, questioning the faith that characterizes the orthodox culture. The resulting tension between the subtext of form and the verbal system energizes the poem, producing two possibilities of interpretation. As we have seen (pages 23–31 above), the poem must then be referred to both the orthodox, logocentric, musical aesthetic as well as the radical, hylocentric, painterly aesthetic.

Petrarch recognized this interplay between the subtext of form and the verbal system in a sonnet, and he found it wondrously suited to the conflict between body and soul that he wished to confess in the *Canzoniere*. The ambivalence in Petrarch as reason struggles with passion has often been noted, especially as it was encapsulated in oxymorons.[25] But the conflict can be detected not only in formulations such as "dear enemy" and "bitter delight," but also in the opposition between language and form. The resultant dynamics are well exemplified by number 101:

> Lasso, ben so che dolorose prede
> di noi fa quella ch' a null'uom perdona

25. See William J. Kennedy, *Rhetorical Norms in Renaissance Literature* (New Haven: Yale University Press, 1978), 20–21; and my "Sequences, Systems, Models: Sidney and the Secularization of Sonnets," in *Poems in Their Place: The Intertextuality and Order of Poetic Collections*, ed. Neil Fraistat (Chapel Hill: University of North Carolina Press, 1986), 73–75.

et che rapidamente n'abandona
il mondo et picciol tempo ne tien fede;

veggio a molto languir poca mercede,
et già l'ultimo di nel cor mi tuona;
per tutto questo Amor non mi spregiona,
che l'usato tributo agli occhi chiede.

So come i dì, come i momenti et l'ore
ne portan gli anni, et non ricevo inganno
ma forze assai maggior che d'arti maghe.

La voglia et la ragion combattuto anno
sette et sette anni, et vincerà il migliore,
s'anime son qua giù del ben presaghe.

Alas, I know well that she who pardons no man [i.e., Death] makes of us her anguished prey, and that the world rapidly abandons us and keeps faith with us but a little while;

I see little reward for much yearning, and already the last day thunders in my heart. But, for all that, Love does not set me free, for he demands the usual tribute from my eyes.

I know how our days, our minutes, and our hours carry off our years, and I am not deceived but beset by forces much greater than magic arts.

Desire and reason have battled for seven and seven years, and the better one will win out, if souls down here can foresee the good.[26]

The verbal system of this quatorzain begins with morbid thoughts of death, the ultimate acknowledgment of mortality. And love provides no comfort, but instead complicates the desolation inflicted by the course of events. The sestet makes overt the theme of mutability, emphasizing the inevitability of death and verging toward despair. Line 12 offers an explanation for this torment in the lover: "Desire and reason have battled for seven and seven years." The language expresses Petrarch's anguish over this conflict between desire and reason.

26. Both the Italian version and its translation come from Robert M. Durling, ed. and trans,, *Petrarch's Lyric Poems* (Cambridge: Harvard University Press, 1976), 204–5. Later citations of Petrarch will include item and line numbers from this edition.

In the final line, however, Petrarch unexpectedly hopes that mortal souls can "foresee the good." Played off against mortality is a vision of beatitude. In the end, the subtext of form with its incipient optimism takes over, and an undeniably happy conclusion is admitted as at least a possibility. Although the eventual outcome is perhaps uncertain, the optimism expressed in the subtext of the quatorzain's form tilts the balance in favor of reason over desire. The verbal system of the quatorzain voices pain and wavering hope; but the form, although inoperative until its completion with the final line, eventually counterbalances the misery and holds out the promise of salvation.

In later quatorzains, however, the force of passion is more compelling. In number 236, for example, Petrarch states flatly: "I used to rein in my hot desire so as not to darken her clear face; I can no longer do it." And in number 240 he confesses to Laura, "I cannot deny, Lady, nor do I deny, that Reason, who reins in every good soul, in me is overcome by Desire." The latter poem ends with questions posed by Laura: "Why is he so desirous, and why am I so beautiful?"—troubling questions that remain unanswered. The conflict between desire and reason has intensified, with the outcome even more doubtful. Representing this ambivalence, the counterpoint between the verbal system and the subtext of form is also strained, and there is no resolution between them. The optimistic form of the quatorzain, though, as well as the spiritual beauty of Laura, is in the end again reassuring that goodness will prevail.

When Wyatt introduced the quatorzain to English audiences, he capitalized upon the generative interplay between verbal and nonverbal signs that the verse embodies. Rebholz assigns twenty-nine quatorzains to Wyatt with assurance (numbers 9–37), one of which is a double quatorzain (number 34).[27] Twenty-one of these were composed in paraphrase of Petrarch or his close followers. Among what we might call Wyatt's original sonnets, then, I take the following (number 30) as my exemplary text:

Each man me telleth I change most my device,	a
And on my faith me think it good reason	b
To change purpose like after the season.	b
For in every case to keep still one guise	a
Is meet for them that would be taken wise;	a
And I am not of such manner condition	b

27. R. A. Rebholz, ed., *Sir Thomas Wyatt: The Complete Poems* (New Haven: Yale University Press, 1981).

But treated after a diverse fashion,	b
And thereupon my diverseness doth rise.	a
But you that blame this diverseness most,	c
Change you no more, but still after one rate	d
Treat ye me well and keep ye in the same state;	d
And while with me doth dwell this wearied ghost,	c
My word nor I shall not be variable	e
But always one, your own both firm and stable.	e

This quatorzain is firmly divided into an octave and a sestet, with the *volta* at line 9 marked by "But," the common indicator. The rhyme scheme is the standard arrangement devised by Wyatt for his quatorzains, with few aberrancies.[28] In all his quatorzains with only two exceptions (numbers 34 and 37), Wyatt adopts the form of Petrarch's octave, rhyming *a b b a a b b a*. Without exception, each of Wyatt's quatorzains ends with a rhyming couplet.

In the verbal system of number 30, as usual, Wyatt puts the language in the mouth of a first-person male speaker. He begins by defending his changeableness, even while admitting that constancy is more consistent with wisdom. His fickleness, though, is brought about by the fickleness of his mistress; so he promises that if she becomes faithful, he too will forgo his variability. This abjuration of change neatly coincides with the stasis achieved in the rhymed couplet that concludes the quatorzain. Verbal and nonverbal signs mutually confirm one another.

Wyatt is known for the roughness of his metrics, and certainly that roughness is evident here. The rhymes are wrenched, so that among the *a* rhymes we find words as different as "reason" and "condition." Furthermore, the lines have varying numbers of syllables. In the first line, for example, there are eleven syllables, unless "telleth" is telescoped into a monosyllable. In the ninth line there are only nine syllables—although, since this line begins the sestet, we might make allowance for the *volta* and count it as some sort of pause to fill out the line. But no matter what accommodations we attempt, the eleventh line is aberrant: eleven low words have crept into that dull line.[29] And so on.

28. The exceptions are as follows: number 10, where the sestet rhymes *c d c c d d;* numbers 28, 29, and 33, where the sestet rhymes *c d c d e e;* number 34, the double quatorzain, where each rhymes *a b b a c d d c e f f e g g;* and number 37, which rhymes *a b a b a b a b a b a b c c.*

29. In his Miscellany, interestingly, Tottel smoothed out the scansion of these lines; see *Songes and Sonettes*, E2v.

The rhetorical organization of Wyatt's quatorzain also is transgressive—that is, the thought-units do not comply with any familiar structure of quatrains, tercets, and couplets in the traditional quatorzain. According to Petrarch's formula, the first four lines should be devoted to one thought-unit and so punctuated, the second four lines should be devoted to another thought-unit and so punctuated, and the sestet, though open to modest variation, should be divided into two tercets by the thought-units as well as the punctuation. In our own time the pattern has been abstracted by Mary Ellen Solt to produce a clever concrete poem (Fig. 7). In Wyatt's quatorzain, by contrast, the first *three* lines comprise one thought-unit with a period at the end. Lines 4–5, introduced by the disjunctive "For," comprise a separate thought-unit and appear as a rhymed couplet. Lines 6–7 comprise yet another thought-unit and appear as a rhymed couplet, while line 8, introduced by the conjunctive "And" and completing the octave, stands alone as an end-stopped line. Although Wyatt follows the rhyme scheme for Petrarch's octave, he plays footloose with its rhetorical organization. In his sestet, though, Wyatt follows Petrarch's model more conventionally—and appropriately so, I would say, because as the quatorzain approaches its closure in the rhymed couplet, Wyatt wishes to produce a sense of increasing orderliness.

The concluding couplet in Wyatt's scheme is important because of its signifying power. Given the metrical and rhetorical anomalies that he introduces to complicate and even obscure the traditional form of the quatorzain, it is all the more necessary that Wyatt ultimately establish its true value as a nonverbal sign of optimism. For that reason, Wyatt replaces Petrarch's form for the sestet with a quatrain rhyming *c d d c* invariably followed by a rhymed couplet *e e*. The previous multeity of the rhyme scheme is reduced to a couplet, and that duality is further resolved by the rhyme into a homogeneous unity. In effect, Wyatt collapses the Petrarchan sestet into a rhymed couplet in order to make clear that despite his sophistication of the familiar arrangement, the optimistic intent of the form remains in force. From this time in England, even though the rhyme scheme of the first twelve lines was subjected to various permutations, the rhymed couplet at the end remained a stock feature and continued to serve as a nonverbal reminder of the quatorzain's grounding in logocentric imperatives.[30] The effect is rather like that achieved by the verbal system alone in Herbert's "The Collar": although the first-person speaker strikes the

---

30. Formal features in other lyrics by Wyatt, such as the refrains in his rondeaus and songs, reveal a similar grounding in the logocentric aesthetic.

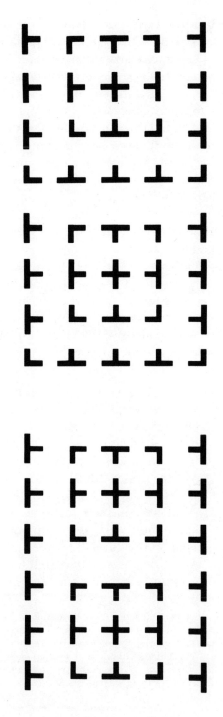

Fig. 7 "Moonshot Sonnet." Mary Ellen
Solt, *Concrete Poetry: A World View*
(Bloomington: University of Indiana
Press, 1968), 242

board and cries out angrily, after testing the limits of his defiance he hears a voice call "Child" and submissively replies, "My Lord."

This intertextual matrix, comprising not only the themes of earlier sonneteers but also the interplay between verbal system and formal properties, provided the coordinates for Elizabethan sonneteering, beginning with Philip Sidney and Thomas Watson but including Spenser, Shakespeare, Daniel, and Drayton. It is almost as though these major poets were obsessed by the possibility of ringing changes on the tradition. The tension between form and language—the opportunity of confrontation between them as well as of mutual confirmation—was seen as an unsurpassed means for expressing the tension between the logocentric and hylocentric imperatives in the contemporary culture. Exemplary texts abound; but I shall choose only one that, though well known, is still not always adequately understood.

Shakespeare's Sonnet 73 demonstrates how exquisitely a poet may for purposes of counterpoint play off the language of a text against the meaning of its formal properties. In this quatorzain, Shakespeare recalls the same topos as Surrey (pages 27–31 above): the lover caught in the seasonal cycle as an ideogram for time.[31] And similarly, the lover describes his landscape in graphic images:

That time of year thou mayst in me behold	a
When yellow leaves, or none, or few, do hang	b
Upon those boughs which shake against the cold,	a
Bare ruin'd choirs, where late the sweet birds sang.	b
In me thou seest the twilight of such day	c
As after sunset fadeth in the west,	d
Which by and by black night doth take away,	c
Death's second self, that seals up all in rest.	d
In me thou seest the glowing of such fire	e
That on the ashes of his youth doth lie,	f
As the death-bed whereon it must expire,	e
Consum'd with that which it was nourish'd by.	f

31. Operative here is the microcosmic analogy between the life of a human, the four times of the day, and the four seasons: "The infancie of man may be resembled to the morning, and to the spring time of the yeere: mans age to midday and to the summer: olde-age to the Evening and to Autumne: and death to night and to winter" (La Primaudaye, *Second part of French academie*, 412). E. K. makes explicit the same analogy in the Argument before the December eclogue of Spenser's *Shepheardes Calender*.

This thou perceiv'st, which makes thy love more strong,   g
To love that well, which thou must leave ere long.   g

Notice how Shakespeare has organized his poem. Each of the three quatrains is given over to a separate image described in extended detail: in the first four lines the lover is seen as autumn, in the second quatrain as twilight, and in the third as a dying fire. Because the number of images is reduced from the plethora of one-line descriptions we saw in Surrey's quatorzain, the effect is more pointed, more personal.

Actually, unlike Surrey's poem, where the speaker does not appear until the final couplet, in Shakespeare's sonnet first-person pronouns indicate the presence of the lover from the start. Moreover, the poem is further personalized by the use of metaphors. Whereas in Surrey's poem the creatures in nature are described as entities quite apart from the lover, in Shakespeare's sonnet the lover *is* a wind-blown tree, a sunset, a smoldering fire. Each of these entities is near the end of its natural cycle, drawing close to its demise; and therefore by these images the speaker announces his own imminent death. The pessimistic message of mutability—that all things must die—is clear and unmistakable.

And yet, because this is a quatorzain, an optimistic message inheres in its form. The relationship of four to three embedded in the octave-sestet arrangement might be obscured by the more complicated rhyme scheme of the English sonnet, but it nonetheless persists. A subtext of form reminds us that, despite the continuous changes wrought by time, an everlasting divinity shapes our end, so that change transmutes to perfection and death leads to eternal life. Shakespeare's poem, like Surrey's, concludes with a rhymed couplet, and this happy stasis represents the abode of heavenly love. This logocentric reality, obtruded into the poem by formal properties, provides the conditions that allow this to be a love poem. The reference to heavenly love makes love possible at the human level; and therefore Shakespeare's poem ends with the lover asking that the loved one intensify his love in the brief interim before death.

Despite the optimistic message immanent in the form of the quatorzain, however, the subject matter of this poem consists of decay, and the language of the final couplet assumes that the lovers, far from being joined in irruptible union, will soon be forever parted. There is no permanent resting place for the faithful lover where his long service will be rewarded with grace. Whatever joy love brings must be realized within the fast-changing world of human time. Implicit is the hedonistic message of carpe diem:

"Gather ye rosebuds while ye may, for Father Time is flying." The comforting message of the quatorzain form is not borne out by the message of the verbal text; indeed, the logocentric reality seems to be invoked as a foil to show how far the hylocentric reality falls short of its promise. Death is not the beginning of eternal life. This end brings no renewal, no reward. Surrey's sunny scene of freshly enlivened bird and beast has darkened to a winter landscape of fading hope, if not despair. While Surrey made the familiar topos of unrequited love into a witty *jeu d'esprit*, Shakespeare remakes it into a cry of anguish in the face of unremitting death.

In this instance, the language of Shakespeare's poem is glaringly at odds with the confident message of the quatorzain form. Verbal system and formal properties do not coincide, but rather confront and subvert one another. There is no resolution. The result is a rich and vibrant interplay that works against any simple reading and engages the reader in a very active role of interpretation.

Shakespeare was a consummate master at playing off the formal mode of signifying against the linguistic mode, although he was not alone in exploiting the difference between formal semantics and verbal semantics. With increasing frequency what the sonnet said through its words began to question and even refute the optimistic message of its form. Renaissance poets became ever more adept at setting up a counterpoint between formal properties and poetic imagery. And poetry became ever more painterly, while still echoing the distant harmony of heavenly beauty. In pretty sonnets, logocentrism and hylocentrism faced one another with fierce intensity and engaged in dynamic dispute.

When the deity created our universe, claims the orthodox cosmogony, he proceeded by imposing upon matter the idea of cosmos that resides eternally in his mind. His benevolent intention literally informs the mathematical order that pervades creation. Particularly the systematic motions of the heavenly bodies are evidence of God's careful planning, proof of his providential scheme; and both Plato's *Timaeus* and the Book of Genesis begin their accounts of creation by noting that the deity placed in the sky a greater light and a lesser light to mark the passage of time (cf. Fig. 5). Timaeus traces the origin of philosophy as well as theology to these manifestations of celestial order:

> The vision of day and night and of months and circling years
> has created the art of number and has given us not only the

notion of Time but also means of research into the nature of the Universe. From these we have procured Philosophy in all its range, than which no greater boon ever has come or will come, by divine bestowal, unto the race of mortals. (47A–B)

According to John Dee, the science of astronomy was instituted at the moment of creation in order to acquaint humankind with this divine intention: "*Astronomie,* was to us, from the beginning commended, and in maner commaunded by God him selfe. In asmuch as he made the *Sonne, Mone,* and *Sterres,* to be to us, for *Signes,* and knowledge of Seasons, and for Distinctions of Dayes, and yeares" (b2v).[32]

The sun and moon "in their perpetual round," to use Milton's phrase,[33] define the daily unit of time, and their complementarity repeated endlessly extrapolates to eternity. Similarly, the four seasons or the twelve months comprising the year are mathematical units of time to be endlessly repeated.[34] They are integers of eternity, and any one of these mathematical units can serve as an ideogram for time itself. Another very special case is the seven days of the week corresponding to the seven days of creation, the sacred heptaemeron of the Book of Genesis, because there, inextricably interlinked, we see our universe, time, God's will, and the providential scheme. Each is a metonym for the others, and the number seven is a nonverbal signifier activating all those interchangeable signifieds.[35]

32. Discussion of the diurnal, weekly, monthly, and annual units of time was commonplace; for seminal treatments, see Augustine, *De civitate Dei,* 11.6; and Valla, 4v–5v. For a volume devoted entirely to the subject, see Lilio Gregorio Giraldi, *De annis et mensibus, caeterisque temporum partibus . . . dissertatio* (Basle, 1541). For Spenser's presentation of this material, see "Cantos of Mutabilitie," 7.28–46.

33. See the epigraph to chapter 4 below.

34. This course of kind, to use the Elizabethan phrase, is concisely delineated by Louis LeRoy:

> The Sunne . . . rising and setting maketh the day and the night, by comming towards us, and going from us, causeth the yeres continually to be renewed, and by the obliquity or crookednes of the Zodiacke with the helpe of the twelve signes which are in it, doth distinguishe by his Solstices and Equinoxes the fower seasons of the sommer and winter, of the spring and harvest: In the which consisteth the vicissitude of life and death, and the change of all thinges: by the mediation of the first qualities, hot and cold, drie and moist, being duely tempered for generation, and unproportionably distempered for corruption. (*Of the interchangeable course, or variety of things in the whole world,* trans. Robert Ashley [London, 1594], fol. 2)

35. While praising number in general, Recorde singles out seven, "in whiche is contained,

This orthodox, logocentric culture gave rise to a topos that fundamentally affected the writing of poetry. In the formulation of Cristoforo Landino, "God is the supreme poet, and the world is His poem."[36] God created the universe in the same way a poet composes a poem, and this belief gave license for the notion of discerning God's will by reading the book of nature. The corollary, of course, is that a poet in composing his poem must follow the example of the deity as revealed in that book of nature. The poet is a mortal maker who emulates the heavenly maker to create a second nature—I take my vocabulary, as well as my argument, from Sidney, who imported this doctrine wholesale from the Continent and gave it great prominence in his *Defence of Poesie* (79.17–23).

So the poet must order his fictive universe according to the mathematical rules of proportion and harmony. He must create his poem according to number, weight, and measure. He must resort to meter and rhyme, and not casually. The metrics are not applied *post facto*, after the subject matter is laid out. That is mere versifying. Rather, meter and verse are integral to the composition, essential from the start. The metrics are, in fact, the raison d'être of the poem, which is intended to reflect God's use of number in creation. The very use of meter and rhyme makes an optimistic statement: it recalls God's benevolence. These formal properties serve as a metonym for God's ordered creation, and thence for the providential scheme. Despite what the *words* of the poem might say, as we have seen, these numbers encode the logocentric ideology. The formal properties of the poem make manifest the "heavenly beauty" that comprises its serious content. Spenser's *Fowre Hymnes* is an exuberant case where the subject matter reiterates the subtext of the tetrad form, arriving ultimately in the divine presence.

The force of this poetics abated during the course of the Renaissance, but certain traditional verse forms retained the power to signify. Terza rima, for example, though used less and less frequently, kept its association with the Trinity.[37] Even at the end of the sixteenth century there lin-

---

not onely the secretes of the creation of all thynges: and the consummation of the whole worlde againe, with the state of eternitie: But also by it is the Sabbothes reste, and thereby the full life and conversation of godlie persones, represented and insinuate" (*Whetstone*, b1v).

36. See my *Touches of Harmony*, 292, and *Sidney and Spenser*, 181. This topos in the same vocabulary persisted well into the seventeenth century; see Abraham Cowley, "Davideïs," in *Poems*, ed. A. R. Waller (Cambridge: Cambridge University Press, 1905), 253. In his notes, Cowley quotes Augustine as authority (*De civitate Dei*, 11.18), as well as Book of Wisdom 11.21 and Psalm 19.

37. For a dazzling combination of terza rima and quatorzains written as four tercets with

gered a general sense that metrics were significative and should be appropriate to the subject matter. In wan echo of the logocentric aesthetic,
Gascoigne wrote: "Ballades are beste of matters of love, and rondlettes
moste apt for the beating or handlyng of an adage or common proverbe:
Sonets serve aswell in matters of love as of discourse: Dizaynes and Sixaines
for shorte Fantazies" (56–57). Remembering the sacred associations of
seven and ten, Puttenham praised Chaucer: "His meetre Heroicall of *Troilus*
and *Cresseid* is very grave and stately, keeping the staffe of seven, and the
verse of ten" (61);[38] and Drayton employed ottava rima in *The barrons wars*
because, by his assertion, "This sort of stanza hath in it majestie, perfection, & soliditie."[39]

One of the more persistent verse forms was the seven-line stanza known
as "rime royal," which continued to suggest the heptaemeron and activate
that ideogram for time. When we examine the dynamics of the stanza, we
can see that the rhyme scheme itself reenacts the starts and hesitations that
mark the seven days of biblical creation, a fact that perhaps accounts for
its long-lived popularity. Although making the pattern explicit is awkward,
and perhaps even offensive—after all, it is the innate forms in our souls
that should respond in sympathetic vibration—I believe the effort to be
worthwhile. So, assuming that the rhyme scheme of the rime-royal stanza
is a nonverbal signifier, I offer this clumsy interpretation:

a   The first line institutes the space of the poem and differen-
    tiates it from infinity, just as God on the first day set apart
    the site of creation from the abyss.

b   The second line, which does not rhyme with the first line,
    distinguishes two entities within the space of the poem, just
    as God on the second day separated the waters below from
    the firmament, thereby initiating duality.

a   The third line produces a third entity that is distinct from
    the second line, but compatible with the first, just as God on
    the third day gathered together the waters so that dry land
    might appear, thereby initiating sameness as well as alterity.

b   On the fourth day God set the sun and moon in the heavens

---

a concluding couplet, see Philip Sidney, *The Countess of Pembroke's Arcadia (The Old Arcadia)*,
ed. Jean Robertson (Oxford: Clarendon, 1973), 124–25.

38. That is, each stanza has seven lines, and each line has ten syllables.

39. See my *Sidney and Spenser*, 343–44.

to institute time, thus making palpable his scheme; so too this line makes apparent for the first time the articulated scheme of sameness and otherness. It is a node in the process. Only at this point, in fact, can we accurately designate a pattern of *a* and *b* rhymes. Until this point, the rhyme scheme is inchoate, just as time did not exist until the fourth day when God set the sun and moon in place to mark its passage.

b   On the fifth day God created the lower creatures to populate his time-space continuum, and the repeated rhyme demonstrates how the creatures amplify and confirm what took place on the fourth day.

c   On the sixth day God created humankind, something new and wonderful, and the introduction of a *c* rhyme represents our novelty and also our superiority.

c   The repeated *c* rhyme announces that creation has reached closure, confirming humankind as the culmination of the system and demonstrating how we fit into the eternal scheme by our co-option into what is final.

By reasoning of this sort, I believe, whether it was consciously articulated or subliminal, Elizabethans assigned significance to rime royal and gave it honored status. According to Gascoigne, for example, "Surely it is a royall kinde of verse, serving best for grave discourses" (54). Spenser saw fit to adapt it as an envoy for his "Epithalamion," and Sir John Davies used it for his *Orchestra*.

When we see the rime-royal stanza as a spatialization and temporalizing of the number seven coordinated with the heptaemeron, we recognize it as a cognate of the quatorzain, which is informed by the sum $4 + 3 = 7$ as well as the proportion $4/3$. The seven double hendecasyllabic lines of Giacomo's sonnet lead us to Augustine's "undisturbed peace and eternity" (page 77 above) just as surely as the seven days of creation culminate in the sabbath. Moreover, we should also recognize the rime-royal stanza and the quatorzain as cognates of the literary calendar employed by Palingenius and Spenser, since $4 \times 3 = 12$, simply a further manipulation of these seminal integers. This sort of platonist mathematics pervaded the Renaissance, not only as a remnant of earlier orthodoxy but also as a continuing tradition refurbished by a line of distinguished theorists that stretched unbroken from Leon Battista Alberti in early fifteenth-century Italy to Thomas Campion at the end of the sixteenth century in England.

Such logocentric imperatives were expressed arithmetically in the metrical forms we have examined. In addition, not surprisingly, they were expressed also in geometry through the relationships perceived between various geometrical figures. Johann Kepler, as a late example, in a supreme effort that involved all the quadrivial disciplines—music and astronomy as well as arithmetic and geometry—determined the intervals between the planetary orbits by circumscribing each of the five regular solids with spheres which he then placed concentrically.[40] Before accepting the distances between the planets that had been calculated from observed data, Kepler required a theory based upon natural principle and grounded in platonist mathematics.

When we take the proportion 4/3 and express it geometrically, we confront a familiar configuration (Fig. 8). The number four is naturally expressed by a square, since a square has four sides and four corners. With equal conviction, though perhaps not so obviously to us, the number three was expressed by a circle. The interchangeability between three and the circle, however, was based upon the notion that each is "perfect." The number three was considered perfect because of its inescapable association with the Trinity, and hence with eternity and infinity. Correspondingly, the circle was declared to be the perfect geometrical figure for a number of reasons, variously adduced to suit the immediate occasion: it has no beginning or end, and therefore evokes eternity; all points on its circumference are equidistant from its center, and therefore it comprises a homogeneous unity; it encloses the maximum area that a line equivalent to its circumference is capable of enclosing, and therefore it represents a limit, like infinity. In geometry, then, the proportion 4/3 was expressed as the relationship between the square and the circle, and we now recognize it as the old problem of squaring the circle that obsessed mathematicians for centuries—by tradition, at least since Archimedes (Figs. 9, 10, and 11).[41]

40. See my *Cosmographical Glass*, 127–32.

41. For history and bibliography, see Jean Etienne Montucla, *Histoire des recherches sur la quadrature du cercle . . . avec une addition concernant les problèmes de la duplication du cube et de la trisection de l'angle* (Paris, 1754), which has been translated in William Alexander Myers, *The Quadrature of the Circle, The Square Root of Two, and the Right-Angled Triangle* (Cincinnati, 1874), 9–33. See also Augustus de Morgan, *A Budget of Paradoxes* (London, 1872); Ernest W. Hobson, *"Squaring the Circle": A History of the Problem* (Cambridge: Cambridge University Press, 1913); my *Touches of Harmony*, 141n88 (cf. 111–15); Paul Lawrence Rose, *The Italian Renaissance of*

The square, because it rests upon a firm base and diagrams the elemental tetrad, represents this world. The circle, because of its associations with divinity, represents heaven.[42] In consequence, the relationship between square and circle that this problem seeks to determine is actually a geometrical formulation of the metaphysical problem of relating the material and the spiritual.[43] Humankind—the essential link in the chain of being, the nexus between the sensible realm and the kingdom of heaven—is the natural meeting-place where divinity and corporeality coalesce (cf. Fig. 12). But this central position in the universe poses practical questions. In one direction, how does the mortal gain immortality? In the opposite direction, how are divine laws introduced into human affairs?

The answer in geometrical terms, which seems no answer at all to us, involves perfecting the square—that is, transmuting the square into a cir-

---

Mathematics: Studies on Humanists and Mathematicians from Petrarch to Galileo, Travaux d'Humanisme et Renaissance 145 (Geneva: Librairie Droz, 1975), 5–6, 30, 49–50; and my *Cosmographical Glass,* 184–91.

For most of those writing on the problem, it was largely a mathematical challenge rather than a metaphysical epiphany: as Hobson observes, "The problem of 'squaring the circle' is roughly that of constructing a square of which the area is equal to that enclosed by the circle" (4). Hobson, though, wrote as a professor of mathemathics at Cambridge during the early decades of our century, very much in the spirit of scientific modernity and out of sympathy with "non-Mathematicians." Nonetheless, he acknowledged the metaphysical dimension of the problem in earlier centuries: "The man of mystical tendencies has been attracted to the problem by a vague idea that its solution would, in some dimly discerned manner, prove a key to a knowledge of the inner connections of things far beyond those with which the problem is immediately connected" (4).

For a convenient compendium of treatises on the topic available during the sixteenth century, see the appendixes to Gregor Reisch, *Margarita philosophica* (numerous editions between 1512 and 1583, and perhaps others). These include tracts by Giovanni Campano, Giorgio Valla, and Charles de Bouelles. Luca Gaurico edited the tract of Campano, *Tetragonismus idest circuli quadratura* (Venice, 1503), augmented with treatises on the topic by Archimedes and Boethius. Jacques le Fèvre d'Etaples edited the tract of Bouelles and appended it to *Epitome compendiosaque introductio in libros Arithmeticos divi Severini Boetii* (Paris, 1503). Other famous writers on the topic include Nicholas of Cusa, "De quadratura circuli," in *Opera,* 3 vols. (Paris, 1514), 2.59–60; Oronce Finé, "De quadratura circuli," in *Protomathesis* (Paris, 1532), fols. 89v–91v; and Joannes Buteo, *Opera geometrica, quorum tituli sequuntur . . . Confutatio quadraturae circuli ab Orontio Finaeo factae* (Lyons, 1554), 42–50. John Dee offers a geometrical solution (fol. 356v–357; cf. also c1v–c2v).

42. On the square and the circle, see Puttenham (98–101): "As the roundell or Spheare is appropriat to the heavens, . . . so is the square for his inconcussable steadinesse likened to the earth" (100).

43. One of the most familiar icons of the Renaissance is Leonardo's version of the Vitruvian motif inscribing a male figure within both a square and a circle, an icon that has only recently been fully explicated by Carman. Geoffroy Tory used a series of similar diagrams to show that his letters of the alphabet and the human body share the same proportions (*Champ Fleury* [Paris, 1529], fols. 17–19).

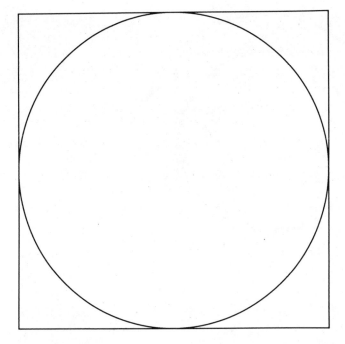

Fig. 8.   The squared circle

cle by transforming it into a polygon with an infinite number of sides. This answer is unacceptable today because it requires a leap across the hiatus between the finite, which we know well enough, and the infinite, which exists not as an actuality for us but only as a convenient concept. In a materialist culture the infinite is by definition an unrealizable alterity that exceeds the summation of finite things, and we are not prepared to make the leap of faith necessary to breach this carefully crafted disjunction between finitude and infinitude. Constricted by our materialist conditioning, we similarly misunderstand the ancient canard about how many angels can dance on the head of a pin—which, properly formulated, should be "How many angels can dance on the *point* of a pin," because this also encapsulates a metaphysical problem about the relation between the spiritual and the material. The right answer is that an infinite number of angels can dance on the point of a pin because angels are insubstantial and therefore take up no space whatsoever. The question seems foolish to us because we subscribe to a culture different from the one reputed to have devised it.

In any case, the problem of squaring the circle involves increasing the

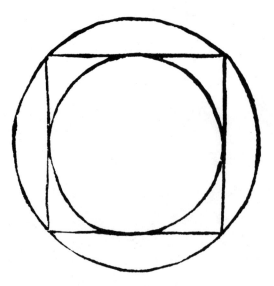

Fig. 9.   Squaring the circle. Charles de Bouelles, "Liber de circuli quadratura," in *Epitome compendiosaque introductio in libros Arithmeticos divi Severini Boetii,* ed. Jacques le Fèvre d'Etaples (Paris, 1503), fol. 87

number of sides in the square from four to infinity; or, conversely, disrupting the perfection of the circle by introducing angles into its circumference. Earthliness is beatified, or divinity is rendered frangible and thereby mutable. Donne toyed with these possibilities. Since God had long been emblematized as a circle with center everywhere and circumference nowhere, Donne saw squaring the circle as a novel way of representing the deity in comprehensible terms. He begins his ode "Upon the translation of the Psalmes by *Sir Philip Sydney,* and the Countesse of Pembroke his Sister" with an address directed heavenward:

> Eternall God, (for whom who ever dare
> Seeke new expressions, doe the Circle square,
> And thrust into strait corners of poore wit
> Thee, who are cornerlesse and infinite). . . .

Donne knew that an adequate depiction of divinity is as difficult as squaring the circle, because in each case the incongruity between the realm of spirit and the realm of matter must be overcome.

The metaphysical issues encoded in the problem of squaring the circle are the same as those we found addressed by the fours and threes inherent in the form of the quatorzain. Because the quatorzain depends upon the prototypical proportion 4/3, thereby reducing the complexity of the

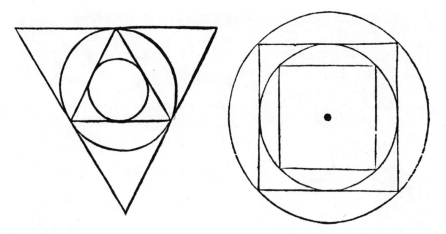

Fig. 10. The inscription and circumscription of triangles and circles, and of squares and circles. Charles de Bouelles, [*De géometrie*] (Paris, 1542), fol. 43v

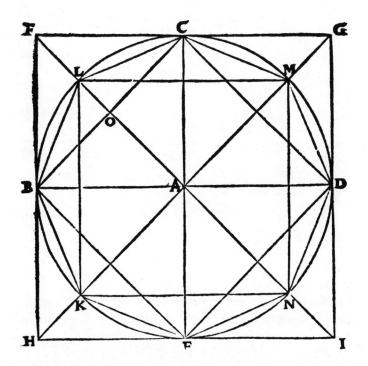

Fig. 11. Squaring the circle. Oronce Finé, "De quadratura circuli," in *Protomathesis* (Paris, 1532), fol. 91

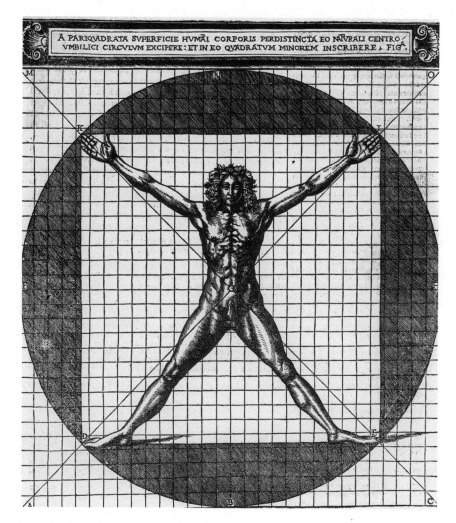

Fig. 12. "Vitruvian man," inscribed within both a square and a circle. Vitruvius, *De architectura libri dece,* ed. and trans. Cesare Cesariano (Como, 1521), fol. 50

many metrical forms that signify to the lowest common denominator, it is the simplest arithmetical statement of the relationship between this world and the divine. Correspondingly, the problem of squaring the circle is the simplest statement of that relationship in geometrical terms.

But other, more elaborate, possibilities exist within the semiotic system of geometrical symbols—for example, the intricate arrangement of circles, triangles, and squares that make up the tracery in stained-glass windows. A magnificent case in point is the early thirteenth-century rose window that still illuminates the south transept of the cathedral at Lausanne, where the integers of eternity that we have noted are embellished with much else to produce an intricate pattern of interlocking geometrical forms (Fig. 13).[44] Among its prominient features, there are four panes in the central square (2–5) depicting the sun, the moon, day, and night which surround a pane (1) representing the year. Immediately outside this square, symmetrically arranged, are four panes (7, 11, 15, 19) representing the seasons; and each season, in turn, is surrounded in its semicircle by three panes representing the months that comprise it (8–10, 12–14, 16–18, 20–22). Outside this configuration, four panes representing the elements are placed strategically as centers of circles (24–27), and they are intermixed with panes depicting the sun at the top (28) and the moon at the bottom (29), the signs of the zodiac (30–41), and the divinatory sciences (63–64). Panes depicting eight winds (54–61) dot the periphery of the construction; while various other sets of panes, such as four depicting the rivers of paradise and eight depicting monsters, provide the necessary fillers to complete the assemblage. Although fours and threes and squares and circles insistently assert themselves, a sense of unity emerges from the multeity. Furthermore, as in all rose windows of the period, the subject matter has been rigorously subordinated to the form, even though labels on many panes provide a verbal component. The geometrical subtext serves as the major mode of signifying.

The logocentric culture relentlessly pressed art into service to the Church, so as a matter of course we find these geometrical principles projected into the three dimensions of religious architecture. The performance of squaring the circle, in fact, becomes a cliché in church building. Whenever a dome is placed over a crossing, we have a representation of the scheme. And when the church is planned in the form of a Greek rather than Roman cross, the relevance of the square cum circle is made even more salient. This is the impetus, I believe, behind the persistent interest in centrally designed churches.

Bramante's plan (c. 1505) for the new Saint Peter's in Rome (Fig. 14), for instance, exemplifies the fascination with squaring the circle and pro-

44. For greater detail, see Ellen J. Beer, *Die Rose der Kathedrale von Lausanne und der Kosmologische Bilderkreis des Mittelalters,* 2 vols. (Bern: Benteli, 1952), vol. 2; and Beer, *Die Glasmalereien der Schweiz vom 12. bis zum Beginn des 14. Jahrhunderts,* Corpus Vitrearum Medii Aevi, Schweiz (Basel: Birkhäuser, 1956), 1.23–72.

Fig. 13.   Plan of the rose window, south transept, Lausanne Cathedral. Ernest Murbach, *La Rose de la Cathédrale de Lausanne,* Guides de Monuments Suisses (n.p.:
Société d'Histoire de l'Art en Suisse, 1970), 3

liferates the principle throughout a multitude of details. A large dome rises
above the central crossing, and this motif is repeated symmetrically in
chapels occupying the four angles, while a variation of it is reenacted in
four towers comprising the extreme corners of the construction. The ichnographic representation of Bramante's proposal for Saint Peter's is little
more than an exercise in the interplay between squares and circles.

Bramante's plan was never implemented. One of the most famous examples of Renaissance architecture, however, similarly incorporates the rela-

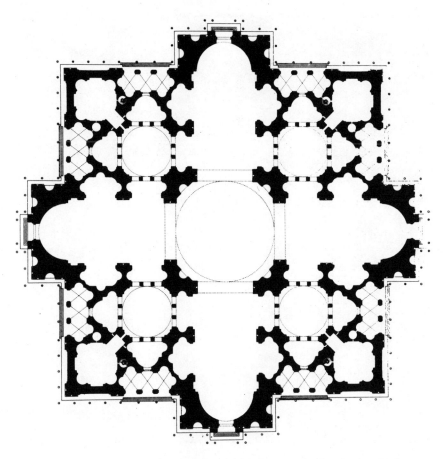

Fig. 14.   Bramante's floor plan for Saint Peter's, Rome. John Barrington Bayley, *Letarouilly on Renaissance Rome,* ed. Henry Hope Reed (New York: Architectural Book Publishing Co., 1984), 121

tionship between square and circle, appropriating it to make a lofty state-ment. The Medici chapel designed by Michelangelo, properly referred to as the new sacristy of San Lorenzo in Florence, appears immediately as a version of squaring the circle. The floor is exactly square, and by a series of architectural accommodations this square is transformed into a circu-lar opening, which is surmounted by a commanding dome (Fig. 15).[45]

45. The configuration of Michelangelo's dome when viewed from below recalls the squared circle of alchemical medicine; cf. Figure 16, and my *Cosmographical Glass,* 184–88.

Fig. 15.   Photograph of the cupola from the inside, Medici Chapel. Photographic
Archives, Joseph C. Sloane Art Library, University of North Carolina, Chapel Hill

Michelangelo could have found this scheme in the old sacristy of San
Lorenzo designed by Brunelleschi a century earlier; but, as I have suggested, it is inherent in any church where a dome caps the crossing.

Michelangelo reinforced this interpretation of his plan by an allusion
to the tetrad explicit in the suite of sculptures he prepared to decorate the
tombs. Known commonly as Day and Night and Dawn and Dusk, the large
human figures by express intention represent the four phases of the diurnal unit of time.[46] In each pair of statues, significantly, one is female and

46. See nn. 31–34 above.

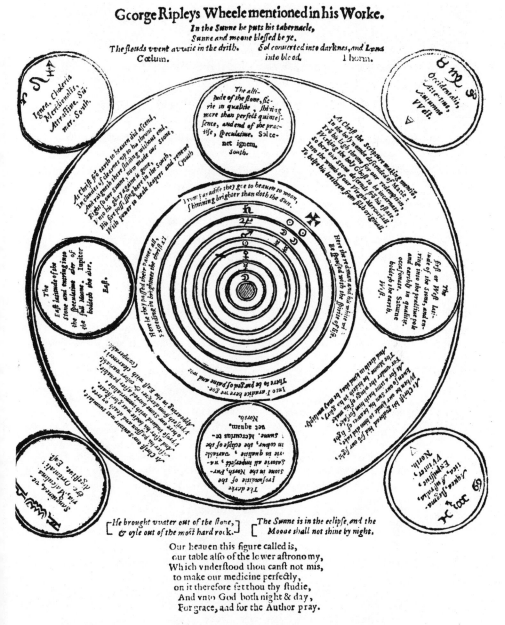

Fig. 16. The squared circle of alchemical medicine. George Ripley, *The compound of alchymy*, ed. Ralph Rabbards (London, 1591), M3

one is male, so that in an almost alchemical fashion alterity and complementarity are carefully played off against one another. Even more important, this sculptural program locates the bottom reaches of the construction (where the tombs reside) firmly within the flow of time. It proclaims
the temporal nature of mortality.[47]

When we look at a wall-section of Michelangelo's construction, though,
we see how he transmutes this mortality into a hopeful ascension toward
immortality (Figs. 17 and 18). He gradually circularizes the square floor
as it rises toward the heavenly dome. The lowest tier of the wall is divided
by strong pilasters, and in actuality the bottom story of the chapel is clut-
tered by the tombs, eight doors, a program of deeply recessed niches, and
extensive statuary. Next comes a much-simplified second tier, where a semicircle is introduced as well as windows symmetrically placed to admit light.
In the third tier, even further simplified, carefully contrived pendentives
provide a harmonious geometry including arcs and circles, and make the
final adjustment for the dome. In the otherwise unadorned lunettes of
this tier, windows providing the main source of light pierce the wall, and
as Ackerman observes, "They are unique in diminishing in breadth toward
the top, as if in a perspective with its vanishing point at the lantern; the
canted lines continue those of the cupola" (1.24). At last, the cupola soars

---

47. Creighton E. Gilbert cites an "iconographic note" by Michelangelo accompanying
some sketches:

> Day and Night, it begins, speak, and say: "We with our swift course have brought
> the Duke Giuliano to death." We are here required to think of Day and Night
> in motion—swift motion—and not of a single day and night but of Day and
> Night as such, alternating days and nights in motion that causes death. This
> is a motion through time, and such motion of day and night is perhaps most
> conventionally imagined as making circles, the endless round of time. (402)

Citing a memoir written in the 1540s by Donato Giannotti in which Michelangelo participates and often quotes Dante, Gilbert then observes:

> It is near the end of the *Convivio* [4.23] that Dante describes life as being an
> arc that rises and then falls and has four segments, the four ages of man, the
> four seasons, the four times of day. Thus the curving line, the times of day
> along it, and their meaning as the course of life, appear both in the Medici
> tombs and in this text of Dante.
> ("Texts and Contexts of the Medici Chapel," *Art Quarterly* 34 [1971]: 391–409)

On the sculptures as a program representing "Time which consumes all," see also Ascanio
Condivi, *The Life of Michelangelo* [1553], trans. Alice Sedgwick Wohl (Baton Rouge: Louisiana
State University Press, 1976), 67.

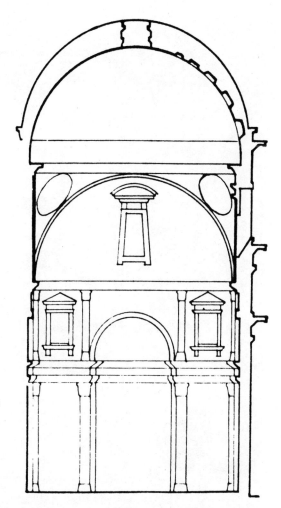

Fig. 17.   Drawing of wall section, Medici Chapel. Johannes
Wilde, "Michelangelo's Designs
for the Medici Tombs," *Journal
of the Warburg and Courtauld
Institutes* 18.1 (1955): 54–66
(plate 22d)

aloft, providing a terminus, but also an invitation to glide from this confined
world to a different order of geometrical perfection. This dome—which,
like that of the Pantheon in Rome, is coffered and hemispherical, almost
exactly so—completes the three-dimensional circularizing of the square.
Thereby the mortal is conclusively rendered immortal, while divine perfection is brought to bear upon the mutability that besets mankind.[48]

48. The Medici chapel, like most of Michelangelo's works, has occasioned fervent scholarly debate. The touchstone for current interpretation is Carlo Tolnay, "Studi sulla Cappella
Medicea," *L'Arte*, n.s., 5 (1934): 5–44, 281–307; repeated in Charles de Tolnay, *The Medici*

Fig. 18.　Photograph of a wall, Medici Chapel. Edizione Brogi 23948

To return to our starting point in this chapter, Giacomo da Lentini "invented" the sonnet, both in the modern sense that he was the first to use the peculiar octave-sestet arrangement and in the literal sense that he "came upon" this form in the larger culture. Giacomo devised this quatorzain form because it facilitated the expression of ennobling love as his culture perceived it. Seemingly, he followed the common technique of the medieval poet, a technique that starts with a fixed metrical form which is then fitted with an integument of words. Of course, when music is the sister art of poetry, formal properties predominate.[49] In such poetry, form is privileged as anterior to language, and therefore dominant over subject matter.

I am not suggesting, of course, that formal features are asemantical. Quite the contrary. They prove to be salient and signify independently of subject matter. The signifying power of the form operates within a semiotic system grounded in platonist mathematics, while the words of the poem operate within the semiotic system of language. It is possible that the meaning generated by the language will accommodate and confirm the meaning generated by the metrical form, but such corroboration is

Chapel, in Michelangelo [1943–60], 5 vols. (Princeton: Princeton University Press, 1948), 3.29–41, 61–75. Tolnay begins with a personal observation: "A visitor in this quiet room, slender and high in its proportions and lighted by a pale diffused light, feels himself carried away from empirical reality and removed to another world"; and he quickly announces his thesis: "The whole chapel was intended to be an abbreviated image of the universe, with its spheres hierarchically ranged one above the other" (3.63). While I do not agree with all elements of Tolnay's neoplatonic interpretation, I am sympathetic to the general thrust of his argument—which, incidentally, does not mention either the squared circle or the tetrad.

Between the article in L'Arte and his book, the interpretation by Tolnay was confirmed and elaborated with much iconographic evidence by Erwin Panofsky, Studies in Iconology: Humanistic Themes in the Art of the Renaissance (New York: Oxford University Press, 1939), 203–12. This neoplatonic reading of the chapel, however, has been severely challenged by Frederick Hartt, "The Meaning of Michelangelo's Medici Chapel," in Essays in Honor of Georg Swarzenski (Chicago: Henry Regnery, 1951), 145–55 (see also Hartt, History of Italian Renaissance Art [New York: Abrams, 1969], 487–89). Separately, John Pope-Hennessy also took Tolnay and Panofsky to task: Italian High Renaissance and Baroque Sculpture [1963], in An Introduction to Italian Sculpture, 3 parts, 2d ed. (London: Phaidon, 1970), 3.22–25.

The confrontation between neoplatonic interpreters of the Medici chapel (Tolnay, Panofsky) and their adversaries (Hartt, Pope-Hennessy) provides an excellent instance of my point that a single Renaissance work produces two discrete readings: one when analyzed according to the orthodox aesthetic, and another when analyzed according to the hylocentric aesthetic. Gilbert (cited in preceding note) exemplifies the current tendency to recognize the validity of both readings without necessarily reconciling them. For a balanced opinion on the topic of "Michelangelo's Platonism," see David Summers, Michelangelo and the Language of Art (Princeton: Princeton University Press, 1981), 14–17 and passim.

49. See James Anderson Winn, Unsuspected Eloquence: A History of the Relations between Poetry and Music (New Haven: Yale University Press, 1981), 85–87.

negotiable. In fact, in greater likelihood the two signifying agents (metrical form and language) will not coalesce. And the poet may indeed intentionally exploit this opportunity for counterpoint. In any case, in this poetics the words are merely the medium of the poem, not its essence.

If we think of this tension between formal properties and verbal integument as a form itself, we have two entities at odds with one another but nonetheless interrelated in never-ending cycles of alternation. Now formal properties predominate; now, verbal integument. The reader may interpret the poem with either one or the other as primary. Reading then becomes a process of interpretation whereby the poem is referred to one or the other semiotic system in order to generate meaning. As we have noted, the metrical form generates meaning according to the orthodox aesthetic, in which music is the sister art of poetry; the verbal system generates meaning according to the radical aesthetic, in which painting is the sister art of poetry. The reader's eventual chore consists of correlating these two meanings. Can they be reconciled to produce an integrated interpretation for the poem as a totalized entity?

It is this challenge, emerging as an insistent crux in our culture during the nineteenth century, that Paul de Man has analyzed as "allegories of reading." In this dynamic superform, according to his thesis, not only do formal features and verbal system subversively counter one another, but there are conflicts within the verbal system itself. Any statement admits of at least two, contrary meanings (8–19), so that "the text . . . leads to a set of assertions that radically exclude each other" (245). These internal contradictions prevent closure, so interpretation is interminably deferred. The only meaning possible for the text, then, is a self-reflexive commentary on the act of reading itself.

De Man draws his conclusions, however, from a body of post-Renaissance literature that, except for Rilke, appears in prose, the end products of a cultural process whereby the subtext of form had been systematically obliterated. His argument is applicable, perhaps, to a canon in which platonist discourse had been silenced—to a canon, in fact, whose ideology rejected logocentric principles. Curiously, however, and tellingly, in other literature of the same period the subtext of form had reappeared with renewed vitality as an urgent riposte against the ideology implied in the use of prose. Early in the nineteenth century the quatorzain made a much-heralded comeback, most notably in the sonnets of Wordsworth and Keats. Tennyson meticulously pursued metrical finesse, Browning sought explicit musical effects in his poetry, and Gerard Manley Hopkins soon followed with an even more introspective approach to metrics. Pater stood ready to proclaim what was obvious to an aesthete: "All art constantly aspires towards the condition of music."[50]

Similar attention to the subtext of form was developing also in poetry's sister art, painting. Artists began again to seek permanence in formal features, recalling the fascination with perspective that marks painting of the Renaissance. Because of the intervening triumph of materialism, however, nineteenth-century painters could not assume an invisible universal order instituted by an all-powerful deity. Single-point perspective may be a fact that seemingly holds in nature; but when transferred to the two-dimensional surface of a painting, it becomes a construction by artifice. So rather than slavishly replicating the appearance of an admittedly transient nature, painters instead sought form by attempting to *look through* external appearance to a hidden infrastructure, hoping to find some fixed points of reference in the kaleidoscope of everyday events.

In still lifes as well as landscapes Cézanne led the way for these cosmologists on canvas, with the cubists Picasso and Braque soon producing the purest results of the new search for a reality of forms. Monet, though, provides the most illuminating case in point, especially his so-called series paintings, because at the start his agenda was to capture as accurately as possible the evanescence of nature. Monet, like his forebears in the Renaissance, was poised on a cusp between realism and idealism.

During the 1890s Monet made a practice of returning to the same subject on several successive occasions, painting it at different times and in different light—different times of the day as well as different times of the year.[51] The most extensive series of these studies include grainstacks, poplars along the Epte River, an obscure mountain in Norway, an almost featureless view of the Seine in the early morning—hardly subject matter of a compelling sort. Even when he painted Rouen Cathedral, which he did some thirty times, Monet reduced this imposing structure to only a fraction of its facade, and he further reduced this fragment to a flat pattern of highlights and shadows in a subdued palette of narrow range. Although the "impressions" he achieved are startlingly realistic when viewed from the appropriate distance, by this time he was not interested in simply repli-

50. Walter Pater, "The School of Giorgione," *Fortnightly Review*, n.s., 22.2 (1877): 526–38.

51. See Grace Seiberling, *Monet's Series* (New York: Garland, 1981); John House, *Monet: Nature into Art* (New Haven: Yale University Press, 1986), esp. chap. 12; and Paul Hayes Tucker, *Monet in the '90s: The Series Paintings* (New Haven: Yale University Press, 1989), the catalog for an exhibition organized by the Museum of Fine Arts, Boston.

cating visible nature, as had been the dominant tradition in painting since the Renaissance.

We might even say that Monet was not much interested in his subject matter as such. Any old thing would do, even subjects as mundane as grain-stacks and poplar trees. Perhaps, even, the more mundane the better, because his pursuit was not the verisimilar representation of some arrest-ing subject. Rather, he was seeking what lay beneath experience. He was looking for that permanent something—that still life—that allowed these items to persist. He was looking for an essence that gave them identity despite the changes of light as time went by in its repetitive cycles. Although an item in nature changes in appearance from one time to another, it is still recognizable as the same item even if the viewer has not stood and watched it during the interim. *La plus ça change. . . .*

Such an interpretation of Monet's series paintings allows them to be read like a sonnet sequence. In a sonnet sequence the essential nature of the lady is revealed cumulatively in a series of short, partial poems report-ing the lover's fleeting perceptions of her: seeing her among other ladies, seeing her on a bridge, in church, on a boat, in a carriage, asleep. Just as the sonnet sequence is devoted to revealing the essence of the lady by recording a discontinuous series of impressions of her, so Monet's series reveal the residual character of the grainstacks or the poplar trees or Rouen Cathedral. The subject itself, although it cannot be known except through engagement with its temporal (and therefore partial) manifestations, dom-inates the series and provides coherence. The series, whether of sonnets or of canvases, is devoted to revealing the true nature of the subject in its perfection, and the outcome is a totalizing concept that subsumes all the preliminary glimpses of it. When first shown, Monet insisted that his series paintings be displayed en suite.

But there is another way of interpreting Monet's series paintings. Perhaps he assumed that there are no recurring phenomena that guarantee a con-tinuing identity to items in nature. So he was demonstrating their evanes-cence, the great differences in their states from one time to another. Each of his representations is a momentary record of a fleeting condition that has no substance—a state that exists only as difference. *His art* is the only reality in a world of conflicting and confusing phenomena.

Or, again, was Monet genuinely ambiguous, presenting at once both permanence and impermanence, inner form and outer illusion? His last series, and his greatest, depicts the surface of the pool in his garden where water lilies floated. These paintings when looked at coolly are a careful study in composition, a delicate arrangement of nebulous forms in an inde-terminate medium without horizon—an abstraction. After visiting Giverny, however, one realizes that these paintings are exactly what the eyes of an old man actually saw when looking down at the water dotted with plants in bloom and reflecting clouds in a blue sky. Nature could not be more accurately recorded. So there is perfect ambiguity in Monet's technique: the painting hovers between an exact replication of a passing scene in objective nature and the subjective abstraction that we associate with expres-sionism.

The abstract expressionists in the middle of the present century responded to Monet's search for inner form and extended it. Increasingly, objective nature was occluded, and the painting became its own justification. Increasingly, paintings ignored, or even denied, the relevance of anything else, and the painterly surface itself became the only reality. Like the deconstructionists in literary theory, the abstract expressionists eschewed even the possibility of an objective reality. The result was a progressive intensifying of abstrac-tion until it reached the dead end of minimalism. At this point the pop artists and others with a political purpose stepped in to endow art with specific content again and thereby rescue it from irrelevance.

The twentieth century has had its own share of conflicting imperatives in the culture, and as an addendum to our consideration of logocentrism versus hylocentrism in the Renaissance we might do well to reflect upon one of the masterworks of abstract expressionism. Barnett Newman's *Stations of the Cross* neatly inscribes a latter-day version of the interplay between inner- and outer-directedness. Like Monet's series paintings, *The Stations of the Cross* comprises a sequence of separate canvases, fourteen variations on a theme that Newman identifies as *Lema sabachthani*—"Why did you for-sake me?"[52] Newman hears this biblical question as the stricken cry of suf-fering humanity that has echoed down through the centuries since the beginning of human history. Each of his panels is a version of this theme, which he has abstracted and visualized in stark terms, producing a sum-mative work that integrates and transcends the individual panels.

In this series Newman paints upon untreated cotton duck, using only black paint and (briefly) white paint (Fig. 19). Alloway notes: "The recur-rent image in the Stations is of two bands, variously defined, that modu-late the field of raw canvas" (15). Between the vertical band anchored

52. See Lawrence Alloway, *Barnett Newman: The Stations of the Cross* (New York: Solomon R. Guggenheim Museum, 1966), 9, a catalog for an exhibition at the Guggenheim Museum; and Thomas B. Hess, *Barnett Newman* (New York: Museum of Modern Art, 1971), esp. 94–107.

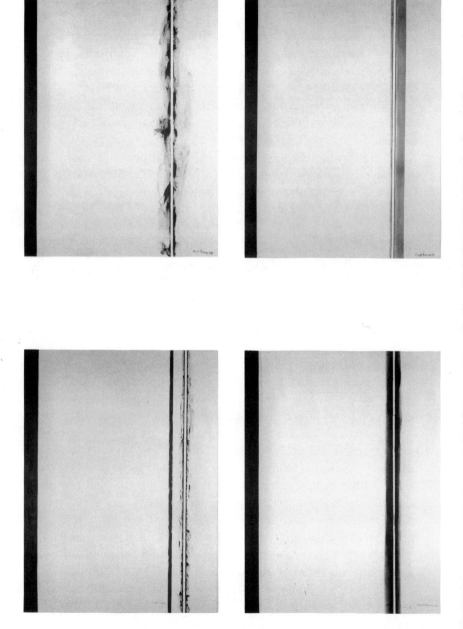

Fig. 19.   Barnett Newman, *Stations of the Cross*. National Gallery of Art, Washington, D.C.   Robert and Jane Meyerhoff Collection

firmly at the left edge of each panel and the band that moves more freely to its far right, a field is set apart which Newman modifies by its relation to the black or white paint that borders it. These modifications among the panels are perceived as shifts in tonality that are analogous to changes of color. A range of color is further suggested by the interplay between the naturalness of the canvas and the white paint that appears in three panels (9–11), and by the subtle modification of black within the series. Not only is the black sometimes solid and sometimes smudged, but Newman used oil paint and two different synthetic paints (magna and acrylic polymer), so that different blacks occur from one panel to another. As Alloway concludes, "The series as a whole, for all its impression of austerity, constitutes a highly nuanced system."

As in Newman's other mature canvases, in each panel there are what Hess calls "secret" symmetries that emerge and retreat—organizing, yet destabilizing the space, energizing the visual field. Extending these dynamics throughout the series, a medley of repetitions and variations among the panels induce the viewer to move backward and forward in a continuous process of cross-reference, recalling what has been seen before and noting what is new. Repeated motifs correlate a number of panels: for example, among the first eight panels, all but one has a dark vertical band that defines the left edge, like a *terminus à quo*. But these motifs are then varied, to suggest change and development within that consistency: for example, the originating black band in some panels is wider than in the first panel, while the black band in the sixth panel is fuzzed at its right edge, and in the seventh panel the motif becomes an unpainted band defined by a thin black line at its right. Furthermore, the second of the two vertical bands that Alloway speaks of—the one filling the right side of each panel—undergoes even greater metamorphosis from one panel to the next, and in the final panel expands to the point of obliteration. The last panel is all white, with only the slightest articulation (except for a narrow band at the left painted with white acrylic polymer, a thin wash of Duco covers the entire surface).

To be in a room surrounded by these panels, progressing from one to the next but aware of their totality, provides an overwhelming experience.[53] Semantics are subliminal, though struggling powerfully toward consciousness and precision. Relevant to the viewer's response, most critics agree, is the

53. The National Gallery of Art in Washington, D.C., has beautifully mounted *The Stations of the Cross* within a separate, circular room in the East Building, but with the questionable addition of an extraneous panel.

fact that Newman did not set out with an intention to paint fourteen panels representing the stations of the cross. Rather, he painted two panels in 1958 that seemed to him in some way related, although as yet he did not associate them with any specific subject matter. He painted two more panels of identical size in 1960, and only then did any idea of the stations come into his mind. It took six more years to complete the series. In his comments at the time, Newman encouraged some notion that the work generated its own form and preserves a record of its own creation. In other words, the work is, in the parlance of the '60s, a "happening," and the viewer should engage it as an active participant.

In my own encounter with the work, what eventually came to mind as I struggled to "read" it was its similarity to the quatorzain. There are, of course, fourteen panels to match the fourteen lines of the quatorzain. More substantively, the organization of Newman's *Stations* reveals an octave/sestet arrangement. When we engage the panels sequentially, the first eight panels cohere by virtue of the black band at their left edge, as we have noted. Furthermore, at panel 9 there is an abrupt change to all white, producing a *volta*. The last six panels are separated as a sestet. And in the final panel, with black paint and raw canvas eliminated, the resultant homogeneity suggests a resolution of conflict. Duality is reduced to sameness, and stasis ensues—as in the rhyming couplet that concludes the sonnet in England after Wyatt.

I am not idiosyncratic in this response. Hess reports that during an interview with the artist in 1966 when the work was first shown to the public, he asked: "It's like doing a sonnet, a given number of lines, and you fit into that form?" Newman replied, "Well, to the extent that a sonnet is an arbitrary poem, and to the extent that the Stations form an arbitrary number of paintings, I felt that it was appropriate to do it" (99). Hess asked if the artist began with a conventional scheme in mind, proceeding then to realize what already existed at least *in potentia*. Although Newman shies away from such prescriptiveness, he does acknowledge an inner form—not dictating that the work unfold in a predetermined manner, but recognizing that upon completion it recalls a familiar analogue. Newman suggests that he fulfilled this potential for form not by intention or even prior awareness, but by an intuition of rightness when it was completed. He knew when to stop, and lo! there were fourteen panels representing the stations of the cross.

Here, as elsewhere in his extensive writings, Newman is wary of formalistic analysis because of its antipathy to subject matter and therefore, in his view, its aridity. Attention to form comes at the expense of content. Nonetheless, in this work he makes his statement through the relationships of stark forms on a bare field. Thanks to his intensity, Newman is the most eloquent of a long line of painters who sought expressiveness through abstraction. Because of this renascent search for meaning through inner form during the last century, perhaps we are newly receptive to an appreciation for the subtext of form in the English Renaissance.

4 Companion Poems
The Discourse About Otherness

> *... light and darkness in perpetual round*
> *Lodge and dislodge by turns, which makes through Heaven*
> *Grateful vicissitude, like day and night.*
> —*John Milton*[1]

The opposition of day and night is a signifying opposition. . . . If I have taken day and night for my model, it is of course because our topic is man and woman. The signifying-man as well as the signifying-woman are nothing other than the passive attitude and the active attitude, the aggressive attitude and the docile attitude— nothing other than modes of behavior.

> —*Jacques Lacan*[2]

lthough they have their roots in the medieval débat,[3] companion poems, like the quatorzain, are a distinctively Renaissance phenomenon. They showcase distinctively Renaissance concerns. They address the relocation of reality that characterizes the

---

1. *Paradise Lost,* 6.6–8.
2. L'opposition du jour et de la nuit est une opposition signifiante. . . . Si j'ai pris pour exemple le jour et la nuit, c'est bien entendu parce que notre sujet est l'homme et la femme. Le signifiant-homme comme le signifiant-femme sont autre chose qu'attitude passive et attitude active, attitude agressive et attitude cedante, autre chose que des comportements. (*Le Séminaire: Livre III, Les Psychoses, 1955–1956,* ed. Jacques-Alain Miller [Paris: Seuil, 1981], 223; my translation).

In order to extrapolate from Lacan to other binary systems, cf. the following statement of Jacques Derrida: "The hierarchical opposition between son and father, subject and king, death and life, writing and speeech, etc., naturally completes its system with that between night and day, West and East, moon and sun" ("Plato's Pharmacy," in *Dissemination,* trans. Barbara Johnson [Chicago: University of Chicago Press, 1981], 92).

3. See Kathryn Hume, *The Owl and the Nightingale: The Poem and Its Critics* (Toronto: University of Toronto Press, 1975), chap. 3. Despite a poststructuralist bias that predicts his conclusions, even more is to be learned from Thomas L. Reed, Jr., *Middle English Debate*

Renaissance and by their very form delineate the range of possible ontologies. In essence, companion poems comprise a binary system that may be holistically integrated or, conversely, irremediably divided. Like other binary systems, they encapsulate a stable arrangement of two halves that overcomes difference; or, conversely, they remain inherently unstable, incapable of internalizing difference. These matters have received renewed attention in the current debate over the psychoanalytical theories of Jacques Lacan, so we may profitably ask: What do companion poems contribute to this ongoing discourse about otherness?

First, a working definition and a few examples.[4] By companion poems, I mean two relatively brief metrical compositions each of which is semi-autonomous, even though they are meant to be read together. Both exhibit the same metrical form and rhetorical organization, and therefore share an identity through their formal properties. However, each has a subject matter and argumentative intent exactly opposite to the other. Many examples appeared during the English Renaissance, but prototypical are two lyrics traditionally assigned to Marlowe and Ralegh, respectively. They were extremely popular and survive in several versions. They are best known, though, as printed in *Englands Helicon* (1600):

The passionate Sheepheard to his love.

Come live with mee, and be my love,
And we will all the pleasures prove,
That Vallies, groves, hills and fieldes,
Woods, or steepie mountaine yeeldes.

And wee will sit upon the Rocks,
Seeing the Sheepheards feede theyr flocks,
By shallow Rivers, to whose falls,
Melodious byrds sing Madrigalls.

And I will make thee beds of Roses,
And a thousand fragrant poesies,

Poetry and the Aesthetics of Irresolution (Columbia: University of Missouri Press, 1990). What Reed fails to understand, however, is that *varietas*, while it implies multeity and even pluralism, militates against disjunction and indeterminacy.

4. There has been no general study of companion poems as a genre; but see E. F. Hart, "The Answer-Poem of the Early Seventeenth Century," *Review of English Studies* 7 (1956): 19–29; and Steven W. May, "Companion Poems in the Ralegh Canon," *English Literary Renaissance* 13 (1983): 260–73.

A cap of flowers, and a kirtle,
Imbroydred all with leaves of Mirtle.

A gowne made of the finest wooll,
Which from our pretty Lambes we pull,
Fayre lined slippers for the cold:
With buckles of the purest gold.

A belt of straw, and Ivie buds,
With Corall clasps and Amber studs,
And if these pleasures may thee move,
Come live with mee, and be my love.

The Sheepheards Swaines shall daunce & sing,
For thy delight each May-morning,
If these delights thy minde may move;
Then live with mee, and be my love.

The Nimphs reply to the Sheepheard.

If all the world and love were young,
And truth in every Sheepheards tongue,
These pretty pleasures might me move,
To live with thee, and be thy love.

Time drives the flocks from field to fold,
When Rivers rage, and Rocks grow cold,
And *Philomell* becommeth dombe,
The rest complaines of cares to come.

The flowers doe fade, & wanton fieldes,
To wayward winter reckoning yeeldes,
A honny tongue, a hart of gall,
Is fancies spring, but sorrowes fall.

Thy gownes, thy shooes, thy beds of Roses,
Thy cap, thy kirtle, and thy poesies,
Soone breake, soone wither, soone forgotten:
In follie ripe, in reason rotten.

Thy belt of straw and Ivie buddes,
Thy Corall claspes and Amber studdes,

> All these in mee no meanes can move,
> To come to thee, and be thy love.
>
> But could youth last, and love still breede,
> Had joyes no date, nor age no neede,
> Then these delights my minde might move,
> To live with thee, and be thy love.[5]

Almost equally well known, and just as exemplary, are the twin songs of spring and winter that Shakespeare uses to conclude *Love's Labor's Lost.* And to indicate the popularity of companion poems into the seventeenth century, there is Milton's labored pair, "L'Allegro" and "Il Penseroso." Companion poems, then, comprise two exact counterparts that interact in a dynamic system of similarities and contrarieties, of sameness and otherness, of identity and difference.[6]

Recently the ambiguity of otherness has attracted considerable atten-

---

5. *Englands Helicon* (London, 1600), Aa1v–Aa2v (see *The Complete Works of Christopher Marlowe,* ed. Fredson Bowers, 2d ed., 2 vols. [Cambridge: Cambridge University Press, 1981], 2.519–37). A truncated version of these poems was printed in *The Passionate Pilgrim* (London, 1599), D5–D5v (William Shakespeare, *The Passionate Pilgrim,* ed. Joseph Quincy Adams, Folger Shakespeare Library Publications 4 [New York: Scribner's, 1939]). Another six-stanza version (with a variant fifth stanza) appeared in parallel columns on a broadside printed by Thomas Symcocke about 1603 (*The Roxburghe Ballads,* ed. William Chappell, Ballad Society, 2 vols. [Hertford: Stephen Austin, 1872], 2.1–6). The first poem bears the heading, "A most excellent Ditty of the Lover's promises to his beloved"; and the second, "The Ladies prudent answer to her Love." Both are to be sung "to a sweet new tune, called *Live with me, and be my Love.*" Beneath the headings are a pair of woodcuts representing a lord and a lady (Fig. 20).

6. The theory and practice of the philosophical dialogue, especially when conceived as dialectic, bears at least tangentially upon the study of companion poems—which, in fact, may be construed as a special case of the philosophical dialogue. For the Renaissance, a prototype of the philosophical dialogue may be found in Petrarch, *De remediis utriusque Fortunae,* translated by Thomas Twyne as *Phisicke against Fortune, as well prosperous, as adverse* (London, 1579); see also Kennedy, *Rhetorical Norms,* 20. In Petrarch the two interlocutors are Joy and Reason, who sound very much like the shepherd and the nymph, though the speeches of Reason are much longer than those of Joy.

The philosophical dialogue during the Renaissance has been studied by several literary scholars. The two most recent books, each with an extensive bibliography, are K. J. Wilson, *Incomplete Fictions: The Formation of English Renaissance Dialogue* (Washington, D.C.: Catholic University of America Press, 1985); and Jon R. Snyder, *Writing the Scene of Speaking: Theories of Dialogue in the Late Italian Renaissance* (Stanford, Calif.: Stanford University Press, 1989). For a cogent discussion of the discipline of dialectic in the sixteenth century, see Lisa Jardine, *Francis Bacon: Discovery and the Art of Discourse* (Cambridge: Cambridge University Press, 1974), chaps. 1–2. For a relevant critique of many of the Platonic materials I use, see Hans-Georg Gadamer, *Dialogue and Dialectic: Eight Hermeneutical Studies on Plato,* trans. P. Christopher Smith (New Haven: Yale University Press, 1980), esp. chaps. 5, 6, 7.

Fig. 20.   Woodcuts from a ballad version of "Live with me, and be my Love." *The Roxburghe Ballads,* ed. William Chappell, Ballad Society, 2 vols. (Hertford: Stephen Austin, 1872), 2.3

tion in anthropological and political as well as psychological contexts, with emphasis upon the indeterminacy of mutuality. This wide-ranging discourse is often grounded in—and certainly nourished by—Lacanian principles describing the means whereby individuals acquire psychic identity in opposition to a "symbolic order," the "other" that surrounds them. By bringing Lacan to bear upon companion poems, therefore, I hope to illuminate more clearly what and how companion poems signified in Elizabethan England. At the same time I hope to reveal the restless ambiguity which permitted them to instantiate the conflict of ontologies that we have seen to prevail in the Renaissance. By their very dynamics, companion poems accomplish an easy accommodation to both the logocentric and the hylocentric realities, and therefore easily adjust to the relocation of reality that was occurring during the period. They were, in fact, designed for this pur-

pose and prove wondrously effective as representations of diverse worldviews. Their power to signify lies in this dynamism. They embody the conundrum of mutuality.

Following Freud, Lacan identifies sexuality as the dominant factor in the
individual personality, and he analyzes sexuality in terms of *jouissance*—a
word, we are told, impossible to translate adequately into English. According
to David Macey, though, *jouissance* "denote[s] an amalgam of enjoyment
and orgasm that is always caught up in a dialectic of desire which defines
the subject in terms of the other and of the desire of and for that other."[7]
The lover—unspecified by gender, though clearly assumed to be male—
confronts an object of desire that is female and therefore different from
himself; nonetheless, he hopes to appropriate and assimilate the female
"other." The sexual politics of this play for power become evident. And
when we add that the male can define himself only by opposition to the
female—a circumstance which, paradoxically, grants control of the male's
identity to the female (a reversal in the usual hierarchy sought by deconstructionists in general and feminists in particular) . . . well, in this game
of mutual dependency and willful struggle, the outcome is anything but
certain. To deconstructionists, in fact, it is patently indeterminate. Difference
defies resolution; otherness refuses to be internalized. The play continues
endlessly and unabated.

Describing otherness in sexual terms, of course, is not new; nor is it new
to describe desire in terms of otherness. Already in the *Symposium* Plato
had offered an extended discussion of desire for the other,[8] most memo-
rably concretized in the myth of the androgyne offered by Aristophanes
in praise of the god of love (189B–93E). In the beginning, says Aristophanes
(improvising a plot in the manner of a dramatist), there were three sorts
of sexual creatures: male, female, and androgyne, which as the name indicates was an integrated composite of the other two. In their self-sufficiency,
however, in their perfection, the androgynes grew impious; so by way of

7. *Lacan in Contexts* (London: Verso, 1988), 203. See also John P. Muller and William J.
Richardson, *Lacan and Language: A Reader's Guide to* Ecrits (New York: International Universities
Press, 1982), 355–414. The most concise account of Lacan's doctrine of otherness, in his
characteristic terms of male and female sexuality, is given by Bice Benvenuto and Roger
Kennedy, *The Works of Jacques Lacan: An Introduction* (London: Free Association Books, 1986),
187–95.

8. For Lacan's appropriation of Plato's *Symposium* to analyze *jouissance* in terms of Alcibiades'
desire for Socrates, see *Ecrits: A Selection*, trans. Alan Sheridan (New York: Norton, 1977),
322–23.

punishment Zeus sliced them in two along the fault-line between their distinguishable genders. Despite the separation into discrete sexes, though, desire for the other persists: "Each half longing for its fellow would come to it again; and then would they fling their arms about each other and in mutual embraces yearn to be grafted together." The resulting circle, formed in the act of intercourse and reproducing the circle of their original bisexuality, provides Aristophanes with his comedic definition of love. While we might see insouciance, and even irony, in Aristophanes' account of the androgyne, others reading it in the larger context of the *Symposium* have regarded it as affirmation of the ennobling completeness that love holds out to mortals—in the words of Aristophanes, "reassembling our early estate and endeavoring to combine two in one."

Whereas the androgyne provides a static model for combining opposites, a totalizing entity, the movement of the platonic dialogue itself provides a paradigm for the kinetic relationships within a binary system. In the dialogues where Socrates engages a single companion, through questioning he leads the other speaker through a series of positions, each of which is challenged in turn and rejected in favor of a position proposed by Socrates. The result is the gradual formulation of an agreement that approaches truth-value. In the dialogues including a larger number than simply Socrates and another speaker, there is a similar pattern of positive assertion, challenge, rejection, reformulation, and conciliation. As each speaker expresses his opinion, one by one, a dialectic is created whereby each possibility is rejected in favor of another, which is more nearly comprehensive. Each possibility is subsumed in an accumulating synthesis that eventuates in a consensus expressed by Socrates—in a consensus that has internalized its opposition.

Nonetheless, each rejected possibility remains as an invisible residue, Derrida's "trace." A deconstructionist would argue, therefore, that any conclusion proposed by Socrates has no positive substance. Since his conclusion has been reached by negating the views of his friends, it exists only by virtue of its differences with the opinions of others. Socrates' view enjoys no more than negative definition in a continuous dialectic with a succession of others. So the current discourse on otherness, clearly, is inscribed in the form of the platonic dialogue itself. Once the totalized model of the androgyne is set in motion, the binary system is subject to difference and consequently disruption. Change, with the multiple states it entails, opens the system to dissolution, dispersion, destruction. Poets since Ovid have denounced time as the insatiable devourer.

Those ages committed to logocentrism, however, were prone to take a positive view of mutability. Rather than lamenting the change that time inevitably occasions, leading to death, the faithful rejoiced in the ordered patterns in nature that, endlessly repeated, lead to a blissful eternity. "The ever-whirling wheele / Of *Change*," to use Spenser's phrase,[9] literally involves each mortal in the course of kind. Paradoxically, therefore, although the passage of time brings death, this death is the beginning of beatified life, since it incorporates the individual into the all-encompassing providential scheme. Multeity and otherness are homogenized in cosmic harmony. As Donne says with his usual wit, "Change is the nursery / Of musicke, joy, life, and eternity."[10]

So in those ages when logocentrism prevailed, discourse about otherness adopted the model of the androgyne, at least as an end result, and proceeded usually in terms of reconciling opposites. Projecting Plato into the realm of Christian ethics, Augustine gave prominence to this synthesizing dialectic in terms of good and evil, and he extended this ethical discourse into cosmology to propose a deific power that forces contraries to coexist. In a notable passage frequently quoted during the Renaissance— and one that we have cited as a touchstone for the topos that the world is God's poem (page 90 above)—Augustine proposes that "God would never create any man, much less any angel, if he already knew that he was destined to be evil, were he not equally aware how he was to turn them to account in the interest of the good" (*De civitate Dei*, 11.18). Augustine ranges evil against good, but places them in a hierarchy. Because of God's benevolence, evil occurs only as the provisional absence of its opposite, good; so evil exists only as a negative, as not being something else. Good always prevails, in accordance with God's will, because evil has no identity of its own.

Although in the providential scheme good eventually and inevitably overcomes evil as the cosmos returns to its pristine norm, evil does intermittently occur. And this disruption temporarily upsetting the norm produces a dynamism that permits change—indeed, accounts for the passage of time. In Augustine's cosmology, this altercation/alternation between good and evil "add[s] lustre to the succession of the ages as if it were an exquisite poem enhanced by what might be called antitheses." Augustine sees this ongoing process of confrontation and resolution as a divine rhetoric, a universal statement of God's goodness, his promise of human salvation: "So,

9. "Cantos of Mutabilitie," 7.6.1.1–2. Cf. Figure 26 in Chapter 5 below.
10. "Change," 35–36.

just as beauty of language is achieved by a contrast of opposites in this way, the beauty of the course of this world is built up by a kind of rhetoric, not of words but of things, which employs the contrast of opposites."[11]

To those in the wake of Augustine, the proper study of mankind was precisely this exquisite poem expressed in the divine rhetoric of contrasted opposites. And right reason is the divine gift that allows mere mortals to perceive the ultimate coincidence of those opposites and gain sustenance from it. "The soule is a manner of spiritual and reasonable substaunce, that GOD maketh of naught for to give lyfe and perfection to mans body," says Bartholomaeus Anglicus late in the Middle Ages; and he continues, "Because it is a substaunce that maye receyve contraryes: It receiveth understanding."[12] In its contest with the fallen flesh, the soul is all too familiar with the rhetoric of opposites, so moral awareness permeated the thinking of Renaissance humanists.

During the early Renaissance, Nicholas of Cusa focused attention upon the dialectic of reconciled opposites and endowed it with the sophistication of paradox. Transferring the locus of action from the universe to the psyche, from the macrocosm to the microcosm, he prescribed "learned ignorance" as the human condition.[13] We are fated to know only that we do not know. Such knowledge, however, serves as the basis of wisdom, because it induces a faith unavailable to reason. Once again, knowledge and ignorance—for the educated, the equivalents of good and evil—are arranged hierarchically; and, once again, the bad is obliterated by being defined in negative terms alone, the absence of learning. Such ignorance, however, if we recognize and profess it, becomes a summum bonum. When logically pursued to a conclusion, this line of thought decrees that the idiot, ignorant by nature and irremediably so, is God's chosen creature.

11. Cf. "The beauty of all things is derived, as it were, from antitheses, or contrasts" (Augustine, *De ordine*, 1.7.18). For an example of this Augustinian discourse in the Renaissance, see LeRoy, who includes a chapter: "How all things in the world are tempered and conserved by unlike, and contrarie things" (fol. 5–7). The force of this Augustinian tenet continued in post-Reformation England; see, for instance, Peter Sterry's religious tract on free will: "The Order and Harmony is there perfect, where the Variety is full. Contrariety is an eminent part of the Variety, which enlargeth the Variety, and heightens the Harmony. *Contraria juxta se posita magis elucescunt*, Contraries illustrate and heighten one another" (*A discourse of the freedom of the will* [London, 1675], 158; cf. 175).

12. *Batman upon Bartholomew*, ed. Stephen Bateman (London, 1582), fol. 13–13v.

13. The crucial study of Nicholas remains Ernst Cassirer, *The Individual and the Cosmos in Renaissance Philosophy*, trans. Mario Domandi (New York: Barnes & Noble, 1963), chap. 1, esp. pages 16–18. But see also Jasper Hopkins, *Nicholas of Cusa on Learned Ignorance: A Translation and an Appraisal of De Docta Ignorantia* (Minneapolis: Banning, 1981).

In the high Renaissance the discipline of alchemy still employed the coincidence of contraries in the discourse on otherness, and by means of the hermaphrodite returned to the theme of sexuality. This symbol for the opus recalls Plato's androgyne and encapsulates the intervening cosmological discourse about reconciling opposites. Figure 21, taken from a Paracelsan handbook of alchemy, provides a typical example.[14]

The central figure, half female and half male, reveals the essential division that the opus is designed to resolve. The female right hand holds a flask facing downward, out of which descends a white dove; the male left hand holds a flask facing upward, out of which ascends a black dove— exact opposites in complementary gestures and performing complementary actions, each symbolizing one of the opposites to be reconciled in the alchemical process. But formidable differences and multeities must be overcome. In the corners of the diagram, the four bodily humours reproduce the elemental tetrad that comprises the microcosm, and they divide the hermaphrodite into equal quarters. A continuous pneuma flows around the central figure, indicating the need to integrate the disparate parts and the constant flux involved in doing so. And surrounding this pneuma, the twelve signs of the zodiac recall the annual unit of time that governs the macrocosm. Arranged sequentially going clockwise, they lay out the orderliness of the sun's yearly journey.

This diagram, dominated by a composite man-woman, delineates the difficulty and dimension of the problem in reconciling opposites, as well as confidently proposes a means of doing so. The cosmos, as God intends, supplies the patterns: the tetrad and the calendar. In the background the heptaemeron—culminating in the creation of man and woman, and crowned by the sabbath—offers a processive account of how God both created difference and overcame the divisiveness of multeity (pages 91–92 above). The alchemical hermaphrodite rests comfortably within this platonist, logocentric discourse about otherness.

There is a precise and limited number of paradigms for interrelating the two counterparts of a binary system such as companion poems. The counterparts may be reconciled in stable union to produce a whole greater than the two parts, a platonist model (Fig. 22a), where the counterparts are firmly integrated.[15] The opposites are reconciled in a totalized entity

14. See also my *Cosmographical Glass*, 188–89.
15. A prototype for this platonist synthesis of opposites is provided in Timaeus' account of how the demiurge generated the world-soul (*Timaeus*, 34C–37C). Cf. also Aristotle, *Physica*,

Fig. 21. The alchemical
hermaphrodite. Leonhard Thurneisser zum
Thurn, *Quinta essentia,
das ist die höchste subtilitet
krafft* (Münster, 1570),
Ffl.

that frustrates their difference. Or, the counterparts may confront and subvert one another to produce an aporia, a deconstructive model (Fig. 22b), where the counterparts are irreconcilably opposed and divided by a rift.[16] In this instance, difference precludes assimilation, stasis is pre-

---

187a12–189b29. For an example of this model in the Renaissance, see Daneau, *Wonderfull woorkmanship*, fol. 84v. In a chapter entitled, "Whether in the first creation of all thinges, God made two Contraries," the Student asks "whether God made two contraries, & the one to strive against an other?"; and the Master responds in a way that explains counterparts as phases in God's plan to provide variety and movement in the universe, but leading to the sabbath. Cf. La Primaudaye, *Third volume of French academie*, 160–61.

16. For this model, we may go directly to Derrida:

> In a classical philosophical opposition we are not dealing with the peaceful coexistence of a *vis-à-vis*, but rather with a violent hierarchy. One of the two

vented, and the resultant ambiguity thwarts any identity beyond indeterminacy itself.

There seem to be other possibilities also. In Figure 22c the counterpart with diagonal lines has overcome the counterpart with horizontal lines; and in Figure 22d, vice versa. But in actuality these two possibilities are simply intermediate versions of Figure 22a or Figure 22b. Looking again at

---

terms governs the other (axiologically, logically, etc.), or has the upper hand. To deconstruct the opposition, first of all, is to overturn the hierarchy at a given moment. To overlook this phase of overturning is to forget the conflictual and subordinating structure of opposition.

(*Positions*, 41; cf. Derrida, "Plato's Pharmacy," 92–93)

Note, however, the hierarchy is overturned only "at a given moment"—that is, the two counterparts engage in a continuous, arhythmic, and never-ending conflict, presumably with one and then the other dominating, and without stasis or predictability as a possible consequence. As Derrida states elsewhere, "Performative supplementarity is thus open to infinity" (*The Truth in Painting* [1978], trans. Geoff Bennington and Ian McLeod [Chicago: University of Chicago Press, 1987], 3).

For the same issue viewed from a logocentric perspective, cf. Dante in his letter to Can Grande della Scala:

Now of things which exist, some are such as to have absolute being in themselves; while others are such as to have their being dependent upon something else, by virtue of a certain relation, as being in existence at the same time, or having respect to some other thing, as in the case of correlatives, such as father and son, master and servant, double and half, the whole and part, and other similar things, in so far as they are related. Inasmuch, then, as the being of such things depends upon something else, it follows that the truth of these things likewise depends upon something else.

(*Epistolae,* ed. and trans. Paget Toynbee, 2d ed. [Oxford: Clarendon, 1966], 198)

According to this logocentric model, the conflict may be never-ending, but there is a truth, residing in the dominant counterpart.

During the Renaissance it is likely that Figure 22b would have been seen in terms of the Manichean dieresis of goodness and evil; see Philippe Duplessis-Mornay, *The Trewnesse of the Christian Religion*, trans. Philip Sidney and Arthur Golding, *The Complete Works of Sir Philip Sidney*, ed. Albert Feuillerat, 4 vols. (Cambridge: Cambridge University Press, 1912–26), 3.266–67, 290–91. For a similar discussion of the mutuality between good and ill—including justice and wrong, health and sickness, pleasure and sorrow—see Castiglione, 89–90. Such discourse was grounded in Socrates' interdependency of pleasure and pain in the *Phaedo* (pages 37–38 above). This platonic/Manichean analysis of the binary system as two equal and complementary components proved viable throughout the Renaissance: cf. a passage with the marginal gloss, "Why God ordained the Night and Day alternately to succeed each other," Guillaume Saluste du Bartas, *Devine weekes & workes*, trans. Joshua Sylvester (London, 1605), 19; and Samuel Pordage, *Mundorum explicatio or, The explanation of an hieroglyphical figure* (London, 1661), 25–27 (Wing P2974).

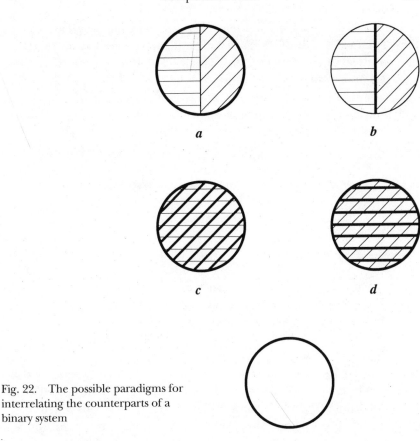

Fig. 22. The possible paradigms for interrelating the counterparts of a binary system

Figure 22c, where diagonal lines dominate, we ask: Has the diagonal counterpart assimilated its opposite, transforming its otherness into a homogeneous sameness; or does the horizontal counterpart retain a suppressed
potency, so that the diagonal half has introduced into itself a subversive
otherness? At this inchoate stage, both are incipient readings. Figures 22c
and 22d, then, represent intermediate stages of either Figure 22a or Figure
22b. Since inevitably they will evolve to something else, Figures 22c and
22d may be disregarded.

When we explore the signifying power of these possibilities, we should
begin with the ambiguities in the word "counterpart" itself. In companion
poems the two parts are "counters" for one another, identical in several
ways, such as vocabulary, metrical form, and rhetorical organization. But

yet, through the overt opposition of their subject matters and arguments, they "counter" one another. They confront, oppose, overturn, and cancel one another. So at all times there is the potential in the system for both synthesis and aporia.

Companion poems are emblematic of this dialectic between identity and difference, presenting the extremes of how the human condition may be viewed. One speaker offers an idealized, logocentric vision, where life is Arcadian joy; the other, an outlook that is hylocentric and pessimistic, where the inevitability of death eclipses life (Et in Arcadia ego). Each speaker has the opportunity of presenting a fully developed point of view. It is the relation between these counterparts, though, that ultimately matters. How the poet weights the balance between the two, or attempts to reconcile them, or accepts their difference—this relationship between the opposites is what reveals the underlying reality the poet is attempting to represent.

Plato, with Christian neoplatonists such as Augustine, presupposes an oxymoronic unity, as we have noted in Figure 22a. Under the auspices of a benevolent deity, opposites are reconciled in stable union, a metonym for heavenly grace. Lacan, however, and the deconstructionists, who follow a linguistic model derived from Saussure and based upon difference, reject the totalizing assumptions of Plato's doctrine and emphasize the aporia, as in Figure 22b. They go further, in fact, and deny even the possibility of a paradigm that invites fulfillment, and therefore which might serve as a teleological goal. They refute positivism and attack logocentrism, -isms associated with humanism and codified in the humanities. In their antitheological moves they deny a prior order of being that preexists human knowing, thereby interchanging epistemology for ontology. They advocate a reality of nothing more than free play, with neither origins nor natural laws.

But the matter is not so simple. Although the deconstructive arguments are ingenious and suasive, they pose a problem: How to avoid the slide into nihilism? Let's look at Figure 22e. If the two counterparts confront one another in a continuous process of subversion, as in Figure 22b, they in effect cancel one another. The net result is mutual negation. Only the bounds of the ensuing chaos remain. Jameson, aware of the problem at an early date, attempted to intervene and save the day by proposing that this mutual annihilation produces a perpetual dialectic with positive value: "In that ephemeral void . . . signification itself as an emergence is to be found."[17] But his argument that "the process of signification" occurs in the void is readily demolished (pages 138–146 below). To talk of a void as something other than nothing is to prevaricate. It is the medieval argument of *creatio ex nihilo*, but without a deity.

If, like so much poststructuralist thought, we begin with Saussure, we can think of these possibilities for interrelating the counterparts of a binary system (Figs. 22a–e) as potentialities for configuration of the sign, comprising signifier and signified. When Saussure introduces his definition of the sign, he pointedly says:

> The linguistic sign is, then, a two-sided psychological entity, which may be represented by the following diagram.

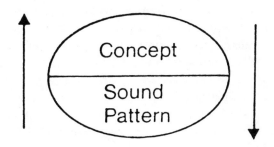

> These two elements are intimately linked and each triggers (s'appelle) the other. (66)[18]

The signifier, here labeled "sound pattern," and the signified, here labeled "concept," exist within a system of mutuality known by the inclusive term "sign."

But when we think of signifier and signified as mutually defining, each recalling the other through complementarity and existing only by virtue of the other's presence, we can identify yet another possibility for the relationship of counterparts in a binary system such as Saussure's sign. In Figures 22a or 22b, signifier and signified define one another, but within a cozily circumscribing boundary. In such a closed system, the counterpart

17. Fredric Jameson, *The Prison-House of Language: A Critical Account of Structuralism and Russian Formalism* (Princeton: Princeton University Press, 1972), 168; cf. 119–20.

18. Precisely because Saussure so intimately and inviolably links sound pattern and concept (speech and logos), Derrida castigates him as a logocentrist (*Of Grammatology*, 30–44).

is what the other is not; and if its other disappears, so does the counterpart we are seeking to individualize, because there is nothing to define it against. But the bounds of the system persevere, as in Figure 22e. In these three figures (22a, 22b, 22e), a boundary for the system is assumed as its precondition, an antecedent circumstance. However, if we obviate this boundary in order to open up the system and allow free play without prior restraint of any sort, as poststructuralists would have it, nothing is left to permit definition of either the system or its components. The entire project collapses and chaos follows. Saussure says as much: "Any linguistic entity exists only in virtue of the association between signal (signifiant) and signification (signifié). It disappears the moment we concentrate exclusively on just one or the other. We are then left with a pure abstraction in place of a concrete object" (101).

In this final configuration, the sign retains no identity except as a dialectic of signified and signifier, which are themselves mutually necessary. So when one goes, the other goes, and the sign as distinct entity also disappears. In the words of Saussure, the sign as concrete object vanishes, leaving only abstraction in its place. Since concrete actuality has been eliminated, we cannot illustrate this possibility by a palpable diagram. The enclosing circle (which gives definition to the preceding diagrams, Figures 22a–e) itself disappears. Here the binary system is totally, absolutely self-annihilating. This is utter nihilism, preserving not even the residue of a limit.[19]

19. Poststructuralists did not invent the problem of indeterminacy. Many in the Renaissance were well aware of it and under the aegis of logocentrism devised a solution that, predictably, exactly counters the nihilistic conclusion of poststructuralists. For logocentrists the inability to reach a stable meaning and produce closure does not indicate the absence of meaning, but just the opposite: the indeterminacy that erases the boundary of a finite system releases its elements to transcend that confinement and expatiate in the infinite and eternal. Rather than nihilism, the net result is unbounded and everlasting blessedness, approaching divinity.

A passage from Lyly's *Euphues and His England* illustrates the point. Euphues and Philautus are on the way to London to see for themselves the peerless English queen. When challenged for this impertinence, on the grounds that Elizabeth's magnanimity defies comprehension, Euphues replies:

> I graunt it, and rejoyce at it, and that is the cause of our comming to see hir, whom none can sufficiently commend: and yet doth it not follow, that bicause wee cannot give hir as much as she is worthy off, therefore wee should not owe hir any. But in this we will imitate the olde paynters in *Greece*, who drawing in theyr Tables the portrature of *Jupiter*, were every houre mending it, but durst never finish it: And being demaunded why they beganne that, which

A crucial question now formulates itself: Is nihilism the inevitable price for rejecting positivism? Spivak, the translator of Derrida, is aware of the problem and states it forthrightly, although she offers no solution:

> To locate the promising marginal text, to disclose the undecidable moment, to pry it loose with the positive lever of the signifier; to reverse the resident hierarchy, only to displace it; to dismantle in order to reconstitute what is always already inscribed. Deconstruction in a nutshell. But take away the assurance of the text's authority, the critic's control, and the primacy of meaning, and the possession of this formula does not guarantee much.

With a certain degree of pride and self-importance (because deconstruction is unique in this), Spivak soon concludes: "Deconstruction can therefore never be a positive science."[20] If deconstruction denies positivism in such definitive terms, rightly noting that as a precondition positivism sets up its own fulfillment, are there any grounds whatever for claiming knowledge or asserting truth-value?

To begin an answer, we must recall the path that led to our poststructuralist premises about what is ultimately real and what we may learn about that reality—that is, the basis for the ontology of free play and the epistemology of indeterminacy. The pertinent starting point is the Renaissance, characterized by a shift in the location of reality. Before the Renaissance, taking Augustine as our benchmark, there was a prior order of being, the deity, that necessarily precedes any human order of being or of knowing. All creatures inhere in his being, and all true knowledge refers to him. We may then characterize the Renaissance as that ontological shift after which

---

they could not ende, they aunswered, in that we shew him to bee *Jupiter*, whome every one may beginne to paynt, but none can perfect. In the lyke manner meane we to drawe in parte the prayses of hir, whome we cannot throughly portraye, and in that we signifie hir to be *Elyzabeth*.

(John Lyly, *Complete Works*, ed. R. Warwick Bond, 3 vols. [Oxford: Clarendon, 1902], 2.40)

The inability to describe definitively does not lead to a denial of meaning, but rather it signifies the transcendence of finitude—that is, it signifies something illimitable. Elizabeth's glory, like Jupiter's majesty, could not be contained within any bounds determined by humans. Spenser agreed—witness Gloriana, who stands outside and above the interminable meanderings of the knights and ladies that populate her epic kingdom and represent her plenitude.

20. Derrida, *Of Grammatology*, lxxvii–lxxviii.

ultimate reality resides not with the deity in a platonic-Christian heaven, but with objective nature. Ultimate reality now resides among the items we perceive with our senses. Although this shift has transpired over a long period of time—and only today is coming to its denouement, with the deconstructionists—the result is known by a generic term, empiricism. It has manifested itself in a succession of transformations with increasing emphasis upon a self-conscious subject: the so-called scientific revolution of the seventeenth century, the reliance upon reason in the Enlightenment, construction of the egotistical sublime during the Romantic movement, the existential angst of the modern period, and the rejection of preemptive paradigms that currently emerges.

In our own century, as the ontic questions have gained new urgency with the rapid advance of technology, they have produced a comparable crisis in the arts. We live in a postmodern, poststructuralist, postpositive environment, and literary theory is struggling to adjust to this fact. It is informative to see what led to deconstruction, so let's review briefly the increasingly rigorous application of empiricism that effected the alteration of literary studies during the last half-century.

Already by the time of the New Critics the author was neutralized as the origin of a text in order to give priority to its phenomena. Authorial intention was sublimated and the textual object was hypostatized in order to submit to empirical analysis, *explication de texte*. Necessarily such empiricism empowers the reader, so a doctrine of reader-response naturally followed. But when each reader reads for her- or himself, the result is pluralism, since no two subjects will read with the same sensibility. Pluralism, however, leads to relativism. Each reader produces a unique reading; but since there is no norm, no authority, by which to adjudicate among the varying results, all interpretations have equal validity. This relativism, though, then leads to indeterminacy: since any interpretation is as valid as any other, there is no way to determine which is better and which is worse, much less which is true and which is false. And this indeterminacy finally leads to nihilism, because when a text can mean anything, it means nothing. There is no stable other against which it can establish its own distinctive identity.

This is what I call the slide into nihilism.[21] Very few (de Man is an excep-

21. Culler explains: "Since deconstruction treats any position, theme, origin, or end as a construction and analyzes the discursive forces that produce it, deconstructive writings will try to put in question anything that might seem a positive conclusion and will try to make their own stopping points distinctively divided, paradoxical, arbitrary, or indeterminate"

tion) want to end up here, with the concomitant skepticism, agnosticism, and atheism. To avoid meaningless chaos, even Derrida in a desperate moment seems to accept a "transcendental signified,"[22] while Lacan resorts to a totalized "symbolic order."[23]

At the end of his influential essay "What Is an Author?" Foucault senses the danger and proposes his concept of "the author-function" as a means of controlling it. "The author," he says, "allows a limitation of the cancerous and dangerous proliferation of significations"; and again, "The author is the principle of thrift in the proliferation of meaning."[24] Foucault seeks to limit the unsanctioned production of meaning precisely because it leads to indeterminacy and nihilism, and because it makes the text available for appropriation by ideologies that are politically incorrect. To prevent such chaos, Foucault reinscribes the author as a boundary around the work. However, since the author, according to Foucault, is a construct by the reader, this proposal does not really solve the problem and avoid the danger of meaninglessness. Each reader according to his or her personal disposition constructs a different author-function for the text, so for each text there is the potential for an infinite number of author-functions. Again, indeterminacy, and eventual nihilism.

Some, like myself, would like to halt the slide into nihilism at the stage where multiple readings are countenanced, each with equal validity—that is, at the stage of pluralism.[25] William J. Kennedy, for example, proposes

---

(*On Deconstruction*, 259–60). John Searle addresses this "persistent confusion between epistemology and ontology," and refutes the now common assertion that there is no "independent reality that exists beyond texts" ("The Storm over the University," *New York Review of Books*, 6 December 1990, 40).

22. *Positions*, 29.

23. Muller and Richardson passim, esp. 19, 402–4. For Derrida's extended critique of Lacan—who, according to Derrida, remains "*inside* the logocentric, that is phonologistic, field that I undertook to delimit and shake"—see *Positions*, 107–13.

24. *Textual Strategies: Perspectives in Post-Structuralist Criticism*, ed. Josué V. Harari (Ithaca: Cornell University Press, 1979), 158–59.

25. Mikhail Bakhtin, recently acclaimed as a major theorist propounding "dialogism," is an unwitting ally of the pluralists. Bakhtin devised a concept of *heteroglossia*, which refutes Saussure's notion of *langue*, the touchstone for structuralism. There is no abstract system of laws that govern a language, says Bakhtin; rather, different people and different groups speak in different ways, reflecting their diverse social experience. Consequently, within a culture there are multiple voices, many unauthorized; and a literary text at all times participates in these numerous languages, so that various meanings continuously arise. See Tzvetan Todorov, *Mikhail Bakhtin: The Dialogical Principle*, trans. Wlad Godzich, Theory and History of Literature 13 (Minneapolis: University of Minnesota Press, 1984), 56–59; and Gary Saul Morson and Caryl Emerson, *Mikhail Bakhtin: Creation of a Prosaics* (Stanford, Calif.: Stanford University Press, 1990), 139–45 and 309–16.

that Petrarch's *Canzoniere* by itself exists as a text *in potentia,* and this potential is then realized in the numerous, widely varying commentaries that
followed in later centuries.[26] This argument is not only ingenious, but reas-
suringly productive when applied. Others, however, would say that Petrarch's
text retains its hegemony over the multiple interpretations found in the
commentaries, and therefore the individuality allowed to the several commentaries must actually give way to an originary authority. Derrida, in
fact, offers a stringent critique of pluralism that exposes it as monism in
disguise, and therefore logocentric: "One makes of art in general an object
in which one claims to distinguish an inner meaning, the invariant, and
a multiplicity of external variations *through* which, as through so many
veils, one would try to see or restore the true, full, originary meaning."[27]
What Derrida is after, of course, implies the impossibility of any stable
meaning.

As a further preventive to halt the slide into nihilism, there has been
talk of "intersubjectivity" among readers. Although different readers come
up with different interpretations, it is argued that all readers conditioned
by the same culture will reveal common elements in their interpretations.
The model is the intelligibility of a language among its community of speakers. But any notion of a homogeneous community of readers as a fixed
entity within which to ground meaning has been exploded as an oppor-
tunistic myth, the figment of desperate theorists. It is impossible to fix the
bounds of such a community, much less explain how it achieves the com-
monality that binds it together. The proposal of intersubjectivity among
readers simply begs the question of how the individual relates to the cultural other, Lacan's "symbolic order."

So how to halt this precipitous decline into nothingness? I have no con-

---

Bakhtin is congenial also to deconstructionists, because the multiple voices in both the
culture and the literary work are unsanctioned by authority, capable of infinite proliferation, and responsive to politics. For Paul de Man on Bakhtin, and the debilitating incon-
sistencies in his theory, see "Dialogue and Dialogism," *Poetics Today* 4 (1983): 99–107: "The
ideologies of otherness and of hermeneutic understanding are not compatible, and therefore their relationship is not a dialogical but simply a contradictory one. It is not a foregone
conclusion whether Bakhtin's discourse is itself dialogical or simply contradictory" (105).

26. "Petrarchan Authorities and the Authorization of Petrarch," Renaissance Society of
America Conference, Duke University, Durham, N.C., 12 April 1991.

27. *Truth in Painting,* 22. Derrida may well have in mind Roman Ingarden, who argues
that a text is constituted by the infinite number of readings ("concretizations") to which it
necessarily submits (*The Literary Work of Art,* trans. George G. Grabowicz [Evanston, Ill.:
Northwestern University Press, 1973], esp. 9–19).

clusive answer to this dilemma—remember, this is a poststructuralist world. But it may at least be informative to note where we made the turn that led to this dead end. Once we contrive a linguistic model teased from Saussure so that meaning is determined by difference alone, we enter upon a course that inevitably brings us to the impasse of indecipherability.

The argument, as briefly as possible, goes something like this. A word has no prescribed and fixed meaning of its own. It retains no positive signification, but rather signifies only by virtue of a value that emanates from its position within a system of differences. A word, then, is defined negatively by difference—Derrida's celebrated *différance*. The meaning of a word is determined by what it is *not* in a system of similar words—in technical parlance, by what it is *not* among a range of paradigmatic options. Therefore the negative—the absent, what the term is *not*—determines its value, its significance.

Furthermore—and it is at this point, it seems to me, that our slide into nihilism becomes irreversible—there are no stable entities to set limits for (and therefore to define) these differences upon which meaning depends. In any language, Saussure concludes, "there are only differences"; and he continues:

> Although in general a difference presupposes positive terms between which the difference holds, in a language there are only differences, *and no positive terms.* Whether we take the signification (signifié) or the signal (signifiant), the language includes neither ideas nor sounds existing prior to the linguistic system, but only conceptual and phonetic differences arising out of that system. (118)

According to this linguistic model, the system is liberated from all prior conditions. A language includes neither ideas nor sounds that preexist it. Being synchronic, the system is self-dependent, totally self-reflexive, and must provide its own bases for generating meaning. Nothing, though, is stable within this system. There are only differences, and these differences occur between indeterminate entities. There appears to be no objective reality.

But let's go back in Saussure's argument. In order to establish the thorough relativity of a word's meaning, Saussure bases that meaning upon the differences within a system. Then he argues that these differences are between terms which are unfixed, completely free. But that is only half true. Although the individual terms may be indeterminate, the range of options within which they have a paradigmatic relationship to the word being assigned value is quite determinate—in fact, predetermined by some undesignated authority. The range of options that comprises the system within which the word acquires meaning is limited, prescribed, and given a positive identity. There is an a priori assumption that the category has already been determined and that it is finite. Let me explain by a familiar example.

According to Saussure's theory, the word "brown" is defined as what is not red, black, tan, yellow, etc. The value of any of these other words is determined in the same way. But the point here is that the value of "brown" is assigned negatively by what it is not within the range of these related possibilities. That range of options, however, is specified in advance as the field of "colors" and is confined to entities within that register. By some unspecified authority, the possibilities have been severely limited. It would not work if we tried to assign value to "brown" within the conceptual field of desserts, say, or birds, even though there are brown desserts and brown birds.

The same is true when value is assigned to words not by what they mean but by how they sound. Again following Saussure (116–17), we determine a b sound by distinguishing it from p and m sounds—that is, from other labials. Gutturals and dentals do not enter into the determination because beforehand we know to limit our search to labials. But if we ignore this exclusivity and include all possible sounds in our range of options—even those not used in English—we have no way of escaping indeterminacy (and the slide into nihilism).[28]

Actually, the example of how "brown" acquires value through a process of differentiation from its paradigmatic fellows is not Saussure's. Rather, it was invented by Culler to illustrate his redaction of Saussure.[29] Tellingly, the argument of Saussure himself is much more cautious and narrow (*Course*, 112–14). He is locally concerned to distinguish between a positive *meaning* for a word and its relational *value*:

> The content of a word is determined in the final analysis not by what it contains but by what exists outside it. As an element in

28. In practice, we should note, Saussure assumes that the number of possible sounds in a language is *not* infinite: "Each language constructs its words out of some fixed number of phonetic units, each one clearly distinct from the others" (117). But what power has fixed the number of phonetic units, and made the distinctions between them?

29. Jonathan Culler, *Saussure* (Hassocks, Sussex: Harvester Press, 1976), 24–26.

a system, the word has not only a meaning but also—above all—
a value. And that is something quite different.

To illustrate his point that a word has a value as well as a meaning, Saussure then gives only two examples: *mutton/sheep* in English; and r*edouter/
craindre/avoir peur* in French. He logically concludes, "In a given language,
all the words which express neighbouring ideas help define one another's
meaning"; and he reiterates, "The value of any given word is determined
by what other words there are *in that particular area of the vocabulary*" (italics mine). That a "particular area of the vocabulary" must be specified in
advance is the delimiting condition that I am pointing to and that the
deconstructionists have overlooked.

When Culler comes to this portion of Saussure's argument, he proceeds
without taking into account the limitation that a word can be assigned
value only within a "particular area of the vocabulary." That limitation,
though, nudges toward the surface repeatedly in his presentation. Culler
begins in close echo of Saussure: "A language does not simply assign arbitrary names to a set of independently existing concepts. It sets up an arbitrary relation between signifiers of its own choosing on the one hand, and
signifieds of its own choosing on the other" (23). What Culler elects to
ignore, however, is Saussure's assertion that when the sign is considered
as a whole—comprising both its necessary parts, signifier *and* signified
(*Course*, 66–67)—the sign itself is no longer arbitrary or subject to indeterminacy:

> To say that in a language everything is negative holds only for
> signification (signifié) and signal (signifiant) considered sepa-
> rately. The moment we consider the sign as a whole, we encounter
> something which is positive in its own domain. A linguistic sys-
> tem is a series of phonetic differences matched with a series of
> conceptual differences. But this matching of a certain number
> of auditory signals and a similar number of items carved out from
> the mass of thought gives rise to a system of values. It is this sys-
> tem which provides the operative bond between phonic and men-
> tal elements within each sign. Although signification and signal
> are each, in isolation, purely differential and negative, their com-
> bination is a fact of a positive nature. (*Course*, 118–19)

The signified by relational differences acquires value in its system, while the signifier similarly by relational differences acquires value in its system. When united in the sign, however, they produce "a fact of a positive nature"—not just shifting values in a larger inclusive system, but presumably a stable meaning (the "mental elements") that can be transferred to the human brain.

Although, as Saussure continues, these combinations of signified and signifier provide "the only order of facts linguistic structure comprises," it is a necessary order. Without this stability a language could not perform its social role: "For the essential function of a language as an institution," Saussure concludes, "is precisely to maintain these series of differences in parallel." The responsibility of a language in actual usage is to insure the coordination of the signified in its relational system with the signifier in its relational system. Therefore, Saussure reiterates, "The moment we compare one sign with another as positive combinations, the term *difference* should be dropped" (119).

This proviso disregarded by Culler (and Derrida) causes difficulty as soon as he begins to give examples illustrating his redaction of Saussure. Culler handily demonstrates how French and English each has a distinctive (and therefore arbitrary) way of organizing the conceptual field that designates flowing bodies of water (i.e., the "particular area of the vocabulary" that covers flowing bodies of water). French uses *fleuve* and *rivière*, the former of which is distinguished from the latter by flowing into the sea; while English uses *river* and *stream*, which are distinguished according to a different criterion, size. Culler concludes, quite rightly:

> The fact that these two languages operate perfectly well with different conceptual articulations or distinctions indicates that these divisions are not natural, inevitable, or necessary, but, in an important sense, arbitrary. Obviously it is important that a language has ways of talking about flowing bodies of water, but it can make its conceptual distinctions *in this area* in any of a wide variety of ways (size, swiftness of flow, straightness or sinuosity, direction of flow, depth, navigability, etc.). (italics mine)

The point to make is that Culler not only designates a particular area of the vocabulary (i.e., "flowing bodies of water"), but also incipiently acknowledges that in order to generate value this designated field must be further subdivided according to even more restrictive criteria (i.e., size, swiftness of flow, etc.). The areas required to assign value become smaller and smaller. To assign value to "lagoon," for example, how many criteria must we spec-

ify? Is size an operative factor? Must it open into the sea? How deep must
it be, and is it navigable? We are caught in an intellectual exercise similar
to Achilles' futile attempt to catch the tortoise. No matter how specifically
we designate the area of the vocabulary in which we are working, there is
always a possible subdivision of it.

Even more debilitating is what happens if we head in the other direction.
What if we expand the range of paradigmatic options, as Saussure invites
us to do: "Any given term acts as the centre of a constellation, from which
connected terms radiate *ad infinitum*" (124). For the conceptual field in
Culler's example ("flowing bodies of water"), we can produce a fairly long
list of possibilities: to "river" and "stream" provided by Culler, we can add
rivulet, brook, creek (crick), bayou, rill, runnel, etc. (cf. Roget!). But what
if we add estuary, firth, cove, inlet, bay—can we exclude gulf, sea, and ocean?
The bodies of water grow larger and larger, less and less distinct—without
end. How about water vapor and clouds and atmosphere and sky and heavens and universe? By such an expansion, obviously, the conceptual field
loses its ability to serve as a range of *paradigmatic* options that negatively
determine a value for the signifier in question. Furthermore, paradigmat-
ically, can we exclude *non*-flowing bodies of water, such as pond and lake
(a bayou or swamp, for instance, is problematically a *flowing* body of water).
Where is the line drawn to delimit the area within which the word acquires
its value? A line must be drawn, or else the possibilities would be limitless;
and in an infinite field, again, meaning becomes impossible because there
is no determinate other against which an entity can define itself.

At a late point, this problem surfaces in Saussure's *Course*, and he addresses
it in a surprisingly self-contradictory manner:

> Everything having to do with languages as systems needs to be
> approached, we are convinced, with a view to examining the
> limitations of arbitrariness. It is an approach which linguists have
> neglected. But it offers the best possible basis for linguistic stud-
> ies. For the entire linguistic system is founded upon the irra-
> tional principle that the sign is arbitrary. Applied without restric-
> tion, this principle would lead to utter chaos. But the mind
> succeeds in introducing a principle of order and regularity into
> certain areas of the mass of signs. (131)

Apparently, it is "the mind" that applies the restrictions to prevent arbitrariness from turning into chaos. The human mind exercises an author-

ity that sets apart "the particular area of the vocabulary" within which a word acquires value (and thence meaning) by virtue of relational differences. Contrary to his usual stance, it seems as though Saussure has adopted here some notion of a universal, unchanging "human nature" with an innate sense of *langage*. Continuing to hedge, Saussure admits, "There exists no language in which nothing at all is motivated [i.e., predetermined]. Even to conceive of such a language is an impossibility by definition." But he pretty much leaves the matter there, nested in the double negatives. Are there fixed signifieds in language? Is there an objective reality to which language refers? This passage suggests an answer of "yes" to both questions, though elsewhere Saussure argues otherwise.

The difficulty does not go away. And we must ask not only *where* the line is drawn to delimit the area within which both signified and signifier acquire their values, but also *who* draws it. Culler asserts: "Not only can a language arbitrarily choose its signifiers; it can divide up a spectrum of conceptual possibilities in any way it likes" (24). But to avoid the notion of language as organism, we must identify a human agency at work here. Who designates that "spectrum of conceptual possibilities" in the first place? By what authority is that circumscribed area of the vocabulary set aside as the appropriate field for determining the differential relations that assign value to the word in question? Is it cultural (society?), natural (human nature?), or personal (the speaker or the listener?). The question is not raised in Saussure's text, and it goes begging in Culler's.

The most devastating critique of Saussurian linguistics has been Derrida's *Of Grammatology*, which first demonstrates that Saussure subscribed, knowingly or not, to the positivist metaphysics of a transcendental signified. Derrida deftly exposes Saussure's phonocentric, and therefore logocentric, assumptions. But the ulterior motive of this exposé is to empower writing and legitimize the vagaries that writing introduces into language. Derrida reverses the Saussurian hierarchy that makes writing simply a derivative image of the spoken language; with Derrida, speech becomes a species of writing, and he thereby liberates the written word from the power of the *logos*. In order to free writing so that it may proliferate without restraint, however, Derrida eventually adopts Saussure's notion of the arbitrary signifier that carries value (not positive meaning) by virtue of its function within a system of differences—in Derrida's words, "the thesis of *difference* as the source of linguistic value" (52; cf. 62–63). As Saussure had said, "The language itself is a form, not a substance" (*Course* 120).

But Saussure had warned (pages 143–144 above) that the linguist must respect "the limitations of arbitrariness" because, "applied without restriction, this principle would lead to utter chaos." Therefore Derrida heeds this warning and attempts to modify the arbitrariness of the signifier by claiming that it retains a "trace" of some previous determinant, a former presence that is now absent. Derrida must not elevate this former presence to the status of a transcendental signified, though, since that is the hallmark of logocentrism. Just as in the linguistics of difference, he must place a limit on its extent. So what he attempts is to turn this limitation into an advantage. Because a limit must be placed upon this former presence, he concludes, there can be no transcendental signified. The trace then serves as vestigial evidence that a transcendental signified does not exist: *"The trace is in fact the absolute origin of sense in general. Which amounts to saying once again that there is no absolute origin of sense in general"* (*Of Grammatology*, 65). After utilizing the transcendental signified as an absent presence, Derrida proceeds to obliterate it. For signification to derive from the emptiness that is *différance*, even the possibility of substance must be denied. But then, as Derrida states succinctly elsewhere, "The absence of the transcendental signified extends the domain and the interplay of signification *ad infinitum.*"[30]

Derrida's presentation is adroit and at first glance seductive, though it hardly holds up. Especially the notion of "the trace" is vulnerable because it is given too much to do. It performs as *une brisure*, to use another Derridean term; it acts like a hinge, attempting to hold together an essentially fractured argument. According to Derrida, the trace, although not controlled by a logocentric agent, preserves an imprint from some past or some other place: "The instituted trace is 'unmotivated' but not capricious" (46).

This attempt to avoid the semantic chaos that Saussure foresaw is a specious splitting of hairs: if something is "not capricious," it must be beholden to something else and therefore cannot be "unmotivated." This and the hemming and hawing that follows, in fact, are unacceptably obscure, dependent upon the literalness of oxymorons such as "an absent presence":

> The instituted trace cannot be thought without thinking the retention of difference within a structure of reference where difference appears *as such* and thus permits a certain liberty of

---

30. "Structure, Sign, and Play in the Discourse of the Human Sciences," in *The Structuralist Controversy: The Languages of Criticism and the Sciences of Man*, ed. Richard Macksey and Eugenio Donato (Baltimore: Johns Hopkins University Press, 1972), 249.

> variations among the full terms. The absence of *another* here-
> and-now, of another transcendental present, of *another* origin of
> the world appearing as such, presenting itself as irreducible
> absence within the presence of the trace, is not a metaphysical
> formula substituted for a scientific concept of writing. (46–47)

The chantlike playing with words, the verbal oppositions and variations
and nuances, cannot gloss over the basic contradiction. The trace may be
either unmotivated and capricious, or motivated and not capricious—but
hardly both unmotivated and not capricious. Moreover, in Derrida's argument, by whom is this trace "instituted"? Again, is it by a cultural, natural,
or personal agent? And finally, if the trace is "not capricious," as Derrida
says, how can it be autonomous and free to play?[31]

Despite his disclaimer that this "is not a metaphysical formula substi-
tuted for a scientific concept of writing," Derrida too suppresses and conceals in order to give the appearance that his metaphysics of absence is a
sustainable substitute for the positivist metaphysics of presence. Or by his
patent abuse of logic is Derrida demonstrating his larger point that logic
is possible only if one submits to logocentric rules? In the end, the trace
becomes inscrutable: "The trace is not more ideal than real, not more
intelligible than sensible, not more a transparent signification than an
opaque energy and *no concept of metaphysics can describe it*" (65). Like epochs
and texts, philosophers too invite "reading."

In any case, if the range of options is not artificially delimited but allowed
to become infinite, meaning cannot be assigned, not even negatively. If
the signifier for its value depends upon not being an infinite number of
other signifiers, it cannot mean anything, because there is nothing left for
it to signify. Infinity does not permit an opposite because, by definition,
nothing can lie outside it. It does not permit an other; it precludes otherness. Therefore it precludes meaning, because in an infinite field there is
no other against which an entity can define itself. Either we slide into
nihilism, or we assume an unacceptable authority and impose limits upon
the system within which the word gains its value and meaning.[32]

31. For the best effort to legitimize Derrida's concept of the trace, see Marian Hobson,
"History Traces," in *Post-structuralism and the Question of History,* ed. Derek Attridge, Geoff
Bennington, and Robert Young (Cambridge: Cambridge University Press, 1987), 101–15.

32. In a later work Derrida at least sniffs around the problem. Despite his contention that
discourse always requires supplementation and therefore always begets more discourse, he
postulates the necessity of a *passe-partout,* a phrase that commonly means "master-key," but
which Derrida associates with a picture-frame, in the sense that a frame opens access to an

All of this is esoteric, maybe boringly so: the learned tradition. The simple point, though, is that companion poems in England became the *popular* way of participating in this discourse about otherness and mutuality. Marlowe's shepherd and Ralegh's nymph, printed in parallel columns as a broadside, configure an alchemical hermaphrodite fit for sale along the thoroughfares. Companion poems provide a ready means for addressing questions of identity and difference in terms of common experience.

The passionate shepherd, representing the acquisitiveness of masculine sexuality, attempts to seduce his counterpart with a menu of Arcadian delights and unending pleasures. He wittily stakes out an aggressive position in sexual politics, presuming to implement the advantage that logocentrism allows to males. But surprisingly—or, perhaps, not so surprisingly—the wary nymph is not docile, as Lacan might have expected, and she refuses to play the usual game. Instead, she stakes out her own position, delineating her otherness, refusing co-option. In fact, cognizant of mutability—"Time drives the flock from field to fold"—the nymph argues restraint, if not abstinence. In this dialogue between body and soul she assumes the rational role in opposition to the fleshly. Since in platonist thought the soul is masculine and superior to feminine matter, the nymph reverses the traditional hierarchy of male and female, thereby exposing the self-contradiction of the pastoral love lyric. The allegiance to logocentrism professed by the male is revealed as a specious ruse in order to exploit his unmerited privilege. In the end, the positions of male and female, though rendered mutual by gendering, prove incompatible.

In this pair of poems, the sexual politics are salient. Rather than achieving the ideal union of the androgyne, shepherd and nymph confront one another across sharply drawn battle lines. In the companion poems that

---

unlimited fictional space of inexhaustible possibilities. With particular reference to Cézanne's sentence, "I owe you the truth in painting and I will tell it to you," Derrida observes: "It does not mean everything and anything. And besides, like every passe-partout (in the strictest sense!), it must formally, i.e., by its forms, answer to a finite system of constraints" (*Truth in Painting*, 8).

Derrida does not, however, delineate these constraints, but instead continues with his own writing generated by "the performance of this [Cézanne's] performative promising another performative saying nothing that will be *there*" (9). Indeed, Derrida soon disavows his intent (at least, as I understand it) and announces: "The passe-partout which here creates an event must not pass for a master key" (12). Later he concludes, laconically: "Deconstruction must neither reframe nor dream of the pure and simple absence of the frame. These two apparently contradictory gestures are the very ones—and they are systematically indissociable—of *what* is here deconstructed" (73). We are left to ponder "*what* is here deconstructed," and *what* results from the deconstruction.

conclude *Love's Labor's Lost,* however, Shakespeare is appreciably more sophisticated in his discourse about otherness. There are no facilely gendered speakers; instead, one group of players performs a spring song presided over by the cuckoo, followed by another group singing a winter song presided over by the owl. The cuckoo and owl, of course, again suggest the frivolous and the ponderous points of view. But in this instance the poems are situated in the larger framework of the seasonal cycle, a truncated calendar:

> When daisies pied, and violets blue,
>   And lady-smocks all silver-white,
> And cuckoo-buds of yellow hue
>   Do paint the meadows with delight,
> The cuckoo then on every tree
> Mocks married men; for thus sings he,
>   "Cuckoo;
> Cuckoo, cuckoo"—O word of fear,
> Unpleasing to a married ear!
>
> When shepherds pipe on oaten straws,
>   And merry larks are ploughmen's clocks;
> When turtles tread, and rooks and daws,
>   And maidens bleach their summer smocks,
> The cuckoo then on every tree
> Mocks married men; for thus sings he,
>   "Cuckoo;
> Cuckoo, cuckoo"—O word of fear,
> Unpleasing to a married ear!
>
>
> When icicles hang by the wall,
>   And Dick the shepherd blows his nail,
> And Tom bears logs into the hall,
>   And milk comes frozen home in pail;
> When blood is nipp'd, and ways be [foul],
> Then nightly sings the staring owl,
>   "Tu-whit, to-who!"—
> A merry note,
> While greasy Joan doth keel the pot.

When all aloud the wind doth blow,
　And coughing drowns the parson's saw,
And birds sit brooding in the snow,
　And Marian's nose looks red and raw,
When roasted crabs hiss in the bowl,
Then nightly sings the staring owl,
　　　　　　　　"Tu-whit, to-who!"—
A merry note,
While greasy Joan doth keel the pot.

$$(5.2.894–929)$$

These two poems are identical in their formal features, and the music that accompanies them would accentuate this sameness. But they present neatly counterposed descriptions of the human condition. The first song depicts an idealized spring world, an Arcadia where flowers adorn the meadows, birds sing and make blameless love in the trees, and shepherds pipe on Vergilian reeds. The second song depicts a grimly realistic winter world, now inhabited by specific individuals with familiar names: Dick, Tom, Joan, Marian. The wind blows, icicles form along the roofline, milk freezes in the short time between shed and kitchen, the roads turn treacherous, and those who make it to church do so at the risk of illness. The snowy scenes so vividly painted delineate nature at its most discomforting and hostile, while the wretched humans repeatedly display the infirmities to which flesh is heir.

As these two poems proceed sequentially, it seems as though the second is ceded an advantage by virtue of spring giving way to winter. Since winter naturally follows spring, a hierarchy is implied by the order of the seasons. At the end, cold and darkness prevail. But that is to halt at a pessimistic reading in accord with the pessimistic view of mutability. Winter is equated with the close of the natural cycle, and each individual must die. This is Colin Clout's earthbound perception in the final eclogue of *The Shepheardes Calender.*

Viewed optimistically, however, *sub specie aeternitatis,* the end of one cycle becomes the beginning of the next, so that spring and winter follow one another in endless alternation. Significantly, when Don Armado announces the songs and organizes the players into two groups, he reverses the order of the songs as they are performed: "This side is Hiems, Winter; this Ver, the Spring. . . . Ver, begin" (5.2.891–93). In this continuous succession, omega becomes alpha; at the end of the sequence, each individual, one short sleep past, awakens to eternity. The calendar serves as an integer of

this eternity, and the individual caught up in its endless repetition participates in the blessedness that God has bestowed upon his creation. This is
the comforting view of mutability.

When we look more closely at the text, we notice that Shakespeare has
carefully included ameliorating elements in each half. The spring song
contains certain unpleasant occurrences, while the harshness of the winter landscape is alleviated by several pleasures. Although those who sing
of the spring-world offer an idealized version of love taken from senti-
mental pastoral, the cuckoo nonetheless insistently shrills a fearful word
that sounds like "cuckold," suggesting that the innocent affection professed in courtship transmutes to something less admirable in sexual practice. More subtly, the lovely flowers of the first few lines, a metonym for
the females who populate this scene, quickly lose their honesty as well as
their beauty. By the end of the first song, as spring ripens toward harvest,
the "lady-smocks" of the second line become "maidens [who] bleach their
summer smocks," presumably to remove the stains from a roll on the
ground. Time passes; humankind reenacts the Fall; the scene darkens.

Comparably, producing an exact symmetry, those who sing of the winter-
world lighten their harsh recital by recalling a number of compensations
for the cold. Tom will build a fire in the common room, and Joan—good
old greasy, compliant Joan—will stir up a cheering brew, perhaps with
roasted crabapples floating on top and bursting with steam. Not a bad
evening at all. And as a climax, although the weather outside is at its worst,
the owl sings a merry note. The bird of darkness and ill omen, strangely,
changes its tune and holds out hope of happiness. Despite their contrariety, then, the spring song and its winter counterpart interlock through
shared elements to form an integrated whole that carefully incorporates
the extremes of both heedless delight and depressing gloom. Good and
ill, in fact, are interfused, mutually necessary—paradoxically, like these
two worldviews, difficult to separate.

The optimism of the spring song is therefore justified, while the pessimism of the winter song is essential as a prelude to happiness. Although
opposite, the two songs are complementary. And in the end both are subsumed within a greater good. As I have argued elsewhere, Shakespeare
devised his two songs to illustrate the wisdom of integrating both the active
and the contemplative in a well-rounded life that realizes the full dimension of human potential.[33] What the noble youths of the play (and we) dis-

33. For the function of these two songs in Shakespeare's dramaturgy, see my "Pattern of
Love's Labor's Lost," *Shakespeare Studies* 7 (1974): 25–53.

cover is that the meditative life of learning must be melded with active involvement through loving.

The concluding lyrics of *Love's Labor's Lost* are differentiated and correlated also by another pair of opposites that regularly appears in the discourse about otherness. The spring song transpires in bright daylight, illuminating the pretty colors of the flowers, requiring larks to summon plowmen to their daily tasks, and bleaching the smocks of the maidens. In contrast, the winter song takes place in darkness, the nighttime realm of the staring owl. Not only are the two poems situated in the seasonal cycle of time, but also in its diurnal cycle. In both ways they exemplify the "grateful vicissitude" that Milton lauds in the epigraph to this chapter.

Which brings us to "L'Allegro" and "Il Penseroso," the companion poems par excellence. The titles explicitly counterpose two mind-sets, and the opening verse-paragraphs of each poem confirm this opposition. Yet, the two poems are also identical in many respects. They share the same metrics, rhetorical structure, vocabulary, and allusive style.

In both poems Milton clearly echoes the passionate shepherd and the nymph, recalling the intertextual matrix of companion poems in Elizabethan England. Early in "L'Allegro" the speaker supplicates his tutelary goddess:

> And if I give thee honor due,
> Mirth, admit me of thy crew,
> To live with her [Liberty], and live with thee,
> In unreproved pleasures free.
>   (37–40)

Repeating the allusion at the end of his performance, the happy man concludes:

> These delights, if thou canst give,
> Mirth with thee I mean to live.
>   (151–52)

Not to be outdone, and providing exact complementarity, the pensive man at the end of his performance makes a parallel appeal to his guiding spirit:

> These pleasures Melancholy give,
> And I with thee will choose to live.
>   (175–76)

The rural mistress of the passionate shepherd has been replaced by Mirth and Melancholy, females of a higher order, but gender is still an issue in the discourse.

Milton's two poems taken together also participate in the passage of time and reflect the ambivalent attitude toward mutability that licensed optimism as well as pessimism. The world of "L'Allegro"—with its "violets blue" (21) and "meadows trim with daisies pied" (75), with its larks singing at dawn (41–44) and whistling plowmen (63–64)—recalls the spring world inhabited by Shakespeare's cuckoo; while the world of "Il Penseroso" recalls the winter world presided over by the owl, although the owl has been replaced by the more elegant Philomel (56–64) and human misfortunes are transformed into urbane tragedy (97–102). Just as Shakespeare's songs are sung in praise of the cuckoo and the owl, so Milton's lyrics take their cue from the lark and the nightingale. Milton's poems echo Shakespeare's and display the seasonal cycle in its common truncated form.

Even more explicitly, however, Milton constructs his two poems and fits them together to represent the diurnal unit of time. "L'Allegro" begins at "dappled dawn," when "the lark begin[s] his flight, / And singing star-tle[s] the dull night" (41–44), and it proceeds through the morning and afternoon until dusk, "Till the livelong daylight fail[s]" (99). Following a correspondent temporal scheme, "Il Penseroso" begins at dusk, when "Philomel will deign a song" (56), and it continues through the evening until dawn, "Till civil-suited Morn appear[s]" (122). The two poems in their entirety complete in small the perpetual round of light and darkness as they lodge and dislodge each other by turns.

To illustrate that configuration and its significance for humankind, we can bring to bear upon it Figure 23, taken from the notorious Robert Fludd's well-known *Utriusque cosmi . . . historia*. This is the seventeenth century's adaptation of an ancient motif, the microcosmos, which often, as here, had been represented as a bipartite creature divided between day and night.[34] "Microcosmic day" comprises the unshaded upper half of the figure, while "microcosmic night" comprises the shaded bottom half. Incorporated into the upper half (which includes the head) and marked along a median down its middle are the proportions of the Pythagorean tuning system: two diapasons, one "corporalis" and the other "spiritualis," each of which comprises a diatesseron and a diapente. These two diapasons make up a "disdiapason," the mutual accord between "corpus" and

34. See my *Cosmographical Glass,* 151–54. For the microcosm as the zodiac or the four seasons, see ibid., 147–50.

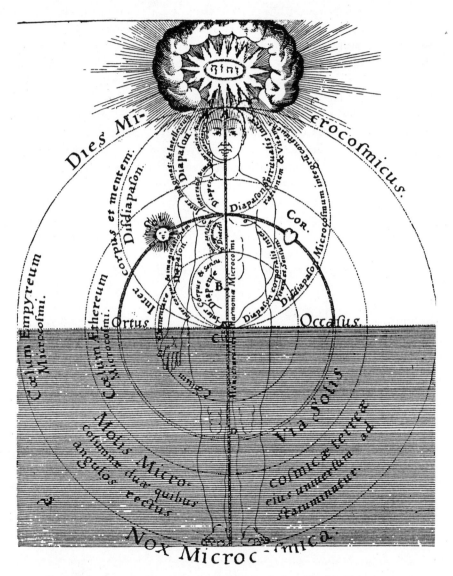

Fig. 23.   The human microcosm as day and night. Robert Fludd, *Utriusque cosmi . . .
historia,* 4 vols. (Oppenheim, 1617–19), 3.275

"mens." In its rational activities, evidently, the human microcosm repeats the musical harmonies of the macrocosm. Equally significant, the sacred tetragrammaton, the unutterable name of the deity, is inscribed in a refulgent aureole immediately above the human figure. This is the surest proof that mankind is created in the image of God and continues to operate under that benign influence. Microcosmic day and night cohere within that larger—indeed, infinite—whole.

We could deconstruct Milton's pair of poems and claim that the happily active man and his meditative counterpart confront one another in unalterable opposition and without stint. We could similarly deconstruct Fludd's icon of human nature, giving separate and equal power to each half. Such an interpretation, though, would ignore the tetragrammaton that caps the diagram. And a deconstructive reading of "L'Allegro" and "Il Penseroso" would be equally contrary to the epigraph from Milton that heads this chapter. The vicissitude of ever-changing moods, like that of night and day, is "grateful," involving us in the patterns necessary to comprehend the sacred knowledge that life leads to:

> Till old experience do attain
> To something like prophetic strain.
> ("Il Penseroso," 173–74)

For Milton—and, I think, for most poets of the English Renaissance—the form of companion poems was overridingly optimistic. The ever-whirling wheel of change in its perpetual round insures that, through God's mercy, difference is subjugated to the perfection of beatitude. It is divinity that serves as the Lacanian "symbolic order," the mirror within whose reflection the individual forms him-/herself. The organs of reproduction are central to human existence, as in Fludd's diagram, because they make offspring possible and thereby insure continuity in the succession of generations. But the self-defining sexuality of *jouissance* is secondary, if recognized at all.

5 Alberti's Window
The Rhetoric of Perspective

I send unto you this booke, as a purtraict in peinctinge of the Court of Urbin: not of the handiwoorke of Raphael, or Michael Angelo, but of an unknowen peincter, and that can do no more but draw the principall lines, without setting furth the truth with beawtifull coulours, or makinge it appeere by the art of Prospective that [which] it is not.

—*Baldassare Castiglione*[1]

n 1933 René Magritte painted a cheeky commentary on the convoluted relationship between art and the actual world (Fig. 24)—a conundrum, really, noting the interchange between these two modes of existence, and yet acknowledging their irrefutable otherness. Not only is art in some way a replication of actuality, a derivative from it, but also art produces an actuality of its own, clearly distinct from its origin in objective nature and counterposed against it. In what sense is art a representation of actuality? Is there a hierarchical arrangement, with one being authoritative and the other supplementary? How do they interface? Is there a clear line of demarcation between them? Do they overlap? Is one real and the other illusory? Are both illusory? These are the teasing questions Magritte poses, with no hint of an answer.[2]

But the questions themselves in Magritte's pictorial formulation per-

---

1. Castiglione's dedicatory epistle to Lord Michael de Sylva, *Courtier,* 10.

2. For a provocative essay that explores how the visual and the verbal in Magritte's paintings interact to produce "similitude" rather than "resemblance" (that is, produce an expanding series of parallel statements about actuality rather than a verisimilar replication of it),

Fig. 24.   René Magritte, *The Human Condition*. National Gallery of Art, Washington, D.C. Gift of the Collectors Committee

petuate a long-standing discourse beginning with a proposal made by Leon Battista Alberti exactly five hundred years earlier in his treatise *On Painting*. When he prepared to paint a picture, Alberti confides, "I draw a rectangle of whatever size I want . . . which I regard as an open window through which the subject to be painted is seen."[3] This statement has been the seminal topos for art theory ever since, suggesting that art replicates a nature which comprises what is ultimately real. This objective nature exists outside a wall that coincides with the plane of the picture's surface and that otherwise separates the space inhabited by the painter from the subject matter of the painting.

Alberti's theory for a new sort of art reflects the relocation of reality that took place as logocentrism gave way to hylocentrism during the Renaissance. "Let us always," he says "take from Nature whatever we are about to paint" (101). His statement underlies a revisionary theory contrived to accommodate this transition in our culture, a theory that makes single-point perspective the sine qua non of painting.[4] The items in a picture—people, buildings, inanimate objects—are arranged in imagined space according to mathematical laws of perspective, and the sight lines (called "orthogonals") converge to a single point on the horizon. In succeeding centuries, as empiricism gained credence, what the painter saw through Alberti's window became increasingly the natural things of the world we perceive with our senses, and realism became the painter's goal, despite the patent illusionism of such painting.[5] Magritte in his turn, marking the end of both

---

see Michel Foucault, *This Is Not a Pipe,* trans. and ed. James Harkness (Berkeley and Los Angeles: University of California Press, 1983).

3. *On Painting and On Sculpture,* ed. and trans. Cecil Grayson (London: Phaidon, 1972), 55. For the later Renaissance, the benchmark text was *De pictura praestantissima, et nunquam satis laudata arte libri tres,* ed. Thomas Venatorius (Basle, 1540). The first vernacular text (Italian) was *La pittura,* trans. Lodovico Domenichi (Venice, 1547).

4. Single-point (or linear) perspective, mathematically determined, must be distinguished from the medieval science of optics called *perspectiva.* For a rudimentary account of this discipline at the beginning of the sixteenth century, see Charles de Bouelles, "Perspectiva introductio," in *Epitome compendiosaque introductio in libros Arithmeticos divi Severini Boetii* et al., ed. Jacques le Fèvre d'Etaples (Paris, 1503), fols. 90–96. For an analysis of *perspectiva* as a science of cognition rather than of perception, see A. Mark Smith, "Getting the Big Picture in Perspectivist Optics," *Isis* 72 (1981): 568–89.

5. Interest in illusionism had begun even before Alberti: "The evidence indicates that beginning with Giotto and continuing with his pupils, there was a continuous experimentation with the role illusionism could play in enhancing realistic effects in painting" (David Wilkins, "The Meaning of Space in Fourteenth-Century Tuscan Painting," in *By Things Seen: Reference and Recognition in Medieval Thought,* ed. David L. Jeffrey [Ottawa: University of Ottawa Press, 1979], 114–15). For a brilliant study of the multiple uses to which illusionism was put in Italy from 1470 to 1524, see Sven Sandström, *Levels of Unreality: Studies in Structure*

realism and illusionism as aims in painting, co-opts Alberti's topos of the window to announce his surrealist theory of art. Magritte thereby partici- pates in the discourse originating with Alberti's statement and intertextu- ally subsumes the intervening variations on Alberti's theme.

Magritte entitled his painting, pointedly, *The Human Condition*, imply- ing that uncertainties about the status of objects in nature as well as of art objects doom us human beings to a quandary. It is the human condition to remain suspended between the actual and the artful, seeking a basis for truth in one or the other, but failing to find grounds for belief and remain-

---

and Construction in Italian Mural Painting During the Renaissance, Acta Universitatis Upsaliensis, Figura n.s. 4 (Uppsala: Almqvist & Wiksell, 1963).

In the eyes of Cristoforo Landino, Masaccio (1401–c. 1428) marked a turning point in the practice of painting because of his mastery of illusionism:

> Masaccio was the best imitator of nature, with full-bodied articulation, some- one extraordinarily good at composition and a purist without ornateness. To him alone we owe the imitation of reality and the projection of figures. He was a sure and accurate perspectivist, like many others of those times, with a great talent for making, a fine young man who unfortunately died in his twenty- sixth year. (my translation)

> Fu Masaccio ottimo imitatore di natura, di gran rilievo, universale buono com- ponitore e puro sanza ornato, perché solo si dette all'imitazione del vero e al rilievo delle figure; fu certo e buono prospettivo quanto altro di quegli tempi e di gran facilità nel fare, essendo ben giovane che morì d'anni ventisei.
> (Dante, *Divina commedia,* ed. Landino [Florence, 1481], [*]5v; also Landino, *Scritti critici e teorici,* ed. Roberto Cardini, 2 vols. [Rome: Bulzoni, 1974], 1.124)

By the end of the sixteenth century, Lomazzo had defined painting as simply the replica- tion of physical nature:

> Painting is an arte, which with proportionable lines, and colours answerable to the life, by observing the Perspective light, doeth so imitate the nature of corporall thinges, that it not onely representeth the thicknesse and round- nesse thereof upon a flat, but also their actions and gestures, expressing more- over divers affections and passions of the minde. (13)

For similar sentiments in a popular text, including a comparison of painting and poetry that echoes Simonides' famous dictum ("[The painter must] bee skilled as a Poete in all thinges, for that paintyng is nothing els, but a deade or dumme poesie"), see Pedro Mexia, *The foreste,* trans. Thomas Fortescue (London, 1571), fol. 65. Mexia also offers descriptions of several examples of trompe l'oeil from the work of Zeuxis and Parrhasius.

For modern studies, see Samuel Y. Edgerton, Jr., *The Renaissance Rediscovery of Linear Perspective* (New York: Basic Books, 1975); and Kemp, *Geometrical Perspective,* esp. 90–91. On illusionism in early seventeenth-century England, see Lucy Gent, "The Self-Cozening Eye," *Review of English Studies* 34 (1983): 419–28.

ing in doubt. Such ontic questions began in the Renaissance, and the arts, especially painting and poetry, began to ponder the epistemology of experience. The most adaptable forum for this discourse was narrative, and storytelling in all media acquired an unwonted importance.

In painting, this radical discourse led to human figures deployed in naturalistic settings devised by the use of perspective, accompanied by the introduction of frames to set apart the art work from actuality. In poetry, it led to comparable fictional spaces with similar framing devices, including the innovative use of titles and enhanced title pages, dedicatory letters to patrons and explanatory letters to readers, and elaborate marginalia. Most interestingly, and most important in cultural history, this radical discourse led to the insertion of a narrator other than the author himself in order to mediate between the narrative fiction and the reader. The parallelism between narrative in painting and literary narrative is striking, evident in their respective strategies and effects.[6]

But to deal with Alberti as an early modern who advocates realism in painting is a gross oversimplification of his doctrine. "The early painter Demetrius failed to obtain the highest praise," Alberti recalls, "because he was more devoted to representing the likeness of things than to beauty" (99). When the painter looks through the hypothetical window that serves as a frame for his painting, he does not see—or even imagine—a simple vista of raw, elemental nature. Quite the contrary. According to Alberti what he sees— or claims to see—is a static tableau of human figures caught in the midst of some dramatic action and expressing intense emotion (79-87). A story from the Bible, perhaps, or a mythological episode or an incident from legend, or maybe even an action imagined by the artist—but always with some implied meaning, usually moral. In any case, the image most often comes from a passage in literature, sacred or pagan, and certainly the best of them do. Alberti notes: "The eminent painter Phidias used to say that

6. For a wide-ranging and still wise essay on this parallelism, see Claudio Guillén, "On the Concept and Metaphor of Perspective" [1966], in *Literature as System: Essays Toward the Theory of Literary History* (Princeton: Princeton University Press, 1971), 283–371. For a suggestive study of how Alberti and some who came after him transformed this parallelism, see Clark Hulse, *The Rule of Art: Literature and Painting in the Renaissance* (Chicago: University of Chicago Press, 1990). For an invaluable bibliography that goes beyond what its title indicates, see Clark Hulse, "Recent Studies of Literature and Painting in the English Renaissance," *English Literary Renaissance* 15 (1985): 122-40. For studies within the temporal and geographic boundaries of my own, see Lucy Gent, *Picture and Poetry 1560–1620: Relations Between Literature and the Visual Arts in the English Renaissance* (Leamington Spa: Hall, 1981); and David Evett, *Literature and the Visual Arts in Tudor England* (Athens: University of Georgia Press, 1990).

he had learned from Homer how best to represent the majesty of Jupiter";[7] and he adds, "I believe that we too may be richer and better painters from reading our poets" (97).

For his exemplary case, Alberti cites a famous painting by the ancient artist Apelles depicting in allegorical fashion a personification of calumny. Alberti paraphrases a well-known dialogue of Lucian (*Dialogues*, 1.365–67), which offers a description of Apelles' long-lost picture:

> In the painting there was a man with enormous ears sticking out, attended on each side by two women, Ignorance and Suspicion; from one side Calumny was approaching in the form of an attractive woman, but whose face seemed too well versed in cunning, and she was holding in her left hand a lighted torch, while with her right she was dragging by the hair a youth with his arms outstretched towards heaven. Leading her was another man, pale, ugly and fierce to look upon, whom you would rightly compare to those exhausted by long service in the field. They identified him correctly as Envy. There are two other women attendant on Calumny and busy arranging their mistress's dress; they are Treachery and Deceit. Behind them comes Repentance clad in mourning and rending her hair, and in her train chaste and modest Truth. (95–97)

The result of such writing is literally a verbal icon, an image constructed of pictorial details.[8] However, it is anything but realistic, drawn from observed nature. Although highly visualized, it is also highly artificial—indeed, blatant artifice. This is art opposed to nature.

Nonetheless, the image purports to contain truth-value. Even though it makes its statement by means of nonexistent abstractions, such as Ignorance and Suspicion, it purveys a moral directed toward and applicable in the everyday world of human affairs. In effect, the image ignores and thereby erases any line of demarcation between art and actuality. What the painter

---

7. Cf. Cicero, *De oratore*, 2.

8. Botticelli presumed to reproduce Apelles' painting from Lucian's description, and his rendition now hangs in the Uffizi at Florence (see Fig. 25). On the topos of Apelles' "Calumny," see Rudolph Altrocchi, "The Calumny of Apelles in the Literature of the Quattrocento," *Publications of the Modern Language Association* 36 (1921): 454–91; David Cast, *The Calumny of Apelles: A Study in Humanist Tradition*, Yale Publications in the History of Art 28 (New Haven: Yale University Press, 1981); and the review of Cast's book by R. W. Hanning in *Art Bulletin* 67 (1985): 690–93.

Fig. 25. Botticelli, *Calumny*

sees when he looks through his framing window is not untrimmed nature itself, but an artifice that suggests a meaning which he imposes upon nature.

Alberti calls this image—what the painter imagines as a visualized object in his frame—a *historia*, and he makes *historia* the substance of the painter's art. "The great work of the painter," he says, "is the *historia*" (71). By using this term Alberti signals his participation in a discourse on the relation between fact and fiction that goes back to Aristotle. Indeed, the wavering interface between fiction and fact—between art and actuality—is recorded most neatly in the changing definitions assigned to this term as our culture has altered over time. In its purest state, uncontaminated by context, *historia* means any narrative, with no indication of whether it is factual or fictitious. *Historia* can be an accurate account of something that has actually happened, or it can be made up—a "feigned history," to use a common Elizabethan phrase.[9] This ambiguity of *historia* is perfectly preserved in its vernacular derivatives: Italian *istoria*, French *histoire*, and English *story*. We can, for example, have a true *story*, as in the statement, "This is the story behind the new degree requirements"; but *story* means also a lie, as in the statement, "He concocted a story about his credentials." It is this flexibility in the term *historia*, however, that has allowed theorists to exploit the interchange between fact and fiction,[10] and it will be worth our while to examine how two of the most influential ancients have handled this issue.

9. See Puttenham's chapter "Of historicall Poesie" (39–42).

10. In her penetrating study of the relationship between narrativity and realism, Wendy Steiner places Alberti in the camp of the realists. But, she argues, Alberti's window requires simultaneity in a picture, thereby ruling out temporality, and consequently (as well as paradoxically) militating *against* realism as well as narrativity: "Though narrative was inextricably connected with realism, paradoxically the strict adherence to the norms of Renaissance realism precluded narrativity from the visual arts" (*Pictures of Romance: Form Against Context in Painting and Literature* [Chicago: University of Chicago Press, 1988], 23). Looking back from a poststructuralist position, Steiner sees Alberti as a theorist with contradictory impulses: to promote realism, but in fact to subvert its implementation. Steiner, however, misreads Alberti's use of the term *historia*, not realizing that it denotes an action which, although depicted instantaneously at its climax, nonetheless implies what came before and what will come after. In literature the parallel of such historiated icons occurs in a classical work popular during the Renaissance, the Εἰκόνες or *Imagines* of Philostratus the Elder, a compendium of sixty-five verbal portraits of such legendary persons as Phaëton and Pasiphaë caught in their most characteristic gesture; cf. Stephen Bateman, *The golden booke of the leaden goddes* (London, 1577). Astigmatically, Steiner imposes her interpretation upon Alberti in order to extol the later narrative and "romance." As a corrective to Steiner, see E. H. Gombrich, "Moment and Movement in Art," *Journal of the Warburg and Courtauld Institutes* 27 (1964): 293–306; and Marilyn Aronberg Lavin, *The Place of Narrative: Mural Decoration in Italian Churches, 431–1600* (Chicago: University of Chicago Press, 1990).

Aristotle in the *Poetics* drew a strong distinction between history and poetry—in his language, ἱστορία and ποιητική, which I have translated as "poetry," though we should note that this poetry is derived from the Greek ποιεῖν, which means "to make," "to fashion," "to fictionalize"—in prose as well as verse. The poet, says Aristotle, "makes" a plot that imitates the actions of human beings. In contradistinction to history, which tells what *has* happened, the poetical plot is a mental construct on the part of the poet that displays what *can* happen according to probability or necessity. So while the truth of history is limited, confined to the particular instance, poetry encapsulates the universal, what may be or should be according to probability or necessity; and therefore the truth of poetry has general applicability. As a result, Aristotle concludes, poetry is more philosophical and more serious than history (1451b6–9). Poetical fiction is privileged at history's expense.

Plutarch, though, in his well-known essay "How the Young Man Should Study Poetry" in effect removes the distinction between history and poetry. He bestows uninhibited ambiguity upon the term *historia*. His purpose is to use narrative, *historia,* as a source for examples of human action that his students can analyze ethically, thereby exercising their moral judgment as preparation for the more difficult discipline of philosophy (25C–27B). For example, in the *Odyssey* when the Phaeacian princess Nausicaa chances upon Odysseus sleeping naked on the beach and becomes enamored of him, is she to be admired as a perspicacious young lady who instinctively recognizes nobility even in a destitute man; or is she to be condemned as an oversexed adolescent indulging her hormones? For Plutarch, it is of no consequence whether the action can be verified historically or whether it is merely the fiction of a poet. He uses the term *historia* for either possibility. *Historia* is narrative of any sort, actual or feigned. Its ontological status is unspecified—whether grounded in the materialism of actual events or in the universals of the poet's making that exist nowhere except in the mind of the poet.

Alberti's *historia* enjoys this same ambiguity. Furthermore, Alberti, like Aristotle, is inclined to give the painter considerable freedom in his making. When he says, "The great work of the painter is the *historia,*" he means that the painting is highly visualized, drawn from and referring to observed nature, but it is not the replication of some actual event. It is not historical fact, but poetical fiction. Alberti's *historia,* like Aristotle's plot, is a construct of the painter's imagination—his ability to conceive images. And the depicted *historia* is organized and made coherent by its composition (103–5), just as a poetical work according to Aristotle is given definition and consistency by its plot.[11] Alberti required some system for imposing organization and coherence upon the painting, hence the necessity for single-point perspective.[12] Similarly, he required some means of giving it definition, of rec-

11. This point is explicit when a painting depicts successive episodes in a narrative—e.g., Sassetta's *Life of Saint Anthony* in the National Gallery of Art at Washington, D.C. For a scholarly discussion of how such paintings signify, see Meyer Schapiro, "On Some Problems in the Semiotics of Visual Art: Field and Vehicle in Image-Signs," *Semiotica* 1 (1969): 230–31.

Despite the pretense of passing time induced by successive episodes, as Jameson has observed (73–74), a plot produces a sense of synchrony in a literary narrative, a sense of unity and simultaneity. The plot supplies an underlying form rendered palpable by its embodiment in sense-perceptible scenes, presented to the eyes of the audience in the theater or to the mind's eye of the reader in printed narrative. As evidence of this constraint, a time limit is imposed upon tragedy (the action must be confined to one day) and upon the short story (the reading must take no longer than one hour). The narrative verges toward the synchrony of single-episode painting—although, of course, it never completely implodes to simple unity. For germane discussion relative to painting, the sister art of poetry, see Rudolf Arnheim, *The Power of the Center: A Study of Composition in the Visual Arts*, new version (Berkeley and Los Angeles: University of California Press, 1988), esp. 55–100, 170–94.

12. For the classic essay making this point, see Erwin Panofsky, "Die Perspektive als 'Symbolische Form,'" in *Vorträge der Bibliothek Warburg, 1924–25*, ed. Fritz Saxl (Leipzig: Teubner, 1927), 258–330. At the end of his book Kubovy supports Panofsky over others: "Perspective often enabled the Renaissance artist to cast the deeply religious contents of his art in a form that could produce in the viewer spiritual effects that could not have been achieved by any other formal means. In that sense, perspective should be viewed as 'symbolic form'" (173). For an important study opposing an Aristotelian tradition against this platonist view, see David Summers: "In the chapters that follow, I shall argue that however great the importance of the Platonic idea of beauty (or beauty of the idea) may have been in the Renaissance, other traditions of meaning shaped the discussion of the art of the period at its deepest levels, at the level of its naturalism" (*The Judgment of Sense: Renaissance Naturalism and the Rise of Aesthetics* [Cambridge: Cambridge University Press, 1987], 2). For a perceptive study detailing Leonardo's "reconciliation of the Platonic and Aristotelian world views," see Kim H. Veltman and Kenneth D. Keele: "The real significance of linear perspective, therefore, was that it introduced a halfway station where geometry and nature could meet" (*Linear Perspective and the Visual Dimensions of Science and Art*, Studies on Leonardo da Vinci 1 [Munich: Deutscher Kunstverlag, 1986], 16).

This latter position was promulgated in the sixteenth century by one of the most extensive and handsome treatises on perspective: Jean Cousin, *Livre de perspective* (Paris, 1560). In a flamboyant woodcut on the title page (Fig. 26), a Christ-like artisan representing the heavenly maker sits at a potter's wheel and fashions a footed bowl, his creation. At the bottom, a caption states: "Stante, et currente rota" (The wheel stands still, and yet is always turning)—the point being that, although time wreaks undeniable changes, mutability by divine intention realizes eternal forms. After the title page comes an extra-size leaf that displays "les cinq Corps Reguliers de Geometrie," the so-called platonic solids, emphasizing the importance of these uniquely perfect forms and grounding this science of perspective in the Pythagorean-platonic tradition (see my *Touches of Harmony*, 107–11). Everywhere in this impressive manual the rules for depicting the universe are in accord with the number, weight, and measure that God used in creating it. The ephemeral data of our mutable world

Fig. 26.   The deity as a
potter at his wheel.
Jean Cousin, *Livre de
perspective* (Paris, 1560),
title page

are placed in the context of a permanent scheme, a providential plan. Indeed, as Cousin
says in his prefatory address "au lecteur," he has set forth these rules "avec l'ayde de Dieu"
(A3). A painting with single-point perspective, then, like a quatorzain, embodies an optimistic form that affirms divine order.

For an example of this theory in practice, see Hieronimo Nadal, *Adnotationes et meditationes in Evangelia*, 2d ed. (Antwerp, 1595), where the ambiguity between platonic-Christian
and empiricist positions is openly exploited in the rhetorical strategy of the engravings. See
also Eugene Cunnar, "Framing Seventeenth-Century Poetics: Liturgical Frames and
Perspectives," in *Perspective as a Problem in the Art, History and Literature of Early Modern England*,
ed. Mark S. Lussier and S. K. Heninger, Jr. (New York: Edwin Mellen, 1992), 27–49.

ognizing limits (as Aristotle said, the plot must have a beginning, middle, and end). Hence the inevitable emphasis upon the frame.

Before Alberti's time, paintings did not have frames. At least, a frame was not applied *post facto,* as we are likely to think of it: a set of moldings placed around the edges of a painting for protection and often for decoration. Of course, a painting had margins, where it ended; but it did not have a frame as a formally recognized element in its own organization.[13] Notice that Magritte's painting within the painting (what stands upon the easel) has no frame, an omission to minimize discontinuity with its surroundings. The painting is susceptible to assimilation.

Similarly, before the Renaissance, paintings were incidental to a larger architectural project, and their borders were determined by what they were fitted into.[14] They existed as parts of something else: as panels in an altarpiece or as frescoes on an articulated wall.[15] Their margins were fashioned in such a way as to facilitate incorporation within a larger whole, confirming a sense of benevolent order in the universe. Paintings reflected a higher reality, and the corporate frame was engineered to allow each panel's participation in that greater truth. Paintings were not self-contained, detachable items that carried their own identities and therefore could be moved about.

But frames make paintings portable—which is another way of saying that frames endow paintings with independence.[16] A frame indicates that a painting is a fictional space which contains its own raison d'être, which requires no extraneous support to substantiate its existence or provide a context for

13. See Claus Grimm, *The Book of Picture Frames,* trans. Nancy M. Gordon and Walter L. Strauss (New York: Abaris Books, 1981), 15–16 and passim; and Richard R. Brettell and Steven Starling, *The Art of the Edge: European Frames, 1300–1900* (Chicago: Art Institute, 1986), 11–13, 27–30.

14. See Henry Heydenryk, *The Art and History of Frames: An Inquiry into the Enhancement of Paintings* (New York: Heineman, 1963), 8–9, 13–15; and Brettell and Starling, 11.

15. To illustrate profusely the appropriation of painting and sculpture by architecture, see Wim Swaan, *The Late Middle Ages: Art and Architecture from 1350 to the Advent of the Renaissance* (Ithaca: Cornell University Press, 1977). For the rhetoric of art in this culture, see Barbara Nolan, *The Gothic Visionary Perspective* (Princeton: Princeton University Press, 1977). For the emerging independence of painting, see Sandström.

16. As Arnheim notes: "Around the fifteenth century the organic connection between artworks and their surroundings began to be loosened in Western art. It is especially true for paintings that the artist's work turned into an ambulant object, made for nobody in particular and at home anywhere. . . . A frame provided the necessary detachment physically and psychologically" (58).

its significance. A framed painting generates its own meaning.[17] A frame asserts the autonomy of the fictional space, affirming its otherness.

Consider, however, the ambiguous status of the frame itself. On the one hand, it has been put in place by the painter and therefore belongs to the fiction. It is part of the artifact. It is integral to the unity of the fictional space, participating in its otherness. But also the frame can be distinguished from the fictional space; it is external to the painting's subject matter. Like the frame of the window through which Alberti's painter looks, it belongs to the space inhabited by the painter. As a result of this ambiguity, the frame serves a dual function: while it separates the painting from its surroundings, the frame also mediates between the fictional space and the actual world, thereby making the painting accessible to the viewer.[18] The frame is Alberti's window that allows us to penetrate the obstructive wall and perceive whatever reality lies beyond.

In Alberti's program for painting, then, the frame is essential to the artifice, as the means both of setting apart the fictional space and of providing access to it. It is the frame that defines a space wherein the mathematical laws of perspective can organize the items of the composition in such a way as to give the illusion of actuality, counterposing this fiction against the actuality of the viewer. Yet, it is the frame that provides access to this fictional space which, though illusory, carries a truth-value perhaps more reliable than actuality itself.

By insisting upon a frame, Alberti devised a new rhetoric for painting. He encouraged an innovative and dynamic relationship between the *historia* and the viewer. While the mathematical exactness of single-point perspective endows the painting with organic unity and sets it apart as a self-consistent entity, the orthogonal lines of the perspectival construct reach out of the painting and incorporate the space inhabited by viewers, thereby situating them in precise relationship to the objects within the frame. The space inhabited by the viewers is rendered continuous with that occupied by the painted objects. The physical demarcation between art and actuality is thereby eradicated. But in this two-way transaction allowing easy com-

17. For a discussion of this point, with a deconstructive bias, see Alfonso Procaccini, "Alberti and the 'Framing' of Perspective," *Journal of Aesthetics and Art Criticism* 40 (1981–82): 29–39. According to Procaccini, a perspective painting can "be about" only its own fictionality.

18. Derrida meditates upon the ambiguity of the frame in his theory of "invagination" (see Culler, *On Deconstruction*, 193–99; cf. also Derrida, *Truth in Painting*, 61–67). For evidence in recent art criticism that the frame continues to be viewed ambiguously, see the review of Svetlana Alpers, *The Art of Describing: Dutch Art in the Seventeenth Century* (Chicago: University of Chicago Press, 1983) by Jan Bialostocki in *Art Bulletin* 67 (1985): 523.

merce between fact and fiction, a delimiting frame, paradoxically, becomes a requisite accessory.

The point is illustrated dramatically by a complex construction devised by Giovanni Bellini in 1488 (Fig. 27), commissioned for the Frari Church in Venice and still there in its original frame.[19] There are three separate panels, arranged in a magnificent frame of vertical piers resting upon a sturdy foundation and supporting a fancy cornice. In the center, a panel with a rounded top, sits a Madonna and child. On the left is a panel of Saints Nicholas and Peter, with a flat top; and on the right, a panel of Saints Mark and Benedict, again with a flat top. In effect, the viewer faces the cross-section of an apse surmounted by a dome and flanked by two side aisles, so the painting iterates in miniature the architecture of the church in which it stands. Single-point perspective is rigorously employed to create an illusion of space within the picture, and an ambulatory wraps behind the central group and joins one outer panel with the other. The viewer looks from slightly below, upward toward the Madonna and child seated upon a prominent pedestal. The vanishing point coincides with the breast of the Madonna, as is common in such paintings of this period.

Despite the insistence upon perspectival correctness and the careful indication of space flowing from panel to panel, the plane of the picture surface is strongly accentuated by the four identical piers of the ornate frame. This frame separates the viewer's space from the holy space of the religious figures, whose divinity (despite their natural demeanor) is insisted upon by the two putti playing heavenly, unheard music. Observe, though, that the piers of the frame are repeated by others in the perspectival construction of the picture, so that the piers of the frame become part of the picture's architecture. As a result, the space inside the painting is made continuous with that inhabited by the viewer. The frame connects what is inside the painting and what is outside. With the aid of the frame, the orthogonal lines of the painting project outward, exceed the plane of the picture's surface, extend into the viewer's world, and encompass the viewer.[20]

19. Only a *very* small number of Renaissance paintings are still in their original frames, so the choice of this example is not wholly gratuitous. The frame is signed by Jacopo da Faenza and dated 1488; see Grimm, 86.

20. In the earliest painting generally agreed to exemplify the mathematical laws of perspective, Masaccio's much-studied *Trinità* in Santa Maria Novella in Florence, the architectural piers that comprise Bellini's frame are painted as part of the picture, which as a mural has no other frame; see Sandström, 28–31. As Sandström notes, the early frescoes of Mantegna in the Chiesa degli Eremitani in Padua are similarly self-framed by pilasters defining a wall/picture surface that human figures within the scene violate and protrude through, as

Fig. 27.   Giovanni Bellini, *The Madonna and Child with Saints*

In accordance with Alberti's scheme, it serves as a window providing access to an alternative reality.

Note the strategy and effect of framing in this elaborate construction. The frame indicates a delimited space with forces of organization and

in Masaccio's *Trinità*. It is as though the wall/picture surface is identified in order for it to be transgressed. See also John White, *The Birth and Rebirth of Pictorial Space*, 3d ed. (London: Faber, 1987), 138–40; and Kubovy, 28–29.

coherence that set it apart from its physical surroundings. The frame is a line of demarcation, a discontinuity, the interface between the fiction and our workaday world. And yet, because of the orthogonal lines that project outward from the perspectival construct, the fictional space and actuality are interrelated. This painting by Bellini with its specially made frame provides a prototype for how frames function in the transaction between art and the actual world, and for how frames participate in the new rhetoric positioning the viewer in relation to the subject matter of art. Seeing the *historia* through Alberti's window—setting aside the fictional space, framing the narrative—remained the basic concept that enabled the dialectic between art and actuality from the Renaissance to the time of Magritte.[21]

And that brings us to the relationship between frames and the fictional spaces they enclose in writing. Framing the narrative in painting occasioned by Alberti's remarks and supported by the larger culture was closely paralleled by developments in literary narrative, where the ambiguity of the term *historia* may be even more readily exploited. A work such as "The History of King Lear," for instance, can be categorized exclusively as neither fictitious nor factual, but rather draws sustenance from both sources. Let's turn our attention, then, to literary narrative and literary framing, especially as it developed in England.

When I speak of "framing the narrative," it should come as no surprise that I am playing with words. The phrase is a pun that submits to various interpretations because "framing" invites several different construals. Before elaborating each, let me quickly identify three distinct senses for the word, each of which is historically justified, though perhaps not all three have been viable at any one time in our culture. First, I use "framing" in the antique sense of "fashioning" or "constructing," so "framing the narrative" is the act of composing it. Second, I use "framing" in the Albertian sense of putting a frame around something, so "framing the narrative" means setting it apart from actuality as a fictional space. Third, I use "framing" in the modern, slang sense of setting someone up to be charged with a crime, so that "framing the narrative" can mean putting it in a position to have

21. In the last few years, after painters boisterously tested the limits of the edge (e.g., Piet Mondrian and Frank Stella), there has been a reactive interest in early frames, with major exhibitions devoted exclusively to them at both the Art Institute in Chicago and the Metropolitan Museum of Art in New York. For catalogs, each with a useful bibliography, see Brettell and Starling (Art Institute, 1986); and Timothy J. Newbery, George Bisacca, and Laurence B. Kanter, *Italian Renaissance Frames* (New York: Metropolitan Musuem of Art, 1990). For the most extensive surveys of frames, see Heydenryk and Grimm.

its veracity challenged. As a culture changes, so do the meanings of words. Ah, those unfixed signifieds!

In its original usage, the verb "to frame," a decent Anglo-Saxon word, meant to shape or to form. In the platonist scheme of things, the demiurge framed the cosmos in compliance with certain mathematical ratios inherent in the world-soul; according to the Bible, God framed our universe in six days of creation. The Book of Wisdom went even further and specified that God framed our universe by number, weight, and measure (11.21). This topos was frequently cited in the Middle Ages and throughout the Renaissance, and was often illustrated, as in Figure 28, an illumination from a late thirteenth-century French Bible. As creator of the world, Christ with extended compasses has just set aside a portion of the abyss so that creation may proceed. Within the circle that he has drawn we can distinguish the emerging contours of the familiar T-shaped world map.[22] In this cosmogony, importantly, a specific space is determined before composition can begin. In order for cosmos to occur and for any value to emerge from chaos, a finite space must be designated and set apart from the amorphous infinite. In an undifferentiated abyss, no order, no value— no meaning—is possible, because the infinite is homogeneous and therefore provides no oppositions by which individual identity can be achieved.

In emulation of the heavenly maker, who has framed the universe, the mortal poet similarly frames his discourse by the disposition of number, weight, and measure. In this orthodox poetics, the narrative is necessarily versified. Indeed, poetry is defined basically as metrified language; and the essence of a poem—its dominant feature—is not the subject matter, but rather its formal properties. Proportion poetical prevails.

In the simplest practice of this platonist poetics, the poet decides upon a metrical form with its own power to signify—such as rime royal or the sestina or the sonnet—and then he fits words to the predetermined metrics. The language reifies a repeated pattern of feet and a rhyme scheme, which provide a subtext of form and serve as the abiding essence of the poem. Since Plato had said that time is the moving image of eternity (*Timaeus*, 37D), the poet adapts this principle to his own making and sees the narrative as a moving, temporal image. What the durational narrative images is the underlying, unchanging form of the poem, usually a repeatable unit of time such as a week or a year, which serves as a synecdoche for eternity itself. The narrative puts into palpable motion the otherwise reces-

22. Lloyd A. Brown, *The Story of Maps* (London: Cresset, 1951), 96-97.

Fig. 28.   Christ creating the universe. *Bible* (late thirteenth century), Paris, Biblio-
thèque Nationale, Cod.fr.12467, fol. 49

sive form, and thereby becomes a moving image of eternity. As Spenser
says in the envoy to *The Shepheardes Calender,* "Loe I have made a Calender
for every yeare, / That steele in strength, and time in durance shall out-
weare."

In its more sophisticated practice, framing the narrative in the sense of
composing a story involves devising a series of episodes with some sort of
linkage to provide an internal consistency. When Aristotle defines poetry
as imitating the actions of human beings, he subscribes to this theory of
narrative. The episodes are to be organized by a frame of cause and effect
to produce what he called the plot, with an organically related beginning,

middle, and end. In this formalist poetics, the plot is paramount, as Aristotle repeatedly insists, taking precedence over characterization and all else in the poetical work. In fact, character is revealed only by participation in the plot, rather than plot stemming from character as in the modern novel. So this plot, the relation between episodes in a formal arrangement, rather than the visualized episodes themselves, proves to be the essence of the poem. Sidney adopts this Aristotelian principle in *The Defence of Poesie;* everyone knoweth, he says, "the skill of each artificer standeth in that *idea* or fore-conceit of the work, and not in the work itself" (79.6–8). And he framed the narrative of the old *Arcadia* in this Aristotelian fashion. The oracle initiates the plot, which unfolds to demonstrate that "all had fallen out by the highest providence" (416.18), despite the human folly occasioned by fear and lust.[23]

The second sense of framing the narrative depends upon Alberti's practice of using a frame to designate a fictional space. The frame is the hypothetical window through which the painter peers in order to visualize the *historia*. Having indicated this frame, the painter then proceeds to fill it with an image, thereby producing a fiction clearly demarcated from his own actuality.

Evidently, this sense of framing is compatible with the first. Just as the creating deity circumscribes his construct with a line of separation and organizes it according to number, weight, and measure, so the painter frames a fictional space and organizes his *historia* by the mathematical laws of perspective. Both resort to proportion poetical.

What is different in this second sense of framing, though, is the importance assigned to the frame. Moreover, there is an intention of counterposing the fictional space and actuality as two distinct, competing entities. In the orthodox system where framing means to compose, the painting is a reflection of the essential reality in which it inheres, a microcosm reproducing the values of the platonic-Christian heaven. For its meaning, the painting refers to that abiding reality of supernal values. In the new system licensed by Alberti, however, where framing means to set apart, the painting is separated from transcendental reality. One practical result of single-point perspective is that it produces an infinite, homogeneous space equivalent to objective nature. As Alberti advises, "The function of the painter is to draw with lines and paint in colours on a surface any given bodies in such a way that, at a fixed distance and with a certain, determined

---

23. See my *Sidney and Spenser,* 401–62; and "Spenser, Sidney, and Poetic Form," *Studies in Philology* 88 (1991): 150–52.

position of the centric ray, what you see represented appears to be in relief and just like those bodies" (95). The painting contains its own raison d'être and provides an alternative to transcendence.

However, since the painting does not simply replicate observable nature, the artificial construct within the frame provides an alternative not only to some notion of "nature," an abstract norm, but also to the actual world itself. Art and the materialist's actuality are counterposed, and it is the frame that establishes and intensifies this opposition. Art thereby engages in dialectic with its own authority. It acquires the power to comment upon actuality.

In the Renaissance, poets also began to use framing devices to set apart their fictional spaces, their *historiae,* and for similar purposes and with comparable results. Poets, in fact, were remarkably ingenious in devising strategies to exploit the potential for dialogue between art and actuality that Alberti's frame encourages. A famous example underlines the point. In his *Utopia* Thomas More begins with a lengthy first book that recounts the major problems in England as he saw them, and this topical recitation serves as a frame for Raphael Hythloday's visit to an imaginary commonwealth in book 2. While book 1 leads the reader into the fictional space of Utopia, Hythloday's narration continually refers across this frame back to More's own world. The fictional space of artificial Utopia comments pointedly upon Tudor actuality. The *Utopia,* in fact, has much more to do with England under Henry VIII than with some abstract notion of an ideal commonwealth, the way it is read when the first book (the frame) is ignored.

While painters were limited in their ways of delineating the fictional space, poets resorted to a variety of devices to frame their narratives. One of the more obvious is the use of attention-getting titles. In earlier centuries, we may say that literary works do not usually display a title as a formal feature of the text. Most often the manuscript opens with an incidental *incipit.* For example, "Here begins the tale of patient Griselda. . . ." Dante claims to have found an entry in his book of memory, *Incipit vita nova.* The title is embedded in the text, and it is later editors who extract a title for the work, *La vita nuova.* Petrarch's comparable sequence of lyrics has no indication of a title, though we retrospectively (and lamely) call it diversely the *Sonetti* or the *Rime sparse* or the *Canzoniere,* titles of our own making to satisfy an imperative of a later period.

Although titles for medieval works are utilitarian at most, Renaissance poets began boldly to introduce their narratives with catchy titles. Consider the impudence of More's "Utopia" (Nowhere), a subversive joke as title for an apparent travel report; or the profound significance of Spenser's "Faerie Queene," a political gesture that positions Elizabeth as a constant presence in the poem despite the looseness of the rambling story. For some poets, the title came to be of such importance and attained such an ability to signify that the poem can hardly be construed without it. Herbert's "The Collar" and "The Pulley" defy comprehension without the point of reference provided by the title. Here the title becomes the very key to meaning.

The increased prominence accorded the title was intensified by an increased attention to the title page. We might even say that the title page as an entity with its own substance was invented at this time. Medieval manuscripts do not normally display an initial page announcing their titles. The sixteenth century, however, is the heyday of the title page with elaborate ornamentation, often with elements that suggest the sort of architectural constructions that sophisticate the frames of Renaissance paintings such as Bellini's (cf. Fig. 29).[24] Although the invention of printing may have encouraged this novel embellishment of the text, it would be wrong, I think, to say that cheaper production was the primary cause of this unwonted fussiness with title pages.

Another sort of framing device used by poets to mediate between their narratives and the reader was the use of prefatory letters: dedicatory letters to a patron, ingratiating letters to the gentle reader, explanatory letters from the printer. In his volume *A Hundreth Sundrie Flowers,* George Gascoigne uses all these plus others to produce a dazzling complex of relationships between the characters in his fictions, the printer, the reader, the author, certain friends of the author, and so forth.[25] Thomas More in the *Utopia* plays a purposeful variation on the introductory letter that frames the narrative: he produces a letter from himself to an actual acquaintance in Antwerp, Peter Giles, a letter that by its evident speciousness (like the title) establishes the fictionality of what follows.

Often authors used other framing devices that function comparably to these prefatory letters. A poet might write an envoy, printed sometimes at the beginning and sometimes at the end of the narrative, existing totally

24. On manuscript forerunners of the architectural title page in printed books, see Margery Corbett, "The Architectural Title-Page," *Motif* 12 (1964): 49–62; and Lilian Armstrong, *Renaissance Miniature Painters and Classical Imagery: The Master of the Putti and His Venetian Workshop* (London: Harvey Miller, 1981), 19–26. On the architectural title page itself, see Margery Corbett and Ronald Lightbown, *The Comely Frontispiece: The Emblematic Title-Page in England, 1550–1660* (London: Routledge & Kegan Paul, 1979), esp. 4–9.

25. See Susan Carol Staub, "George Gascoigne's *A Hundreth Sundrie Flowers:* 'The Method and Maner' of the Poet" (Ph.D. diss., University of North Carolina at Chapel Hill, 1987).

VIRESCIT VVLNERE VIRTVS

ORONTII
FINEI DEL
PHINATIS, LIBE-
RALIVM DISCIPLI-
NARVM PROFESSO-
RIS REGII,
PROTOMATHESIS:
Opus uarium, ac scitu non minus utile
quàm iucundum, nunc primùm in
lucem sœliciter emissum.
Cuius index uniuersa-
lis, in uersa pagina
continetur.

PARISIIS ANNO
1532.

Cum gratia & priuilegio Christianissimi
Francorum Regis, ad Decennium.

CHAMILLY.

Hunc Author propriopingebat marte figuram.

Fig. 29. A title page architecturally constructed. Oronce Finé, *Protomathesis* (Paris, 1532), title page

neither inside nor outside the text but on its threshold. What the poet says as he sends his little book to seek its fortune indicates how he sees its interaction with the actual world. An epigraph or "emblem," printed either first or last, serves a similar purpose and functions in much the same way.

Yet another device used by Renaissance poets literally frames the narrative and occupies its margins. The use of marginal annotation perpetuates an old and revered tradition—surrounding classical texts, preserving talmudic and biblical scholarship, instructing schoolchildren what is most memorable in their textbooks.[26] But marginalia appear sometimes in unexpected places and produce sophisticated results. In some instances, the marginal annotation is incongruous with the main text; in the *Poly-Olbion*, for example, Selden's historical sidenotes provide an unsettling counterpoint for Drayton's poetizing.[27] In some instances, the marginal annotation converts the text to irony; in William Baldwin's early prose memoir *Beware the Cat*, for example, inflated marginalia ridicule the learned tradition and signal the outrageousness of the narrative.[28]

Most interesting and subtlest of the framing devices newly used by poets, however, is the designated narrator other than the author. In earlier periods, the author was both the composer and the subject of the literary work. Dante, for example, both writes the *Vita nuova* and serves as its protagonist. The reader is invited to assume that the text is autobiographical. The same may be said of Petrarch and his *Canzoniere*. But note the different assumption about author and protagonist in Sidney's *Astrophil and Stella*.

26. See William W. E. Slights, "The Edifying Margins of Renaissance English Books," *Renaissance Quarterly* 42 (1989): 682–716.

27. See Anne Lake Prescott, "Marginal Discourse: Drayton's Muse and Selden's 'Story,'" *Studies in Philology* 88 (1991): 307–28.

28. Ed. William A. Ringler, Jr., and Michael Flachmann (San Marino, Calif.: Huntington Library, 1988). In a dedicatory epistle the author claims to be an accurate "reporter," faithfully recording the words of "Master Streamer," the imputed narrator, who is clearly fictitious (3); yet, in "An Exhortation" at the end, the author reiterates his claims of complete truthfulness (54). Other personages, such as George Ferrers, and most places, such as Aldersgate and Kankwood, are actual. The profuse marginalia soon become parodic of learned annotation, often explaining the obvious or offering irrelevant information, and sometimes appearing in Latin. In the sidenotes there is the simulation of sententiousness, with a liberal use of maxims: "Experience is an infallible persuader" (12); "A little sufficeth him that hath enough" (15); "All is fish that cometh to the net" (40). But the relationship between marginalia and text is so tenuous that the commentary proves gratuitous, and therefore tends to be discredited. The net effect is comedic and satiric, with a large element of the ribaldry of jestbooks. For example, when a cat fastens upon the genitals of a seducer attempting to hide from the cuckolded husband and therefore needing to remain silent, the sidenote with mock sententiousness reads: "Fear overcometh smart" (50).

While the persona in that work, Astrophil, bears the personal signature of Philip Sidney, it is a gross oversimplification to read the text as a factual account of Sidney's pursuit of Penelope Devereux. Sidney has created an alter ego, Astrophil, to frame his narrative, setting it apart from actuality in order to allow a meaningful dialectic between Astrophil's fiction and Sidney's fact. The personal signature, like the orthogonal lines of a perspective painting, reaches out of the *historia* into the actual world; but while transgressing the boundary between art and actuality, it also prevents the too-easy conflation of the two worlds. Astrophil as narrator provides a frame for the fiction that guarantees its otherness.[29]

Gradually, as the reading audience was educated to accept the credibility of a designated narrator, the dimension of the framing narrator is diminished. Eventually, the framing narrator is reduced to a disembodied voice, an omniscient but essentially absent presence; and the author in propria persona does not appear at all. Pure fiction—what Sidney calls an "absolute poem"—is born.[30] As Touchstone says, with a pun on *truest*, "The truest poetry is the most feigning"—that is, since poetry is feigning, the truest poetry is that which feigns the most.[31]

During the Renaissance, however, in the early stages of this transformation toward full-fledged fiction, a designated narrator was introduced, counter to medieval practice, to frame the narrative: to set it apart from actuality, and yet to mediate between the fictional world and the reader. This imputed narrator imposes perspective on the characters and episodes, organizing them into a plot, lining them up so they lead toward a single point on the horizon—the end of the story. As an early but splendid example, in the complex construction of *The Canterbury Tales* the narrator enjoys a dual status: he participates in the artificial space of the artifact, yet he addresses an audience as fellow members of his own community. Is this first-person speaker Chaucer himself, or a pilgrim as fictitious as the others? The answer is, of course, both; and this ambiguity of its frame is a measure of the work's success as fiction.

---

29. A transformation similar to that in the sequence of sonnets occurred also in the medieval dream poem, another lyric genre, as it metamorphosed from allegory into narrative fiction. In its original form, the dream allegory does not distinguish between author and dreamer. Chaucer's *Boke of the Duchesse* and Skelton's *Bowge of Court* are cases in point. The pretense is that the poet falls asleep, has a fantastic vision, and then awakens. See J. Stephen Russell, *The English Dream Vision: Anatomy of a Form* (Columbus: Ohio State University Press, 1988), 5–7, 115ff.

30. *Defence*, 81.30–31, 87.1.

31. *AYLI*, 3.3.19–20.

To underline parallel developments in painting and in literary narrative, it is worth noting that Alberti posits a figure like a narrator to inhabit the *historia* of his painting and relate it to the viewers: "I like there to be someone in the *historia* who tells the spectators what is going on, and either beckons them with his hand to look . . . or by his gestures invites you to laugh or weep with them" (83). This commentator, who functions both within and without the picture, negotiates the interaction between painting and viewers. In Bellini's picture (Fig. 27), Saint Benedict performs this role. He is at the far right, with his Bible open to a passage pertinent to the *historia*.[32]

In this second sense—where framing sets the narrative apart, but the use of perspective encourages interplay between the fictional space and its surroundings—art and actuality enjoy equal validity. Both have authority; neither dominates in the exchange. Art has gained an independence from the actual world, so that fiction can now be counterposed against objective nature. Art, in fact, can replace actuality as the more dependable representation of truth. Although the actual world evidently preexists the art, through the ingenuity of the painter/poet the *historia* acquires the capacity to generate truth-value of its own.

Under both of our first two senses of framing it is assumed that the work of art, painting or literary fiction, derives from actuality and in some way represents it. In our first sense, the work of art is a direct representation of the actuality in which it inheres; the content of the artifice is a metaphor for an underlying form, which is the work's abiding essence. In our second sense, the work of art is set apart from what it represents by a frame, and because of its otherness is able to enter into dialogue with actuality and comment upon it, often negatively. In both cases, actuality enjoys the privilege of the original, and the work of art is derivative, a supplement of what already exists.

When we reverse this hierarchy, however, we arrive at our third sense of framing.[33] The *historia* purports to be an account of actuality, a representation of it. But this is a frame-up. The story is open to challenge and to charges of fraud, and thereby it calls into question the actuality it repre-

32. See Rona Goffen, *Giovanni Bellini* (New Haven: Yale University Press, 1989), 161.

33. Friedrich Nietzsche over a hundred years ago was already assigning to art a role as replacement for actuality: "Art is not an imitation of nature but its metaphysical supplement, raised up beside it in order to overcome it" (*The Birth of Tragedy and The Genealogy of Morals*, trans. Francis Golffing [New York: Doubleday/Anchor, 1956], 142).

sents. The discrepancies in the story call for an investigation. We find that what has been omitted from the story is more important than what has been revealed. What has been left in shadow is essential to establishing the truth. The work of art as a potent other deconstructs actuality. But to achieve this purpose, the work of art itself must be deconstructed in order to expose its deficiencies.

In painting the vulnerability of the actual world is most readily apparent in the technique known as chiaroscuro, a deployment of light and dark whereby the shape of an object is indicated by the shadows it throws.[34] Highlighted areas are defined negatively, by darkened areas where light is withheld. Dürer's woodcut of Saint George fighting the dragon exemplifies the technique (Fig. 30). The body of the horse, for example, is defined by the shadows it makes. The presence of light is indicated perversely, by its absence; the positive is given definition only by what is not illuminated—a compelling instance of the deconstructive paradigm derived from Saussurian linguistics, where meaning comes only from difference. Tellingly, Alberti has a long passage on chiaroscuro (87–89), and its development as a common practice coincided with the widespread adoption of his advice about visualizing the painting as though looking through a window.

A notable example of chiaroscuro in literature is provided by Sidney's *Astrophil and Stella.* There the *historia* purports to tell the tale of Astrophil's pursuit of a mistress with Petrarch's code for courtship providing the rules. The usual elements of Petrarchismo are present: a lovesick poet writes sonnets in ritual praise of an unattainable lady. The narrative pretends to represent favorably this convention in Elizabethan society, with all its freezing and frying. But as it unfolds, Astrophil's *historia* challenges the viability of the Petrarchan code and reveals its contradictions.

In Petrarchan discourse the lover claims to be selfless and appears to be self-deprecating; while the lady is idealized, intellectualized to such an extent that she exists only as a perfected male, a man who has overcome male weaknesses, such as passion or appetite or self-doubt.[35] *La mia donna* represents this desire for perfection. In his sequence of sonnets, however, Sidney makes Astrophil a lover whose libido oversways reason. And he gives

34. For a history of this technique, which admits greater variation than one might think, see Walter L. Strauss, *The Clair-Obscur Woodcuts by the German and Netherlandish Masters of the XVIth and XVIIth Centuries* (Greenwich, Conn.: New York Graphic Society, 1973), vii–xiii.

35. Euphues makes the point when in an assemblage of ladies he claims that, "being framed as it were of the perfection of men, they [women] be free from all such cogitations as may any way provoke them to uncleanenesse" (*Euphues,* in *Works of Lyly,* ed. Bond, vol. 1, 204.18–20). Shortly thereafter Euphues again praises women at greater length:

Fig. 30.   Albrecht Dürer, Saint George

Stella just enough substance to suggest a full-bodied woman who, though repressed by the social order, is nonetheless capable of responding to Astrophil's sexual advances.

The point is neatly made by an examination of song 4, a lyric that occurs about two-thirds through the sequence. In the story, Astrophil has induced Stella to meet him secretly in a garden under the cover of darkness. There, impelled by sexual urgency, Astrophil professes his love, which Stella reluctantly rejects; and when importunity fails, he resorts to physical force, at which time Stella indignantly departs. Employing the unusual mode of dramatic dialogue, the poem reduces the entire narrative of the sequence to a vignette: Astrophil's pursuit of Stella, her resistance, and the final separation.

Song 4 comprises nine stanzas, each carefully contrived of six lines in a striking display of metrical ingenuity. In every instance Astrophil speaks the first five lines, followed by a single, invariant line assigned to Stella. The opening stanza is typical:

Onely joy, now here you are,	a
Fit to heare and ease my care:	a
Let my whispering voyce obtaine,	b
Sweete reward for sharpest paine:	b
Take me to thee, and thee to me.	c
'No, no, no, no, my Deare, let be.'	c

In each stanza the first four lines are trochaic tetrameter catalectic, while the last two lines are iambic tetrameter. There are in effect three rhymed couplets, with the two lines of the last couplet distributed between Astrophil and Stella. Their roles are similar to the relationship between the passionate shepherd and the philosophical nymph, with Stella in each stanza countering Astrophil's invitation by a provisional denial.

God when he had made all thinges, at the last, made man as most perfect, thinking nothing could be framed more excellent, yet after him hee created a woman, the expresse Image of Eternitie, the lyvely picture of Nature, the onely steele glasse for man to beholde hys infirmities, by comparinge them wyth woemens perfections. (216.36–217.5)

After the infidelity of Lucilla, however, Euphues sees women as fallen creatures: "I had thought that women had bene as we men, that is true, faithfull, zealous, constant. . . . I was halfe perswaded that they were made of the perfection of men, and would be comforters, but now I see they have tasted of the infection of the Serpent" (241.12–17). The cataclysm of the Fall wrenches the man-woman relationship along with the rest of nature.

From the start, Astrophil addresses Stella as a mistress in the Petrarchan mold. She is his "onely joy," so his pain must be assuaged by her acquiescence. And he rapidly calls into play the other clichés of Petrarchismo. Not surprisingly, Astrophil defines Stella primarily in terms of his desire and sees her as his accessory: she is "fit to heare and ease my care," no more than a "sweete reward" for his "paine" (2–4). Although he suggests a reciprocal relationship in the fifth line of each stanza, which serves as a refrain in his performance ("Take me to thee, and thee to me"), that invariant line does indeed change at the end, becoming "Soone with my death I will please thee" (53). Not only does this change expose Astrophil's opportunism, but also the language exposes his duplicity. Although the sentiment, if taken in a refined sense, is at basis Petrarchan, there lurks in addition the slang sense of death as sexual intercourse. So beneath this punning statement lies a crude reference to Stella's capacity for sensual fulfillment: by his "death," Astrophil can "please" her. This obscene reading of the line is supported by the immediately previous complaint of Astrophil: "Cursed be my destines all, / That brought me so high to fall." Again, if taken in a refined sense, the statement seems innocent enough; but with double-entendre it rails against the thwarting of his sexual arousal. Petrarchan elegance is subverted by the ambiguity of its own terms, and its pretense of nicety is disclosed as salacious.

Most interesting, though, is the role assigned to Stella in this encounter. She is created for the reader almost entirely through Astrophil's words, so that, as we have noted, she appears at first as a figment of his desire. But, unlike most sonnet mistresses, Stella is given a voice. In each stanza of this song she does speak one line—in fact, she has the final word. And like the reply of the philosophical nymph, it is strongly negative: an emphatic "no" repeated four times, culminating in a firm "let be." Nonetheless, this iterated refusal in every instance is tempered by a term of endearment, "my Deare"; and while this indication of affection may reveal no more than feminine compassion, to the inflamed mind of Astrophil it sounds like encouragement. Furthermore, if we wish to empower Stella and see her as a woman enacting her own will, we can read the phrase as a subtext expressing her attraction to Astrophil, her latent sexuality.[36]

But Stella speaks only rarely, and for the most part we can only surmise her attitudes. Even so, the unwritten Stella, the lively one who remains in

36. Despite the considerable attention to Stella in recent feminist discourse, the comprehensive essay remains Nona Fienberg, "The Emergence of Stella in *Astrophil and Stella*," *Studies in English Literature 1500-1900* 25 (1985): 5–19.

shadow, is more significant than the conventional mistress that Astrophil customarily addresses in his text. We the readers are apprised of the truth by what is hinted, but largely left unsaid. In this instance, as in chiaroscuro, the negative defines the positive. Stella highlights the deficiencies of Astrophil as a lover, and she rather than he represents what it is to love in truth. The supplement ultimately provides the definition, the meaning, the value. The deconstructive paradigm—whereby authority is vested in the suppressed—is fulfilled. The social code that Astrophil professes has been framed, judged, and condemned.

In this last sense of framing, the frame sets apart a fictional space that purports to replicate the actual world; but eventually the art opposes actuality, challenges its appearances, and proves them to be false. Rather than art representing a preexistent actuality and therefore being dependent upon that world, it is art that embodies the true and endows an otherwise chaotic world with meaning. Art is more real than the actual world, which is bewilderingly unstable—not only fleeting, but indeterminate. The work of art, whether painting or literary fiction, makes sense of actuality, which otherwise would be a pointless concurrence of disparate, unrelated phenomena. With this slang sense of framing, we approach the conundrum of Magritte's *Human Condition.*

Few works of sixteenth-century fiction are more assiduously framed than Lyly's *Euphues: The anatomy of wyt* (1578). The quickly told story of Euphues' disillusioning experience with Neapolitan society takes up only sixty-two pages of a 144-page text.[37] The rest is given over to prefatory letters before the story begins, and then a plethora of appendages at the end. Although the central tale taken alone has the appearance of simplicity approaching an exemplum, it is encased in a series of framing devices that interact with it and produce complex circumstances that condition its significance. Not least important is the artifice of an officious designated narrator other than the author himself.

The plot of the main narrative, however, is free of complexity and fairly predictable. Euphues, a well-born Athenian youth, willfully travels to Naples, where he pledges an unstinting friendship with Philautus, an equally fortunate young man of the court there. Philautus has gained the consent of a beautiful heiress, Lucilla, whom he plans to marry. But Euphues, when introduced to Lucilla, falls in love with her and, using the

37. *Works of Lyly,* ed. Bond, vol. 1, 184–246, out of 177–323. Hereafter, citations are made by page and line numbers to this text. Quotations are limited to the *editio princeps* (1578).

deception of courting another lady, Livia, soon betrays his friendship with Philautus and wins the affection of Lucilla. After a brief period, though, the fickle mistress ditches Euphues also and chooses yet another suitor, the unworthy Curio, at which point Euphues and Philautus resume their friendship.

That is the apparent end of the narrative. Both before and after returning to Athens, however, Euphues engages in correspondence with Philautus, Livia, and others not mentioned in the central story, and these letters along with sundry other addenda make up the last seventy-seven pages of text.[38] From these supplements we learn, among other things, that Lucilla did indeed marry Curio, but through an unexplained reversal in fortune she soon died on the street, a penniless harlot (311–12). The plot, then, does not really conclude in the main narrative itself, but relevant information continues through various additions that fudge the ending. The edge of the fictional space is complicated by several enhancements that, like mats around a picture, complement certain portions of it and bring them into prominence.[39] A definitive frame, being repeatedly deferred, begins to waver. Indeed, the text concludes with a promise by the author to provide yet more narrative: "I have finished the first part of *Euphues* whome now I lefte readye to crosse the Seas to *Englande*, if the winde sende him a shorte cutte you shall in the seconde part heare what newes he bringeth and I hope to have him retourned within one Summer" (323.15–20). Scarcely more than a year later, as promised, Lyly published the equally successful *Euphues and His England* (1580).

Furthermore, while the plot of the central narrative of *Euphues* is simple enough, the means of unfolding it are anything but straightforward.

38. At the end of the main narrative a remarkable number of cumbersome framing devices engage the reader in a drawn-out denouement. First comes a lengthy moralistic letter from Euphues to Philautus, written just before returning to Athens. This is followed by Euphues' letter "to the grave Matrones and honest Maydens of Italy," a retraction of the misogynistic sentiments he had just expressed to Philautus. Then comes a long-winded paraphrase of Plutarch's treatise on the education of children, entitled "Euphues and his Ephoebus" and clumsily introduced by the narrator, followed by a letter "to the Gentlemen schollers in Athens," in which Euphues exhorts them to study and be religious. Next comes a platonic dialogue, "Euphues and Atheos," in which Euphues converts the atheist to Christianity. And the work concludes with a packet of "Letters writ by Euphues to his friendes," including Philautus, Eubulus, and Livia. In a final paragraph, given distinction by anomalous typesetting, the narrator returns and announces that he is already busy on a "seconde part."

39. For example, the letters of Euphues to Philautus dissuading him from a dissolute life focus the satire against the wickedness of the court (246.13–257.16, 312.18–313.2), and the letters between Euphues and Livia clarify the antifeminism that is everywhere incipient (319.9–322.18).

The storytelling begins in a conventional way when an omniscient but invisible (and certainly male) narrator introduces the main character in his identifying milieu: "There dwelt in *Athens* a young gentleman of great patrimonie, & of so comely a personage, that it was doubted whether he were more bound to Nature for the liniaments of his person, or to fortune for the encrease of his possessions" (184.1–4). Although the titular character is "a young gentleman of great patrimonie"—that is, a *euphues,* meaning in Greek "well-born"—what follows is a lengthy portrait of him as a headstrong wastrel, a "younge gallant, of more wit then wealth, and yet of more wealth then wisdome" (184.9–10). In order to move the narrative forward, the narrator reports that Euphues turned his back upon his old acquaintances and quit his own country, setting out on life's journey. The disapproving narrator, though, adapting the epic forecast, warns in advance: "Leaving the rule of reason, [Euphues] rashly ranne unto destruction" (185.8). But there is an upside to Euphues' folly, and soon the moralistic narrator tosses out a familiar platitude: "It hath bene an olde sayed sawe, and not of lesse truth then antiquitie, that witte is the better if it bee the deerer bought"; and he announces: "as in the sequele of thys historie shall moste manifestlye appeare" (185.20–22). Even though Euphues runs into trouble, he eludes a cloistered virtue and eventually attains a keener wit. Throughout, the narrator is busily—officiously—at work, manipulating the perceptions of the reader.

With equal purposiveness, though with flourishes of the style popularized by this text, the narrator then transfers the ambience from learned Greece to dissolute Italy: "It happened thys young Impe to arive at *Naples* (a place of more pleasure then profite, and yet of more profite then pietie) the very walles and windowes whereof shewed it rather to bee the Tabernacle of *Venus,* then the Temple of *Vesta*" (185.22–26). Now the story begins in earnest as Euphues surrounds himself with freeloaders. Soon he is accosted by an old gentleman, Eubulus, and the mode of narration turns from storytelling to prosopopoeia as Eubulus offers sage advice about temptations to the flesh in Naples and Euphues snidely rejects it (187.1–194.33).

At the conclusion of this balanced exchange, the narrator resumes control of the narration and steps forward to address his implied readership. He emerges from anonymity and begins to acquire a distinct personality as he launches into a finger-wagging diatribe against the pigheadedness of youth: "Heere ye may beholde gentlemen, how lewdly wit standeth in his owne lyght," etc., etc. (195.15–16). We might possibly succumb to laxity here and equate this narrator with Lyly, the author himself, although to do so impoverishes the text and undermines the rich potential for meaning provided by the numerous framing devices, as we shall see.

With an implied narrator and an implied readership now established, the plot moves briskly forward. Gathering us "gentlemen" under his wing (196.17ff.) and with a conspiratorial "we," the narrator announces this intention: "But retourne we agayne to *Euphues*" (196.30).[40] After meeting Philautus, Euphues delivers a conventional praise of friendship (197.3–21) and determines to become his friend. From here, the plot is realized largely through interior monologues,[41] through prosopopoeiac exchanges between two characters,[42] and occasionally through stichomythic dialogue.[43]

The narrator stage-manages these set pieces, efficiently stringing them together by means of necessary information and wry social commentary. On several occasions, he fussily intrudes and calls attention to himself. For example, after Euphues elaborately praises friendship and vows to "have *Philautus* for my pheere," the narrator piques our interest by a promise of juicy bits to come: "Whosoever shall see this amitie grounded upon a little affection, will soone conjecture that it shall be dissolved upon a light occasion: as in the sequele of *Euphues* & *Philautus* you shall see, whose hot love waxed soone colde" (197.30–33). And the narrator continues, before the fact, with a mixture of teasing and moralizing:

> Who deserved the most blame in mine opinion, it is doubtful, and so difficult, that I dare not presume to give verdit. For love being the cause for which so many mischiefes have ben attempted, I am not yet perswaded, whether of them was most to be blamed, but certeinly neither of them was blamelesse. (197.35–198.2)

Then the narrator again addresses his implied audience: "I appeale to your judgement gentlemen, not that I thincke any of you of the lyke disposition able to decide the question, but beeing of deeper discretion then I am, are more fit to debate the quarrel" (198.3–5; cf. 215.8–12). Even if we mistake this meddling narrator for Lyly himself, it is an author who has for-

40. For a similar use of this storyteller's ploy, cf. 207.34–36 and 218.2–3.

41. E.g., by Lucilla (205.4–207.35), by Euphues (208.2–211.24; 240.30–242.31), by Philautus (232.4–233.13).

42. E.g., Euphues and Philautus (211.24–215.7), Euphues and Lucilla (218.7–224.25), Ferardo and Lucilla (227.8–229.16; 242.32–245.17). There is also a notable exchange of letters between Philautus and Euphues (233.13–237.3).

43. E.g., between Euphues and Lucilla (224.26ff. and 237.13ff.).

gone his unassailable authority, an author who invites a challenge to his competence.

In any case, we are continually aware of a narrator's presence, and therefore of the text's fictionality. For instance, after a long interior monologue by Lucilla rationalizing her new preference for Euphues over Philautus, the narrator bustles in to move us toward another episode: "She having thus discoursed with hir selfe hir owne miseryes, cast hir selfe on the bedde: and there lette hir lye, and retourne wee to *Euphues*" (207.34–36). Similarly after a prosopopoeiac exchange between Euphues and Philautus, following Euphues' decision to betray his friend by wooing Lucilla, the narrator again bustles in:

> Heere you may see gentlemen the falshood in felowship, the fraude in friendship, the painted sheth with the leaden dagger, the faire woords that make fooles faine, but I will not trouble you with superfluous addition unto whom I feare mee I have bene tedious, with the bare discourse of this rude historie. (215.8–12)

It is clear that this narrator functions as a frame, delineating the fictional space while making it accessible to us. The opening sentence uttered by the narrator—"There dwelt in *Athens* a young gentleman . . ."—locates the action in a distant city and resorts to the past tense, thereby providing geographical and temporal distancing, while the typography changes from a font of Roman to blackletter, reinforcing the sense of framing.

But let's revert to the very beginning of this text and look in turn at the several framing devices encountered by the gentleman reader even before he is admitted into the narrative. First, of course, comes the title page (Fig. 31), relatively unadorned though surrounded by a border of ornamental devices and heavy with language. At the top is the name of the titular character, preceded by a printer's ornament and italicized to lend it distinction. Then comes a subtitle: "The anatomy of wyt," establishing an association between Euphues and wit, almost as though he personifies wit in an allegorical way. The subtitle suggests also that wit as embodied in Euphues will be submitted to intense scrutiny, even murderous dissection. The next autonomous phrase indicates the genre of the text: it is a comedy, or at least "very pleasant," and an exemplum, "most necessary to remember." It also designates a readership: the growing number of "Gentlemen," both those recognized as such and those lesser folk who aspired to the honor.

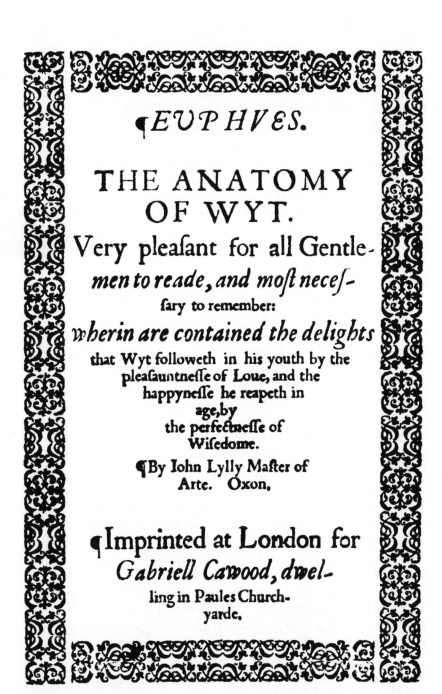

¶EVPHVES.

THE ANATOMY OF WYT.

Very pleaſant for all Gentlemen to reade, and moſt neceſ-
ſary to remember:
wherin are contained the delights
that Wyt followeth in his youth by the
pleaſauntneſſe of Loue, and the
happyneſſe he reapeth in
age, by
the perfectneſſe of
Wiſedome.
¶By Iohn Lylly Maſter of
Arte.   Oxon.

¶Imprinted at London for
Gabriell Cawood, dwel-
ling in Paules Church-
yarde.

Fig. 31.   The title page of *Euphues*

Next comes further information about the subject matter of the narrative—in effect, a summary of its meaning—what Sidney would have called its "*idea* or fore-conceit" (*Defence*, 79.7–8); and here again the talk about Wit and Love and Wisdom smacks of allegory. The contrast between youth and age also activates the semantics of binary systems investigated in the last chapter. The author is then recognized, and his literary credentials as a Master of Arts from Oxford are displayed. Finally, potential buyers are told where the volume is available for sale: at the shop of Gabriel Cawood in the churchyard of Saint Paul's. The title page has accomplished a great deal, not only announcing the title of the work, but also indicating its generic affinities, its intended audience, and even its meaning. The title page opens a door for the reader and serves as a formative rite of passage. Furthermore, by claiming that the text is an "anatomy" of wit, it invites careful interrogation of the subject matter.

Before the story begins, however, there are still two prefatory letters: an obsequious dedication to Sir William West, Lord Delaware, and a jocular address "to the Gentlemen Readers." The first is longer and more important because it comments pointedly upon the nature of the narrative that follows. Especially the opening sentences suggest the several ways of engaging the artifice of literary works and paintings.

Lyly begins his dedicatory epistle in a conventional fashion by stringing together a series of classical allusions. The first word is "Parrhasius," a famous painter of antiquity, and Lyly mentions several of his portraits and the various modes by which they generate meaning:

> Paratius drawing the counterfaite of Helen (right honorable) made the attier of hir head loose, who being demaunded why he dyd so, he aunswered, she was loose. Vulcan was painted curiously, yet with a polt foote. Venus cunningly, yet with hir Mole. (179.7–10)

In the case of Helen's portrait, her licentiousness is indicated directly and accurately by the looseness of her headdress. There is an immediate correlation between signified and signifier, following the Cratylian paradigm of language. When questioned, Parrhasius made this point.

A similar semiotics prevails in the portrait of Vulcan, although the relation between signifier and signified is not so straightforward. The picture is painted "curiously," which I gloss as "strangely" or "unconventionally," and yet it retains Vulcan's "polt" (that is, chicken-like) foot. This defect is his distinctive feature. But exactly what quality does the lame foot signify? Nothing precise, as in the case of Helen's loose tiara. Rather, it seems, the lameness indicates the god's general deformity. If pressed for precision, we can best explain it by means of a story, the myth of how Jupiter cast Vulcan out of heaven in anger when Vulcan took the part of his mother Juno in a quarrel.[44] Cratylian linguistics is strained, since the signified resists exactness. Indeed, when the originary tale is brought to bear upon Vulcan's lameness, it evokes sympathy and perhaps admiration.

The disjunction between signified and signifier is widened even further in the next example of Parrhasius' art. Venus is painted "cunningly"—that is, with great skill. In this case the subject is commonly characterized by her ability to love and be loved. The quality of the goddess to be fore-grounded in the portrait is her loveliness as manifested in beauty. According to Cratylian semiotics we should expect this signified to be rendered by a heavenly smile or sparkling eyes. Instead, her distinctive feature in the painting is a mole, a flaw in her beauty. What we have, of course, is an aesthetic grounded in the contrast of opposites, the mode of chiaroscuro. As Lyly comments later in this letter, "We commonly see that a black ground doth best beseme a white counterfeit [i.e., portrait]" (181.7–8). When applied in the *toilette*, this aesthetic culminated in the use of black patches by eighteenth-century belles. The "beauty spot" was the artificial impair-ment that emphasized the natural "perfections" of the lady who displayed it. So Venus' mole, perversely, calls attention to her celestial beauty.

But the relationship between signified and signifier is now a negative one. We have progressed from positive signification in the case of Helen through indirect signification achieved by narrative in the case of Vulcan to inverse signification in the case of Venus. Lyly has offered a complete range of options in relating signifiers to signifieds—that is, in the inter-pretation of textual data. Applying this semiotics to Euphues, do his rep-rehensible actions reveal otherwise hidden vices, as in the case of Helen, or should they be interpreted as harbingers of inner perfection, as in the case of Venus? We are invited to analyze the story of Euphues as though it were a Plutarchan *historia*, the same action being the occasion for either blame or praise.[45] As Lyly soon says, "In the discourse of Euphues I have aswel touched the vanities of his love, as the vertues of his lyfe" (179.22–23).

From his discussion of paintings by Parrhasius, Lyly proceeds to a dis-

---

44. For the locus classicus, cf. Homer, *Iliad*, 1.590–94. In Homer, of course, the name of the blacksmith god is Hephaestus rather than Vulcan.

45. See my *Sidney and Spenser*, 172–76, and pages 162–163 above.

cussion of a portrait by Apelles, another famous painter of the classical world. His anecdote of how Apelles painted Alexander the Great is more extended and presents even further complications in the hermeneutics of deducing character from depictive details. It moves from accoutrements to actions:

> Alexander having a Skar in his cheeke helde his finger upon it that Appelles might not paint it. Appelles painted him with his finger cleaving to his face, why quod Alexander I layde my finger on my Skarre bicause I would not have thee see it, (yea sayd Appelles) and I drew it there bicause none els should perceive it, for if thy finger had bene away, either thy Skarre would have ben seene, or my arte myslyked. (179.11–17)

Alexander, wishing to present an image of invincibility to the public, chose to cover a scar with his finger in order to hide it and prevent its representation. But out of fidelity to his craft Apelles drew Alexander's finger in that position. Otherwise, he said when queried, this important feature would have been omitted from the portrait and no one would know about it. If Apelles had completed the portrait without Alexander's finger in place, either he would have had to depict the scar as regularly observed, or his art could be chastised for inaccuracy.

What is implied here, and what Alexander is objecting to, is the painting's disclosure of a quality not visible to the eye: Alexander's distaste for appearing vulnerable, his compulsion to achieve perfection. The scar serves as a metonym for Alexander's vain deceit, and his attempt to hide the physical defect exposes a deeper flaw. Apelles has reproduced the telling gesture, the finger that points to the very thing the subject wishes to conceal and thereby exclude. The painter in effect deconstructs the appearance of his subject and produces a true portrait that goes beyond mere visibilia. But note that this semiotics requires a negative relation between signifier and signified. Just as Venus' mole, a flaw, affirms her perfection, so Alexander's act of covering the scar, an attempt at perfection, attests to his deceptiveness, a flaw. "Whereby I gather," Lyly concludes, "that in all perfect workes aswell the fault as the face is to be showen."

Of course, no paintings by Parrhasius or Apelles have survived from the ancient world, and what we know of their work comes entirely from writers such as Pliny and Plutarch. In the case of Apelles, as we have seen, Lucian provides a detailed account of his depiction of Calumny (page

160 above). But nowhere do we have any reference to a portrait of Alexander by Apelles—or to paintings of Helen, Vulcan, or Venus by Parrhasius. These are figments of Lyly's inventive mind, created to serve a purpose. Quite simply, Lyly fabricated these allusions in order to lay forth a hermeneutics for representing character, a correlation between visible features and essential personality.[46] And just as clearly, he prepared such an introduction to his fictional tale of Euphues because he believed in the parallelism between pictorial narrative and narrative in fiction: "For as every Paynter that shadoweth a man in all parts, giveth every peece his just proporcion, so he that desciphereth the qualities of the mynde, ought aswell to shew every humor in his kinde, as the other doth every part in his colour" (180.2–5). Lyly saw the hermeneutics of portraits as a valid method of communicating character in the plot of a story.

So this dedicatory epistle serves as a frame to provide instruction about the processing of textual data, mediating what readers draw from the narrative. Lyly reinforces this instruction by carrying it over into the main narrative. In its first paragraph, he repeats:

> Some men write and most men beleeve, that in all perfecte shapes, a blemmish bringeth rather a liking every way to the eyes, then a loathing any waye to the minde. *Venus* had hir Mole in hir cheeke which made hir more amiable: *Helen* hir scarre on hir chinne which *Paris* called *Cos amoris,* the Whetstone of love. *Aristippus* his wart, *Lycurgus* his wenne. (184.19–24)

In these instances, a defect is a complement to perfection; vice, to virtue. Simplicity is to be avoided: "In the disposition of the minde, either vertue is overshadowed with some vice, or vice overcast with some vertue" (184.24–26). Examples flock to mind: "*Alexander* valiaunt in warre, yet gyven to wine. *Tullie* eloquent in his gloses, yet vayneglorious: *Salomon* wyse, yet to too wanton: *David* holye but yet an homicide" (184.26–28; cf. 179.24–27). Completion requires the assimilation of a negative, an other, and consequently every entity is subject to deconstruction. In this advice about the interpretation of character, the narrator finally narrows his point to the case in hand: "None more wittie then *Euphues,* yet at the first none more

46. Alberti sometimes comments upon the attention paid in ancient paintings of the gods "to representing what was necessary according to function, kind and dignity," including the representation of Vulcan's limp (77); cf. also 79–81. Lyly's passage, however, is more usually referred to Cicero (cf. *Works of Lyly,* ed. Bond, vol. 1, 328 [n. on 179.9]).

wicked" (184.29). No wonder that Euphues, "leaving the rule of reason, rashly ranne unto destruction" (185.8). Thereby hangs the tale.

When reading about Euphues, then, we must not simplistically construe his flaws as direct signifiers of inner defects. The hermeneutics of portraits provides a wide latitude for the assignment of motive, and even provides for an inverse relationship between signifier and signified. As Lyly comments in his dedicatory epistle, "In every counterfaite as well the blemish as the bewtie is coloured" (179.20–21): We must become readers as Plutarch counseled, recognizing the ambivalence of human actions and admitting the difficulty of making moral judgments. Defects may even be precursors of perfection. Although in his opening description the narrator carefully enumerates Euphues' silly mannerisms—his "fine phrases, smoth quipping, merry taunting, using jesting without meane, and abusing mirth without measure" (184.14–16)—there is an overt apology for these vanities. The narrator generously concludes: "As therefore the sweetest Rose hath his pricket, the finest velvet his brack, the fairest flowre his bran, so the sharpest witte hath his wanton will, and the holiest heade his wicked waye." And the narrator later comments (precursing the deconstructionists): "For neyther is ther any thing, but that hath his contraries" (196.12–13). The narrative begins with a portrait of Euphues (184.1–185.8), and in this "counterfeit" Lyly provides all the contrarious materials required to implement the range of readings that his letter addressed to Lord Delaware enumerates.

The other letter preceding the narrative is addressed "to the Gentlemen Readers," with whom Lyly obviously felt great rapport. In this spirited performance Lyly affects an unwonted rakishness and makes the expected appeals for the attention of his mercurial audience. He claims no great profundity, however, but rather admits that fiction is little more than fashion:

> We commonly see the booke that at Christmas lyeth bound on the Stacioners stall, at Easter to be broken in the Haberdasshers shop, which sith it is the order of proceeding, I am content this winter to have my doings read for a toye, that in sommer they may be ready for trash. . . . A fashion is but a dayes wearing, and a booke but an howres reading. (182.5–21)

Like other trivia à la mode, fiction is ephemeral and subject to the whims of its consumer group. Particularly germane to our interests, though, this letter identifies that clientele, the implied readership of the tale that immediately follows. The narrative of Euphues is juxtaposed with the actual world populated by upwardly mobile Elizabethan males, and it comments pointedly upon this world.

Female readers also crowded into that readership, though, either titillated by the naughtiness of the masculine milieu or offended by its mores, and insured the popularity of *Euphues*. By way of apology—but really, I suspect, to capitalize upon this expanded readership—Lyly prefaced the sequel *Euphues and His England* not only with a letter addressed "To the Gentlemen Readers," but also with another "To the Ladies and Gentlewoemen of England."[47] Like orthogonal lines extending beyond the frame of a painting, these letters, in addition to the change in locale, relate Lyly's fiction even more directly to the men and women of the English court he was seeking so actively to engage as patrons. Yet, when the narrative itself begins on the next page, what we hear is not the intimate voice of Lyly the obsequious author, but rather once more the distancing tone of an omniscient narrator speaking in the past tense: "*Euphues* having gotten all things necessary for his voyage into *England*, accompanied onelye with *Philautus*, tooke shipping the first of December, 1579. . . ." A fictional space opens before the reader. It is an imagined world that, with a steady gaze toward actuality, nonetheless proceeds according to its own laws.

The use of framing devices, then, allowed the literary maker to set aside a fictional space that acquired sufficient autonomy to serve as an alternative reality. Especially the use of a designated narrator—or at least the exclusion of the author as the purported speaking voice—introduced a disjunction between the actual world and the world of the narrative, and removed the fictional space from the reader's personal experience. As though seen through an Albertian window, the storytelling provided a hypothetical venue and produced a viable other to enter into dialogue with the familiar. Freestanding fiction as we know it in our hylocentric culture was born. Increasingly, as hylocentrism extended its hegemony, the materialist ontology certified the primary existence of the artifact, so that it acquired an independent identity. Eventually, fiction as a potent other became the more credible reality and imposed its vision upon actuality. The supplement in this inverted hierarchy authorizes the original. But, of course, that usurpation of control was the function of fiction from its beginnings. Fiction by intention is subversive.

47. *Works of Lyly*, ed. Bond, vol. 2, 8–12.

WORKS CITED

Unless otherwise specified, citations of Greek and Roman authors refer to texts in the Loeb Classical Library.

Abulafia, David. *Frederick II: A Medieval Emperor*. London: Allen Lane/Penguin, 1988.

Ackerman, James S. *The Architecture of Michelangelo*. Studies in Architecture 4. 2 vols. London: Zwemmer, 1961.

Agrippa, Heinrich Cornelius. *De occulta philosophia libri tres*. Cologne, 1533.

———. *Three books of occult philosophy*. Trans. John Freake. London, 1651.

Alberti, Leon Battista. *De pictura praestantissima, et nunquam satis laudata arte libri tres* [1434]. Ed. Thomas Venatorius. Basle, 1540.

———. *De re aedificatoria opus* [1452]. Ed. Angelo Poliziano. Florence, 1485.

———. *La pittura*. Trans. Lodovico Domenichi. Venice, 1547.

———. *L'Architettura*. Trans. Cosimo Bartoli. Florence, 1550.

———. *Ten Books on Architecture*. Trans. James Leoni [1726]. Ed. Joseph Rykwert. London: Alec Tiranti, 1955.

———. *On Painting and On Sculpture*. Ed. and trans. Cecil Grayson. London: Phaidon, 1972.

Allen, Don Cameron. *The Legend of Noah: Renaissance Rationalism in Art, Science, and Letters*. Urbana: University of Illinois Press, 1949.

Alloway, Lawrence. *Barnett Newman: The Stations of the Cross*. New York: Solomon R. Guggenheim Museum, 1966.

Alpers, Svetlana. *The Art of Describing: Dutch Art in the Seventeenth Century.* Chicago: University of Chicago Press, 1983.

Altrocchi, Rudolph. "The Calumny of Apelles in the Literature of the Quattrocento." *Publications of the Modern Language Association* 36 (1921): 454–91.

Arator. "In apostolorum acta, libri duo." In *C. Juvenci, Coelii Sedulii, Aratoris sacra poësis.* Lyons, 1553.

Armstrong, Lilian. *Renaissance Miniature Painters and Classical Imagery: The Master of the Putti and His Venetian Workshop.* London: Harvey Miller, 1981.

Arnheim, Rudolf. *The Power of the Center: A Study of Composition in the Visual Arts.* New version. Berkeley and Los Angeles: University of California Press, 1988.

Attridge, Derek, Geoff Bennington, and Robert Young, eds. *Post-structuralism and the Question of History.* Cambridge: Cambridge University Press, 1987.

Augustine, Saint. *De libero arbitrio voluntatis: St. Augustine on Free Will.* Trans. Carroll Mason Sparrow. University of Virginia Studies 4. Charlottesville: University of Virginia Press, 1947.

———. "The Magnitude of the Soul (De quantitate animae)." Trans. John J. McMahon, S.J. In *The Immortality of the Soul* et al. Trans. Ludwig Schopp, 49–149. New York: Fathers of the Church, 1947.

———. "On Music." Trans. Robert C. Taliaferro. In *Writings of St. Augustine.* Fathers of the Church. 6 vols, 2.153–379. Washington, D.C.: Catholic University of America Press, 1947.

Baldwin, William. *Beware the Cat.* Ed. William A. Ringler, Jr., and Michael Flachmann. San Marino, Calif.: Huntington Library, 1988.

Bartholomaeus Anglicus. *Batman upon Bartholomew.* Ed. Stephen Bateman. London, 1582.

Bateman, Stephen. *The golden booke of the leaden goddes.* London, 1577.

Baxandall, Michael. *Painting and Experience in Fifteenth-Century Italy* [1972]. Oxford: Oxford University Press, 1983.

Bayley, John Barrington. *Letarouilly on Renaissance Rome.* Ed. Henry Hope Reed. New York: Architectural Book Publishing Co., 1984.

Bede. "Musica theorica." In *Opera.* 8 vols. Basle, 1563. Vol. 1.

Beer, Ellen J. *Die Rose der Kathedrale von Lausanne und der Kosmologische Bilderkreis des Mittelalters.* 2 vols. Bern: Benteli, 1952. Vol. 2.

———. *Die Glasmalereien der Schweiz vom 12. bis zum Beginn des 14. Jahrhunderts.* Corpus Vitrearum Medii Aevi, Schweiz. Basel: Birkhäuser, 1956.

Beilin, Elaine V. *Redeeming Eve: Women Writers of the English Renaissance.* Princeton: Princeton University Press, 1987.

Bennington, Geoff, and Robert Young. "Introduction: Posing the Question." In *Post-structuralism and the Question of History.* Ed. Derek Attridge, Bennington, and Young, 1–11. Cambridge: Cambridge University Press, 1987.

Bentley, Richard. *A dissertation upon the Epistles of Themistocles, Socrates, Euripides, &c. and the Fables of Aesop.* In *Reflections upon Ancient and Modern Learning* [1698]. By William Wotton. 3d ed. London, 1705.

Benvenuto, Bice, and Roger Kennedy. *The Works of Jacques Lacan: An Introduction.* London: Free Association Books, 1986.

Biadene, Leandro. "Morfologia del Sonetto nei sec. XIII e XIV." *Studi di Filologia Romanza* 4 (1889): 1–234.

Bialostocki, Jan. Review of Svetlana Alpers, *The Art of Describing: Dutch Art in the Seventeenth Century. Art Bulletin* 67 (1985): 520–26.

Blanc, Paul. "Sonnet des origines, origine du sonnet: Giacomo da Lentini." In *Le son-*

net à la Renaissance: Des origines au XVIIe siècle. Ed. Yvonne Bellenger, 9–18. Paris: Aux Amateurs de Livres, 1988.

Bouelles, Charles de. "Liber de circuli quadratura." "Perspectiva introductio." In *Epitome compendiosaque introductio in libros Arithmeticos divi Severini Boetii.* Ed. Jacques le Fèvre d'Etaples, fols. 85–87v, 90–96, respectively. Paris, 1503.

———. [*De géometrie*]. Paris, 1542.

Bowers, Fredson, ed. *The Complete Works of Christopher Marlowe.* 2d ed. 2 vols. Cambridge: Cambridge University Press, 1981. Vol. 2.

Boyle, Charles. *Dr. Bentley's Dissertations on the Epistles of Phalaris, and the Fables of Aesop, Examin'd.* London, 1698.

Brettell, Richard R., and Steven Starling. *The Art of the Edge: European Frames, 1300–1900.* Chicago: Art Institute of Chicago, 1986.

Brown, Lloyd A. *The Story of Maps.* London: Cresset, 1951.

Bukofzer, Manfred F. "Speculative Thinking in Mediaeval Music." *Speculum* 17 (1942): 165–80.

Burckhardt, Jacob. *The Civilization of the Renaissance in Italy: An Essay* [1860]. Trans. S.G.C. Middlemore. 3d ed., rev. London: Phaidon, 1950.

Buteo, Joannes. *Opera geometrica, quorum tituli sequuntur . . . Confutatio quadraturae circuli ab Orontio Finaeo factae,* 42–50. Lyons, 1554.

Campano, Giovanni. *Tetragonismus idest circuli quadratura* et al. Ed. Luca Gaurico. Venice, 1503.

Carman, Charles. "Leonardo's 'Vitruvian Man': A Renaissance Microcosm." Forthcoming.

Cassirer, Ernst. *The Individual and the Cosmos in Renaissance Philosophy.* Trans. Mario Domandi. New York: Barnes & Noble, 1963.

Cast, David. *The Calumny of Apelles: A Study in Humanist Tradition.* Yale Publications in the History of Art 28. New Haven: Yale University Press, 1981.

Castiglione, Baldassare. *The Book of the Courtier.* Trans. Sir Thomas Hoby. Ed. W.H.D. Rouse. Everyman's Library. London: Dent, 1928.

Chappell, William, ed. *The Roxburghe Ballads.* Ballad Society. 2 vols. Hertford: Stephen Austin, 1872. Vol. 2.

Cheney, Iris. "The Galleria delle Carte Geografiche at the Vatican and the Roman Church's View of the History of Christianity." Southeastern Renaissance Conference. University of Kentucky, Lexington. 8 April 1989.

Ciapponi, Lucia. "Il 'De Architectura' di Vitruvio nel primo Umanesimo." *Italia medioevale e umanistica* 3 (1960): 59–99.

Coates, Kevin. *Geometry, Proportion and the Art of Lutherie.* Oxford: Clarendon, 1985.

Cohen, Ralph, ed. "Is Literary History Obsolete?" *New Literary History* 2.1 (1970–71): 7–192.

———, ed. "On Writing Histories of Literature." *New Literary History* 16.3 (1984–85): 447–679.

Colie, Rosalie L. *Paradoxia Epidemica: The Renaissance Tradition of Paradox.* Princeton: Princeton University Press, 1966.

Condivi, Ascanio. *The Life of Michelangelo* [1553]. Trans. Alice Sedgwick Wohl. Baton Rouge: Louisiana State University Press, 1976.

Corbett, Margery. "The Architectural Title-Page." *Motif* 12 (1964): 49–62

Corbett, Margery, and Ronald Lightbown. *The Comely Frontispiece: The Emblematic Title-Page in England, 1550–1660.* London: Routledge & Kegan Paul, 1979.

Cousin, Jean. *Livre de perspective.* Paris, 1560.

Cowley, Abraham. "Davideïs." In *Poems.* Ed. A. R. Waller. Cambridge: Cambridge University Press, 1905.

Culler, Jonathan. *Saussure.* Hassocks, Sussex: Harvester Press, 1976.

——. *The Pursuit of Signs: Semiotics, Literature, Deconstruction.* Ithaca: Cornell University Press, 1981.

——. *On Deconstruction: Theory and Criticism after Structuralism.* Ithaca: Cornell University Press, 1982.

——. "Criticism and Institutions: The American University." In *Post-structuralism and the Question of History.* Ed. Derek Attridge, Geoff Bennington, and Robert Young, 82–98. Cambridge: Cambridge University Press, 1987.

Cunnar, Eugene. "Framing Seventeenth-Century Poetics: Liturgical Frames and Perspectives." In *Perspective as a Problem in the Art, History and Literature of Early Modern England.* Ed. Mark S. Lussier and S. K. Heninger, Jr., 27–49. New York: Edwin Mellen, 1992.

Daneau, Lambert. *Physicà Christiana.* Geneva, 1576.

——. *The wonderfull woorkmanship of the world.* Trans. Thomas Twynne. London, 1578.

Dannenfeldt, Karl H., ed. *The Renaissance: Medieval or Modern?* Boston: Heath, 1959.

Dante. *Epistolae.* Ed. and trans. Paget Toynbee. 2d ed. Oxford: Clarendon, 1966.

——. *Dante in Hell: The* De Vulgari Eloquentia. Trans. Warman Welliver. Ravenna: Longo, 1981.

Danti, Vincenzio. *Il primo libro del trattato delle perfette proporzioni di tutte le cose che imitare, e ritrarre si possano con l'arte del disegno.* Florence, 1567.

De Bruyne, Edgar. *The Esthetics of the Middle Ages.* Trans. Eileen B. Hennesy. New York: Frederick Ungar, 1969.

Dee, John. "A mathematicall praeface." In *The elements of geometrie.* By Euclid. Trans. Henry Billingsley. London, 1570.

De Grazia, Margreta. "The Secularization of Language in the Seventeenth Century." *Journal of the History of Ideas* 41 (1980): 319–29.

de Man, Paul. *Blindness and Insight: Essays in the Rhetoric of Contemporary Criticism.* New York: Oxford University Press, 1971.

——. *Allegories of Reading: Figural Language in Rousseau, Nietzsche, Rilke, and Proust.* New Haven: Yale University Press, 1979.

——. "The Resistance to Theory." In *The Pedagogical Imperative: Teaching as a Literary Genre.* Ed. Barbara Johnson, 3–20. Yale French Studies 63. New Haven: Yale University Press, 1982.

——. "Dialogue and Dialogism." *Poetics Today* 4 (1983): 99–107.

De Morgan, Augustus. *A Budget of Paradoxes.* London, 1872.

Derrida, Jacques. *Of Grammatology* [1967]. Trans. Gayatri Chakravorty Spivak. Baltimore: Johns Hopkins University Press, 1976.

——. "Plato's Pharmacy" [1968]. In *Dissemination.* Trans. Barbara Johnson. Chicago: University of Chicago Press, 1981.

——. *Positions* [1972]. Trans. Alan Bass. Chicago: University of Chicago Press, 1981.

——. "Structure, Sign, and Play in the Discourse of the Human Sciences." In *The Structuralist Controversy: The Languages of Criticism and the Sciences of Man.* Ed. Richard Macksey and Eugenio Donato, 247–65. Baltimore: Johns Hopkins University Press, 1972.

——. *The Truth in Painting* [1978]. Trans. Geoff Bennington and Ian McLeod. Chicago: University of Chicago Press, 1987.

Diehl, Patrick S. *The Medieval European Religious Lyric: An Ars Poetica.* Berkeley and Los Angeles: University of California Press, 1985.

Doczi, Gyorgy. *The Power of Limits: Proportional Harmonies in Nature, Art and Architecture.* Boulder, Colo., and London: Shambhala, 1981.

Draper, John W. "The Origin of Rhyme." *Revue de littérature comparée* 31 (1975): 74–85.

Du Bartas, Guillaume Saluste. *Devine weekes & workes.* Trans. Joshua Sylvester. London, 1605.

Dubrow, Heather, and Richard Strier, eds. *The Historical Renaissance: New Essays on Tudor and Stuart Literature and Culture.* Chicago: University of Chicago Press, 1988.

Duplessis-Mornay, Philippe. *The Trewnesse of the Christian Religion.* Trans. Philip Sidney and Arthur Golding. In *The Complete Works of Sir Philip Sidney.* Ed. Albert Feuillerat. 4 vols. Cambridge: Cambridge University Press, 1912–26. Vol. 3.

Dürer, Albrecht. *De symmetria partium in rectis formis humanorum corporum, libri in Latinum conversi.* Trans. Joachim Camerarius. Nuremberg, 1532. [Books 1 and 2].

———. *De varietate figurarum et flexuris partium ac gestibus imaginum, libri duo.* Trans. Joachim Camerarius. Nuremberg, 1534. [Books 3 and 4].

———. *Les quatres livres . . . de la proportion des parties & pourtraicts des corps humains.* Trans. Loys Meigret. Paris, 1557.

———. *Woodcuts and Wood Blocks.* Ed. Walter L. Strauss. New York: Abaris Books, 1979.

Ebhardt, Bodo. *Vitruvius: The "Ten Books of Architecture" of Vitruvius and Their Editors Since the Fifteenth Century.* Ossining, N.Y.: William Salloch, 1962.

Eco, Umberto. *Art and Beauty in the Middle Ages.* Trans. Hugh Bredin. New Haven: Yale University Press, 1986.

Edgerton, Samuel Y., Jr. *The Renaissance Rediscovery of Linear Perspective.* New York: Basic Books, 1975.

Edwards, Robert R. *Ratio and Invention: A Study of Medieval Lyric and Narrative.* Nashville, Tenn.: Vanderbilt University Press, 1989.

Egidi, Francesco, et al., ed. *Il libro de varie romanze volgare: Cod. Vat. 3793.* Documenti di storia letteraria. Rome: Società filologica Romana, 1908.

Ellis, John M. *Against Deconstruction.* Princeton: Princeton University Press, 1989.

Elton, G. R. *Return to Essentials: Some Reflections on the Present State of Historical Study.* Cambridge: Cambridge University Press, 1991.

Elyot, Thomas. *The castel of helth.* London, 1534.

Englands Helicon. London, 1600.

Evett, David. *Literature and the Visual Arts in Tudor England.* Athens: University of Georgia Press, 1990.

Ferguson, Margaret W., Maureen Quilligan, and Nancy J. Vickers, eds. *Rewriting the Renaissance: The Discourses of Sexual Difference in Early Modern Europe.* Chicago: University of Chicago Press, 1986.

Ferguson, Wallace K. *The Renaissance in Historical Thought: Five Centuries of Interpretation.* Boston: Houghton Mifflin, 1948.

———. "The Reinterpretation of the Renaissance." In *Facets of the Renaissance.* Ed. William H. Werkmeister, 1–17. New York: Harper/Torchbooks, 1963.

Fienberg, Nona. "The Emergence of Stella in *Astrophil and Stella.*" *Studies in English Literature 1500–1900* 25 (1985): 5–19.

Finé, Oronce. "De quadratura circuli." In *Protomathesis,* fols. 89v–91v. Paris, 1532.

Firenzuola, Agnolo. "Dialogo . . . delle belleze delle donne." In *Prose,* fols. 61–89. Florence, 1548.

Fludd, Robert. *Utriusque cosmi . . . historia.* 4 vols. Oppenheim, 1617–19.

Foucault, Michel. *The Order of Things: An Archaeology of the Human Sciences.* New York: Pantheon/Random, 1970.

———. "What Is an Author?" In *Textual Strategies: Perspectives in Post-Structuralist Criticism.* Ed. Josué V. Harari, 141–60. Ithaca: Cornell University Press, 1979.

———. *This Is Not a Pipe.* Trans. and ed. James Harkness. Berkeley and Los Angeles: University of California Press, 1983.

Fowler, Alastair. *Triumphal Forms: Structural Patterns in Elizabethan Poetry*. Cambridge: Cambridge University Press, 1970.

Freccero, Carla. "The Other and the Same: The Image of the Hermaphrodite in Rabelais." In *Rewriting the Renaissance: The Discourses of Sexual Difference in Early Modern Europe*. Ed. Margaret W. Ferguson, Maureen Quilligan, and Nancy J. Vickers, 145–58. Chicago: University of Chicago Press, 1986.

Fussell, Paul, Jr. *Poetic Meter and Poetic Form*. New York: Random House, 1965.

Gadamer, Hans-Georg. *Dialogue and Dialectic: Eight Hermeneutical Studies on Plato*. Trans. P. Christopher Smith. New Haven: Yale University Press, 1980.

Gascoigne, George. "Certayne Notes of Instruction Concerning the Making of Verse or Ryme in English" [1575]. In *Elizabethan Critical Essays*. Ed. G. Gregory Smith. 2 vols., 1.46–57. London: Oxford University Press, 1904.

Gent, Lucy. *Picture and Poetry, 1560–1620: Relations Between Literature and the Visual Arts in the English Renaissance*. Leamington Spa: Hall, 1981.

———. "The Self-Cozening Eye." *Review of English Studies* 34 (1983): 419–28.

Giacomo da Lentini. *The Poetry of Giacomo da Lentino*. Ed. Ernest F. Langley. Cambridge: Harvard University Press, 1915.

———. *Poesie*. Ed. Roberto Antonelli. Rome: Bulzoni, 1979.

Gilbert, Creighton E. "Texts and Contexts of the Medici Chapel." *Art Quarterly* 34 (1971): 391–409.

Gilson, Etienne. *Painting and Reality* [1957]. Bollingen Series 35. 2d printing. Princeton: Princeton University Press, 1968.

Giraldi, Lilio Gregorio. *De annis et mensibus, caeterisque temporum partibus . . . dissertatio*. Basle, 1541.

Goffen, Rona. *Giovanni Bellini*. New Haven: Yale University Press, 1989.

Gombrich, E. H. "Moment and Movement in Art." *Journal of the Warburg and Courtauld Institutes* 27 (1964): 293–306.

Gouws, John. "Fact and Anecdote in Fulke Greville's Account of Sidney's Last Days." In *Sir Philip Sidney: 1586 and the Creation of a Legend*. Ed. Jan van Dorsten, Dominic Baker-Smith, and Arthur F. Kinney. Leiden: Brill, 1986.

Grimm, Claus. *The Book of Picture Frames* [1978]. Trans. Nancy M. Gordon and Walter L. Strauss. New York: Abaris Books, 1981.

Guillén, Claudio. "On the Concept and Metaphor of Perspective" [1966]. In *Literature as System: Essays Toward the Theory of Literary History*, 283–371. Princeton: Princeton University Press, 1971.

Hall, William Keith. "A Topography of Time: Historical Narration in John Stow's *Survey of London*." *Studies in Philology* 88 (1991): 1–15.

Hanning, R. W. Review of David Cast, *The Calumny of Apelles: A Study in Humanist Tradition*. *Art Bulletin* 67 (1985): 690–93.

Harington, Sir John. "Preface to the Translation of *Orlando Furioso*." In *Elizabethan Critical Essays*. Ed. G. Gregory Smith. 2 vols., 2.194–222. London: Oxford University Press, 1904.

Hart, E. F. "The Answer-Poem of the Early Seventeenth Century." *Review of English Studies* 7 (1956): 19–29.

Hartt, Frederick. "The Meaning of Michelangelo's Medici Chapel." In *Essays in Honor of Georg Swarzenski*, 145–55. Chicago: Henry Regnery, 1951.

———. *History of Italian Renaissance Art*. New York: Abrams, 1969.

Haskins, Charles Homer. *Studies in the History of Mediaeval Science*. Cambridge: Harvard University Press, 1924.

Heninger, S. K., Jr. "The Pattern of *Love's Labor's Lost*." *Shakespeare Studies* 7 (1974): 25–53.

———. *Touches of Sweet Harmony: Pythagorean Cosmology and Renaissance Poetics*. San Marino, Calif.: Huntington Library, 1974.

———. *The Cosmographical Glass: Renaissance Diagrams of the Universe*. San Marino, Calif.: Huntington Library, 1977.

———. "Sequences, Systems, Models: Sidney and the Secularization of Sonnets." In *Poems in Their Place: The Intertextuality and Order of Poetic Collections*. Ed. Neil Fraistat, 66–94. Chapel Hill: University of North Carolina Press, 1986.

———. *Sidney and Spenser: The Poet as Maker*. University Park: Pennsylvania State University Press, 1989.

———. "Spenser, Sidney, and Poetic Form." *Studies in Philology* 88 (1991): 140–52.

Hess, Thomas B. *Barnett Newman*. New York: Museum of Modern Art, 1971.

Heydenryk, Henry. *The Art and History of Frames: An Inquiry into the Enhancement of Paintings*. New York: Heineman, 1963.

Hobson, Ernest W. *"Squaring the Circle": A History of the Problem*. Cambridge: Cambridge University Press, 1913.

Hobson, Marian. "History Traces." In *Post-structuralism and the Question of History*. Ed. Derek Attridge, Geoff Bennington, and Robert Young, 101–15. Cambridge: Cambridge University Press, 1987.

Hollanda, Francisco de. *Four Dialogues on Painting* [1558]. Trans. Aubrey F. G. Bell [1928]. Westport, Conn.: Hyperion, 1979.

Hopkins, Jasper. *Nicholas of Cusa on Learned Ignorance: A Translation and an Appraisal of De Docta Ignorantia*. Minneapolis: Banning, 1981.

House, John. *Monet: Nature into Art*. New Haven: Yale University Press, 1986.

Howard, Jean E. "The New Historicism in Renaissance Studies." *English Literary Renaissance* 16 (1986): 13–43.

Hughes, Andrew. "Music, Western European." In *Dictionary of the Middle Ages*. Ed. Joseph R. Strayer. 13 vols., 8.578–95. New York: Scribner's, 1982-89.

Huillard-Bréholles, Jean Louis Alphonse. *Vie et correspondance de Pierre de la Vigne* [1865]. Reinheim: Scientia Verlag Aalen, 1966.

Hulse, Clark. "Recent Studies of Literature and Painting in the English Renaissance." *English Literary Renaissance* 15 (1985): 122–40.

———. *The Rule of Art: Literature and Painting in the Renaissance*. Chicago: University of Chicago Press, 1990.

Hume, Kathryn. *The Owl and the Nightingale: The Poem and Its Critics*. Toronto: University of Toronto Press, 1975.

Hylles, Thomas. *The arte of vulgar arithmeticke*. London, 1600.

Ingarden, Roman. *The Literary Work of Art*. Trans. George G. Grabowicz. Evanston, Ill.: Northwestern University Press, 1973.

Ingpen, William. *The secrets of numbers: According to theologicall, arithmeticall, geometricall and harmonicall computation*. London, 1624.

Jameson, Fredric. *The Prison-House of Language: A Critical Account of Structuralism and Russian Formalism*. Princeton: Princeton University Press, 1972.

Jardine, Lisa. *Francis Bacon: Discovery and the Art of Discourse*. Cambridge: Cambridge University Press, 1974.

Jeffrey, David L., ed. *By Things Seen: Reference and Recognition in Medieval Thought*. Ottawa: University of Ottawa Press, 1979.

Jensen, Frede, ed. and trans. *The Poetry of the Sicilian School*. Garland Library of Medieval Literature, ser. A, 22. New York: Garland, 1986.

Jost, François. "Le sonnet: Sens d'une structure." In *Le sonnet à la Renaissance: Des origines au XVIIe siècle*. Ed. Yvonne Bellenger, 57–65. Paris: Aux Amateurs de Livres, 1988.

Kantorowicz, Ernst. *Frederick II, 1194–1250* [1931]. Trans. E. O. Lorimer. Rev. ed. New York: Frederick Ungar, 1957.

Kelly, Joan. "Did Women Have a Renaissance?" In *Women, History and Theory: The Essays of Joan Kelly*. Ed. Catherine R. Stimpson, 19–50. Chicago: University of Chicago Press, 1984.

Kemp, Martin. *Geometrical Perspective from Brunelleschi to Desargues: A Pictorial Means Or an Intellectual End?* Proceedings of the British Academy 70, 95–101. London: Oxford University Press, 1985.

———. *The Science of Art: Optical Themes in Western Art from Brunelleschi to Seurat*. New Haven: Yale University Press, 1990.

Kennedy, William J. *Rhetorical Norms in Renaissance Literature*. New Haven: Yale University Press, 1978.

———. "Petrarchan Authorities and the Authorization of Petrarch." Renaissance Society of America Conference. Duke University, Durham, N.C. 12 April 1991.

Kerrigan, William, and Gordon Braden. *The Idea of the Renaissance*. Baltimore: Johns Hopkins University Press, 1989.

Kleinhenz, Christopher. *The Early Italian Sonnet: The First Century (1220–1321)*. Lecce: Milella, 1986.

Klemp, P. J. "Numerology and English Renaissance Literature: Twentieth-Century Studies." *Bulletin of Bibliography* 40 (1983): 231–41.

Knowlton, Edgar C., Jr. "Jacopo da Lentini's Sonnet 'Of His Lady in Heaven.'" *Allegorica* 6.2 (1981): 95–101.

Kubovy, Michael. *The Psychology of Perspective and Renaissance Art*. Cambridge: Cambridge University Press, 1986.

Lacan, Jacques. *Ecrits: A Selection*. Trans. Alan Sheridan. New York: Norton, 1977.

———. *Le Séminaire: Livre III, Les Psychoses, 1955–1956*. Ed. Jacques-Alain Miller. Paris: Seuil, 1981.

Landino, Cristoforo. *Scritti critici e teorici*. Ed. Roberto Cardini. 2 vols. Rome: Bulzoni, 1974.

———, ed. *Divina commedia*. By Dante. Florence, 1481.

La Primaudaye, Pierre de. *The French academie* [1577]. Trans. Thomas Bowes. London, 1586.

———. *The second part of the French academie*. Trans. Thomas Bowes. London, 1594.

———. *The third volume of the French academie*. Trans. R. Dolman. London, 1601.

Lavin, Marilyn Aronberg. *The Place of Narrative: Mural Decoration in Italian Churches, 431–1600*. Chicago: University of Chicago Press, 1990.

LeRoy, Louis. *Of the interchangeable course, or variety of things in the whole world*. Trans. Robert Ashley. London, 1594.

Letarouilly, Paul. *The Vatican and the Basilica of St. Peter, Rome*. Ed. Alphonse Simil. London: Alex Tiranti, 1963.

Libro de varie romanze volgare: Cod. Vat. 3793. Ed. Francesco Egidi et al. Documenti di storia letteraria. Rome: Società filologica Romana, 1908.

Lomazzo, Giovanni Paolo. *The artes of curious paintinge, carvinge & buildinge*. Trans. Richard Haydocke. Oxford, 1598.

Lyly, John. *Euphues: The anatomy of wyt*. London, 1578.

———. *Complete Works*. Ed. R. Warwick Bond. 3 vols. Oxford: Clarendon, 1902.

Macey, David. *Lacan in Contexts*. London: Verso, 1988.

McLane, Paul E. *Spenser's Shepheardes Calender: A Study in Elizabethan Allegory*. Notre Dame, Ind.: University of Notre Dame Press, 1961.

Manuzio, Aldo Pio. *Poetae Christiani veteres*. 3 vols. Venice, 1501–4.

Marcus, Leah. "Disestablishing the Renaissance: New Directions in Early Modern Studies." In *Redrawing the Boundaries of Literary Studies*. Ed. Stephen Greenblatt et al. Modern Language Association, forthcoming.

Martianus Capella. "The Marriage of Philology and Mercury." Trans. William Harris Stahl and Richard Johnson. In *Martianus Capella and the Seven Liberal Arts*. 2 vols. New York: Columbia University Press, 1971–77. Vol. 2.

May, Steven W. "Companion Poems in the Ralegh Canon." *English Literary Renaissance* 13 (1983): 260–73.

Mexia, Pedro. *The foreste*. Trans. Thomas Fortescue. London, 1571.

Minturno, Antonio. *L'Arte poetica*. Venice, 1564.

Montrose, Louis. "The Elizabethan Subject and the Spenserian Text." In *Literary Theory/Renaissance Texts*. Ed. Patricia Parker and David Quint, 303–40. Baltimore: Johns Hopkins University Press, 1986.

———. "Renaissance Literary Studies and the Subject of History." *English Literary Renaissance* 16 (1986): 5–12..

———. "Professing the Renaissance: The Poetics and Politics of Culture." In *The New Historicism*. Ed. H. Aram Veeser, 15–36. New York: Routledge, 1989.

Montucla, Jean Etienne. *Histoire des recherches sur la quadrature du cercle . . . avec une addition concernant les problèmes de la duplication du cube et de la trisection de l'angle*. Paris, 1754.

Morson, Gary Saul, and Caryl Emerson. *Mikhail Bakhtin: Creation of a Prosaics*. Stanford, Calif.: Stanford University Press, 1990.

Muller, John P., and William J. Richardson. *Lacan and Language: A Reader's Guide to Ecrits*. New York: International Universities Press, 1982.

Murbach, Ernst. *La Rose de la Cathédrale de Lausanne*. Guides de Monuments Suisses. N.p.: Société d'Histoire de l'Art en Suisse, 1970.

Murphey, Murray G. *Our Knowledge of the Historical Past*. Indianapolis: Bobbs-Merrill, 1973.

Myers, William Alexander. *The Quadrature of the Circle. The Square Root of Two, and the Right-Angled Triangle*. Cincinnati, 1874.

Nadal, Hieronimo. *Adnotationes et meditationes in Evangelia*. 2d ed. Antwerp, 1595.

Natta, Marcantonio. "De poëtis liber." In *Opera*, fols. 110–14. Venice, 1564.

Newbery, Timothy J., George Bisacca, and Laurence B. Kanter. *Italian Renaissance Frames*. New York: Metropolitan Museum of Art, 1990.

Nicholas of Cusa. "De quadratura circuli." In *Opera*. 3 vols., 2.59–60. Paris, 1514.

———. *On Learned Ignorance: A Translation and an Appraisal of De Docta Ignorantia*. Ed. and trans. Jasper Hopkins. Minneapolis: Banning, 1981.

Nichols, Stephen G., Jr. *Romanesque Signs: Early Medieval Narrative and Iconography*. New Haven: Yale University Press, 1983.

Nietzsche, Friedrich. *The Birth of Tragedy and The Genealogy of Morals*. Trans. Francis Golffing. New York: Doubleday/Anchor, 1956.

Nolan, Barbara. *The Gothic Visionary Perspective*. Princeton: Princeton University Press, 1977.

Nyquist, Mary. "Textual Overlapping and Dalilah's Harlot-Lap." In *Literary Theory/Renaissance Texts*. Ed. Patricia Parker and David Quint, 341–73. Baltimore: Johns Hopkins University Press, 1986.

O'Connell, Robert J., S.J. *Art and the Christian Intelligence in St. Augustine*. Cambridge: Harvard University Press, 1978.

Oppenheimer, Paul. "The Origin of the Sonnet." *Comparative Literature* 34 (1982): 289–304.

———. *The Birth of the Modern Mind: Self, Consciousness, and the Invention of the Sonnet*. New York: Oxford University Press, 1989.

Pacioli, Luca. *Summa de arithmetica, geometria, proportioni & proportionalita*. Venice, 1494.
———. *Divina proportione*. Venice, 1509.
Pahlka, William H. *Saint Augustine's Meter and George Herbert's Will*. Kent, Ohio: Kent State University Press, 1987.
Palfreyman, Thomas. *The treatise of heavenly philosophie*. London, 1578.
Palisca, Claude V. *Humanism in Italian Renaissance Musical Thought*. New Haven: Yale University Press, 1986.
Panofsky, Erwin. "Die Perspektive als 'Symbolische Form.' " In *Vorträge der Bibliothek Warburg, 1924–25*. Ed. Fritz Saxl, 258–330. Leipzig: Teubner, 1927.
———. *Studies in Iconology: Humanistic Themes in the Art of the Renaissance*. New York: Oxford University Press, 1939.
———. "The History of the Theory of Human Proportions as a Reflection of the History of Styles." In *Meaning in the Visual Arts*, 55–107. Garden City, N.Y.: Doubleday/Anchor, 1955.
———. *Renaissance and Renascences in Western Art* [1960]. 2d ed. New York: Harper/Torchbooks, 1969.
Passionate Pilgrim. London, 1599.
Pater, Walter. "The School of Giorgone." *Fortnightly Review*, n.s., 22.2 (1877): 526–38.
Peacham, Henry. *The art of drawing with the pen, and limming in water colours*. London, 1607.
Peck, Russell A. "Number as Cosmic Language." In *By Things Seen: Reference and Recognition in Medieval Thought*. Ed. David L. Jeffrey. Ottawa: University of Ottawa Press, 1979.
Perkins, David. *Is Literary History Possible?* Baltimore: Johns Hopkins University Press, 1992.
Petrarch. *Phisicke against Fortune, as well prosperous, as adverse*. Trans. Thomas Twyne. London, 1579.
———. *Petrarch's Lyric Poems*. Ed. and trans. Robert M. Durling. Cambridge: Harvard University Press, 1976.
Plato. *His Apology of Socrates, and Phaedo*. Trans. anon. London, 1675.
Plutarch. *The morals*. Trans. Philemon Holland. London, 1603.
Pope-Hennessy, John. *Italian High Renaissance and Baroque Sculpture* [1963]. In *An Introduction to Italian Sculpture*. 3 parts, 2d ed. London: Phaidon, 1970. Part 3.
Pordage, Samuel. *Mundorum explicatio or, The explanation of an hieroglyphical figure*. London, 1661. (Wing P2974)
Pötters, Wilhelm. "La natura e l'origine del sonetto: Una nuova teoria." In *Miscellanea di studi in onore di Vittore Branca*. 5 vols., 1.71–78. Florence: Olschki, 1983.
Prescott, Anne Lake. "Marginal Discourse: Drayton's Muse and Selden's 'Story.' " *Studies in Philology* 88 (1991): 307–28.
Procaccini, Alfonso. "Alberti and the 'Framing' of Perspective." *Journal of Aesthetics and Art Criticism* 40 (1981–82): 29–39.
Puttenham, George. *The Arte of English Poesie*. Ed. Gladys Doidge Willcock and Alice Walker. Cambridge: Cambridge University Press, 1936.
Quint, David. "Introduction." In *Literary Theory/Renaissance Texts*. Ed. Quint and Patricia Parker, 1–19. Baltimore: Johns Hopkins University Press, 1986.
Rebholz, R. A., ed. *Sir Thomas Wyatt: The Complete Poems*. New Haven: Yale University Press, 1981.
Recorde, Robert. *The castle of knowledge*. London, 1556.
———. *The whetstone of witte*. London, 1557.
Reed, Thomas L., Jr. *Middle English Debate Poetry and the Aesthetics of Irresolution*. Columbia: University of Missouri Press, 1990.

Reisch, Gregor. *Margarita philosophica*. Ed. Oronce Finé. Basle, 1583.

Renwick, W. L., ed. *The Shepherd's Calendar by Edmund Spenser*. London: Scholartis Press, 1930.

Ripley, George. *The compound of alchymy*. Ed. Ralph Rabbards. London, 1591.

Rose, Paul Lawrence. *The Italian Renaissance of Mathematics: Studies on Humanists and Mathematicians from Petrarch to Galileo*. Travaux d'Humanisme et Renaissance 145. Geneva: Librairie Droz, 1975.

Roxburghe Ballads. Ed. William Chappell. Ballad Society. 2 vols. Hertford: Stephen Austin, 1872. Vol. 2.

"Rudimenta musicae figuratae." By anon. In *Margarita philosophica*. By Gregor Reisch. Ed. Oronce Finé. Basle, 1583.

Russell, J. Stephen. *The English Dream Vision: Anatomy of a Form*. Columbus: Ohio State University Press, 1988.

Sagredo, Diego de. *Raison d'architecture antique, extraicte de Victruve, et aultres anciens architecteurs*. Paris, 1539.

Sandström, Sven. *Levels of Unreality: Studies in Structure and Construction in Italian Mural Painting During the Renaissance*. Acta Universitatis Upsaliensis, Figura n.s. 4. Uppsala: Almqvist & Wiksell, 1963.

Sansovino, Francesco. *L'Edificio del corpo humano*. Venice, 1550.

Saussure, Ferdinand de. *Course in General Linguistics*. Trans. Roy Harris. London: Duckworth, 1983.

Scaliger, Julius Caesar. *Poetices libri septem*. Lyons, 1561.

Schapiro, Meyer. "On Some Problems in the Semiotics of Visual Art: Field and Vehicle in Image-Signs." *Semiotica* 1 (1969): 223–42.

Schneiderman, Stuart. *Jacques Lacan: The Death of an Intellectual Hero*. Cambridge: Harvard University Press, 1983.

Searle, John. "The Storm over the University." *New York Review of Books*, 6 December 1990, 34–42.

Seiberling, Grace. *Monet's Series*. New York: Garland, 1981.

Sessions, William A. *Henry Howard, Earl of Surrey*. Twayne Series. Boston: G. K. Hall, 1986.

Shakespeare, William. *The Passionate Pilgrim*. Ed. Joseph Quincy Adams. Folger Shakespeare Library Publications 4. New York: Scribner's, 1939.

Shapiro, Marianne. *Hieroglyph of Time: The Petrarchan Sestina*. Minneapolis: University of Minnesota Press, 1980.

Shute, John. *The first and chief groundes of architecture*. London, 1563.

Sidney, Sir Philip. *The Poems*. Ed. William A. Ringler, Jr. Oxford: Clarendon, 1962.

———. *The Countess of Pembroke's Arcadia (The Old Arcadia)*. Ed. Jean Robertson. Oxford: Clarendon, 1973.

———. *A Defence of Poetry*. In *Miscellaneous Prose of Sir Philip Sidney*. Ed. Katherine Duncan-Jones and Jan van Dorsten, 59–121. Oxford: Clarendon, 1973.

Simpson, David. "Literary Criticism and the Return to 'History.'" *Critical Inquiry* 14 (1987–88): 721–47.

Simson, Otto Georg von. *The Gothic Cathedral: Origins of Gothic Architecture and the Medieval Concept of Order*. 2d ed. Bollingen Series 48. New York: Pantheon Books, 1962.

Slights, William W. E. "The Edifying Margins of Renaissance English Books." *Renaissance Quarterly* 42 (1989): 682–716.

Smith, A. Mark. "Getting the Big Picture in Perspectivist Optics." *Isis* 72 (1981): 568–89.

Smith, Bruce R. "The Contest of Apollo and Marsyas: Ideas about Music in the Middle Ages." In *By Things Seen: Reference and Recognition in Medieval Thought*. Ed. David L. Jeffrey, 81–107. Ottawa: University of Ottawa Press, 1979.

Snyder, Jon R. *Writing the Scene of Speaking: Theories of Dialogue in the Late Italian Renaissance.* Stanford, Calif.: Stanford University Press, 1989.

Solt, Mary Ellen. *Concrete Poetry: A World View.* Bloomington: University of Indiana Press, 1968.

Spanos, Margaret. "The Sestina: An Exploration of the Dynamics of Poetic Structure." *Speculum* 53 (1978): 545–57.

Spenser, Edmund. *The Works: A Variorum Edition.* Ed. Edwin Greenlaw et al. 11 vols. Baltimore: Johns Hopkins University Press, 1932–57.

Staub, Susan Carol. "George Gascoigne's *A Hundreth Sundrie Flowers:* 'The Method and Maner' of the Poet." Ph.D. diss., University of North Carolina at Chapel Hill, 1987.

Steiner, Wendy. *Pictures of Romance: Form Against Context in Painting and Literature.* Chicago: University of Chicago Press, 1988.

Sterry, Peter. *A discourse of the freedom of the will.* London, 1675.

Stevens, John. *Words and Music in the Middle Ages: Song, Narrative, Dance and Drama, 1050–1350.* Cambridge: Cambridge University Press, 1986.

Stone, Lawrence. Review of G. R. Elton, *Return to Essentials: Some Reflections on the Present State of Historical Study. Times Literary Supplement,* 31 January 1992, 3–5.

Strauss, Walter L. *The Clair-Obscur Woodcuts by the German and Netherlandish Masters of the XVIth and XVIIth Centuries.* Greenwich, Conn.: New York Graphic Society, 1973.

Summers, David. *Michelangelo and the Language of Art.* Princeton: Princeton University Press, 1981.

———. *The Judgment of Sense: Renaissance Naturalism and the Rise of Aesthetics.* Cambridge: Cambridge University Press, 1987.

Sunderland, Elizabeth Read. "Symbolic Numbers and Romanesque Church Plans." *Journal of the Society of Architectural Historians* 18 (1959): 94–103.

Swaan, Wim. *The Late Middle Ages: Art and Architecture from 1350 to the Advent of the Renaissance.* Ithaca: Cornell University Press, 1977.

Symonds, J. A. *Renaissance in Italy* [1875–86]. 2 vols. New York: Modern Library, n.d.

Thurneisser zum Thurn, Leonhard. *Quinta essentia, das ist die höchste subtilitet krafft.* Münster, 1570.

Todorov, Tzvetan. *Mikhail Bakhtin: The Dialogical Principle.* Trans. Wlad Godzich. Theory and History of Literature 13. Minneapolis: University of Minnesota Press, 1984.

Tolnay, Carlo. "Studi sulla Cappella Medicea." *L'Arte,* n.s., 5 (1934): 5–44, 281–307.

———. *The Medici Chapel. Michelangelo* [1943–60]. 5 vols. Princeton: Princeton University Press, 1948. Vol. 3.

Tory, Geoffroy. *Champ Fleury.* Paris, 1529.

Tottel, Richard, ed. *Songes and sonettes.* London, 1557.

Trinkaus, Charles. "Renaissance Ideas and the Idea of the Renaissance." *Journal of the History of Ideas* 51 (1990): 667–84.

Tucker, Paul Hayes. *Monet in the '90s: The Series Paintings.* New Haven: Yale University Press, 1989.

Valla, Giorgio. *De expetendis, et fugiendis rebus opus.* Venice, 1501.

Van Cleve, Thomas Curtis. *The Emperor Frederick II of Hohenstaufen: Immutator Mundi.* Oxford: Clarendon, 1972.

Veltman, Kim H., and Kenneth D. Keele. *Linear Perspective and the Visual Dimensions of Science and Art.* Studies on Leonardo da Vinci 1. Munich: Deutscher Kunstverlag, 1986.

Vickers, Brian, ed. *Occult and Scientific Mentalities in the Renaissance.* Cambridge: Cambridge University Press, 1984.

Vitruvius. *De architectura libri decem* et al. Rome, 1486.

———. *[De architectura libri decem] per Jocundum solito castigatior factus cum figuris et tabula.* Ed. Fra Giovanni Giocondo. Venice, 1511.

———. *De architectura libri dece.* Ed. and trans. Cesare Cesariano. Como, 1521.

———. *I dieci libri dell'architettura.* Ed. and trans. Daniello Barbaro. Venice, 1556.

Waller, Gary F. "Author, Text, Reading, Ideology: Towards a Revisionist Literary History of the Renaissance." *Dalhousie Review,* 61 (1981–82): 405–25.

Waswo, Richard. *Language and Meaning in the Renaissance.* Princeton: Princeton University Press, 1987.

White, Hayden. "The Historical Text as Literary Artifact." In *The Writing of History: Literary Form and Historical Understanding.* Ed. Robert H. Canary and Henry Kozicki, 41–62. Madison: University of Wisconsin Press, 1978.

———. "New Historicism: A Comment." In *The New Historicism.* Ed. H. Aram Veeser, 293–302. New York: Routledge, 1989.

White, John. *The Birth and Rebirth of Pictorial Space.* 3d ed. London: Faber, 1987.

Wick, Peter A., ed. *Sixteenth-Century Architectural Books from Italy and France.* Cambridge, Mass.: Harvard College Library, 1971.

Wilde, Johannes. "Michelangelo's Designs for the Medici Tombs." *Journal of the Warburg and Courtauld Institutes* 18.1 (1955): 54–66.

Wilkins, David. "The Meaning of Space in Fourteenth-Century Tuscan Painting." In *By Things Seen: Reference and Recognition in Medieval Thought.* Ed. David L. Jeffrey, 109–21. Ottawa: University of Ottawa Press, 1979.

Wilkins, Ernest Hatch. "The Invention of the Sonnet." In *The Invention of the Sonnet and Other Studies in Italian Literature,* 11–39. Rome: Edizioni di Storia e Letteratura, 1959.

Wilkinson, Catherine. "Proportion in Practice: Juan de Herrera's Design for the Façade of the Basilica of the Escorial." *Art Bulletin* 67 (1985): 229–42.

Wilson, K. J. *Incomplete Fictions: The Formation of English Renaissance Dialogue.* Washington, D.C.: Catholic University of America Press, 1985.

Winn, James Anderson. *Unsuspected Eloquence: A History of the Relations Between Poetry and Music.* New Haven: Yale University Press, 1981.

Wittkower, Rudolf. *Architectural Principles in the Age of Humanism.* New York: Random House, 1965.

Wotton, Sir Henry. *The elements of architecture.* London, 1624.

Wyatt, Sir Thomas. *The Complete Poems.* Ed. R. A. Rebholz. New Haven: Yale University Press, 1981.

INDEX